Thorsten Barnickel

Semantic Relation Extraction for Systems Biology

Thorsten Barnickel

Semantic Relation Extraction for Systems Biology

The development of a semantic search engine and lexicon based on the processing of large biomedical text corpora by a fast SRL engine

Südwestdeutscher Verlag für Hochschulschriften

Impressum/Imprint (nur für Deutschland/ only for Germany)
Bibliografische Information der Deutschen Nationalbibliothek: Die Deutsche Nationalbibliothek verzeichnet diese Publikation in der Deutschen Nationalbibliografie; detaillierte bibliografische Daten sind im Internet über http://dnb.d-nb.de abrufbar.

Alle in diesem Buch genannten Marken und Produktnamen unterliegen warenzeichen-, markenoder patentrechtlichem Schutz bzw. sind Warenzeichen oder eingetragene Warenzeichen der jeweiligen Inhaber. Die Wiedergabe von Marken, Produktnamen, Gebrauchsnamen, Handelsnamen, Warenbezeichnungen u.s.w. in diesem Werk berechtigt auch ohne besondere Kennzeichnung nicht zu der Annahme, dass solche Namen im Sinne der Warenzeichen- und Markenschutzgesetzgebung als frei zu betrachten wären und daher von jedermann benutzt werden dürften.

Verlag: Südwestdeutscher Verlag für Hochschulschriften Aktiengesellschaft & Co. KG
Dudweiler Landstr. 99, 66123 Saarbrücken, Deutschland
Telefon +49 681 37 20 271-1, Telefax +49 681 37 20 271-0
Email: info@svh-verlag.de
Zugl.: München, TU München, Dis., 2009

Herstellung in Deutschland:
Schaltungsdienst Lange o.H.G., Berlin
Books on Demand GmbH, Norderstedt
Reha GmbH, Saarbrücken
Amazon Distribution GmbH, Leipzig
ISBN: 978-3-8381-1518-4

Imprint (only for USA, GB)
Bibliographic information published by the Deutsche Nationalbibliothek: The Deutsche Nationalbibliothek lists this publication in the Deutsche Nationalbibliografie; detailed bibliographic data are available in the Internet at http://dnb.d-nb.de.

Any brand names and product names mentioned in this book are subject to trademark, brand or patent protection and are trademarks or registered trademarks of their respective holders. The use of brand names, product names, common names, trade names, product descriptions etc. even without a particular marking in this works is in no way to be construed to mean that such names may be regarded as unrestricted in respect of trademark and brand protection legislation and could thus be used by anyone.

Publisher: Südwestdeutscher Verlag für Hochschulschriften Aktiengesellschaft & Co. KG
Dudweiler Landstr. 99, 66123 Saarbrücken, Germany
Phone +49 681 37 20 271-1, Fax +49 681 37 20 271-0
Email: info@svh-verlag.de

Printed in the U.S.A.
Printed in the U.K. by (see last page)
ISBN: 978-3-8381-1518-4

Copyright © 2010 by the author and Südwestdeutscher Verlag für Hochschulschriften Aktiengesellschaft & Co. KG and licensors
All rights reserved. Saarbrücken 2010

ACKNOWLEDGEMENTS

First and foremost, I would like to express my deep gratitude to my promoter Dr. Volker Stümpflen. Without his continuing, stimulating encouragement and his excellent background in Enterprise technologies still being predominantly used in the IT-industry rather than in academic research, I would not have been able to finish my doctorate in the presented form. Facing the tremendous amount of data that was generated by gathering the positional information of millions of biomedical terms, I was close to cutting the project down to a notably smaller version compared to the text mining system presented in this thesis. Volkers knowledge on database servers and performance tuning significantly contributed to the development of a database schema finally being able to cope with the immense amount of data.
I would also like to cordially thank Prof. Dr. Hans-Werner Mewes, head of the Institute for Bioinformatics and Systems Biology (IBIS), for giving me the opportunity to do my doctorate at his institute and for his friendly support and encouragement all along my time at IBIS. His critical and constructive reviewing of my paper submissions helped me a lot to structure my writings and lines of thought. I would like to thank Prof. Mewes especially for his continuous support and trust in my work and for providing me with two high performance database servers without which my text mining system would not be able, despite the database schema, to process the generated amount of data in an acceptable frame of time.
At this place I also want to thank Prof. Dr. Ralf Zimmer who, together with Prof. Mewes, supported my work by participating in the Ph. D. committee and by reviewing the presented thesis.

My particular thanks to my former and present colleagues for valuable suggestions, discussions and the inspiring, cooperative working atmosphere here at MIPS: Dr. Karamfilka Nenova, Dr. Thorsten Schmidt, Roland Arnold, Florian Büttner, Mara Hartsperger, Dr. Thomas Rattei, Dr. Matthias Oesterheld, Sebastian Toepel, Dr. Gabi Kastenmüller, Daniel Ellwanger, Richard Gregory, Dr. Igor V. Rodchenkov, Octave Noubibou, Martin Münsterkötter, Nadine Albrecht and Benedikt Wachinger. I also would like to thank all other staff members for the good atmosphere, especially Petra Fuhrmann and Elisabeth Noheimer for their support regarding all administrative issues and Dr. Corinna Montrone and Irmtraud Dunger for their help in evaluating my system.

I owe my deepest gratitude to my parents for their continuous encouragement and support, in particular for giving me the opportunity to study three additional semesters of bioinformatics at the TFH Berlin. For the same reason, I would like to sincerely thank Prof. Dr. Ina Koch, head of the bioinformatics course at the TFH Berlin, for establishing this field of study at the TFH and for guiding my first steps in this new domain, and to Dr. Bertram Weiss, the supervisor of my master thesis at the Schering AG, for his excellent support and his encouragement to apply to Prof. Hans-Werner Mewes for a postgraduate position.

DEDICATION

To my father.

For perpetual support, encouragement and arousing my curiosity for science

ABSTRACT

Due to the growing amount of literature, the need for automated extraction of relations between genes, metabolites and phenotypes from natural language text has steadily been increasing over the last years. A number of tools addressing this task has been developed ranging from document clustering to relation extraction approaches based on cooccurrence or syntactical information. Several algorithms for each of the many steps required for extracting knowledge from natural language texts have been developed and improved. In order to bring text mining from theory to practice, developing optimized solutions for the individual tasks of text mining does not suffice. Problems regarding the processing speed on large text corpora such as MEDLINE, of adequate data integration and representation also have to be addressed. There exist a couple of text mining solutions for a variety of specialized relation extraction tasks making use of a broad range of different approaches. However, the number of freely available, ready-to-use text mining systems is comparatively limited and the number of relation- and entity- types covered by existing systems does not meet the demands of biologists and medical practitioners trying to understand complex biological processes and multifactorial diseases.

This doctorate aimed at the development of a broad scale text mining approach covering a multitude of relation as well as entity types. The resulting text mining system EXCERBT was developed, optimized and evaluated in hindsight on practical usability rather than on optimized precision or recall values for a singular relation extraction task. These usability criteria include relation extraction accuracy and processing time but also data integration, coverage and extensibility aspects. EXCERBT is a dictionary based text mining system based on Semantic Role Labeling in combination with cooccurrence. The system covers a wide range of biomedical entity and relation types. It allows semantic queries for genes causing a certain phenotype or miRNAs inhibiting a certain gene. EXCERBT has been implemented as a component of the GeKnowME information integration system developed by Dr. Karamfilka Nenova. The extracted relations are presented in a subject-centric way and linked to their original ontological as well as textual resources. In addition to relation extraction, EXCERBT also comprises a new approach for automatically generating biomedical lexica linking terms to facts in literature by means of Semantic Role Labeling.

CONTENTS

1. **INTRODUCTION** 1
   1.1. From Data to Knowledge 1
   1.2. Evolutionary Roots of Human Mental Ontologies 2
   1.3. Systems Biology – the Science of Integrating Biological Data ... 3
   1.4. GeKnowME 4
   1.5. Literature Mining: Mapping Textual Data to Ontological Models ... 5
   1.6. Motivation 9
2. **TEXT MINING FOR LIFE SCIENCE** 11
   2.1. Why Text Mining 11
      2.1.1. The Flood of Publications 11
      2.1.2. Linking Text to Primary Databases and Ontologies 12
      2.1.3. Accuracy Augmentation By Superposing 'Omics' Data 13
   2.2. Peculiarities of Biomedical Literature 14
   2.3. Three Levels of Textual Analysis 16
   2.4. Evolutionary View on Human Grammar 19
   2.5. Key Steps in Literature Mining 21
      2.5.1. Information Retrieval 22
      2.5.2. Named Entity Recognition 22
      2.5.3. Relation Extraction 25
      2.5.4. System Integration 28
3. **RELATION EXTRACTION BASED ON SEMANTIC ROLE LABELING** ... 31
   3.1. Introduction to SRL 31
   3.2. Biomedical SRL systems 33
   3.3. SRL Based Relation Extraction 33
   3.4. SENNA: A Neural Network Based SRL Program 34
   3.5. Algorithm 34
   3.6. Evaluation of SRL processing times 35
   3.7. Evaluation of SRL based RE accuracy 36
4. **THE EXCERBT TM SYSTEM** 43
   4.1. Data Generation in EXCERBT 46
      4.1.1. Usecase View 46
      4.1.2. Logical View 47
      4.1.3. Developmental View 57
      4.1.4. Physical and Process View 61
   4.2. Data Representation in EXCERBT 64
      4.2.1. Usecase View 67
      4.2.2. Logical View 70
      4.2.3. Developmental View 71

	4.2.4. Physical and Process View	73
4.3.	**EXCERBT Graphical User Interface**	**75**
	4.3.1. Relation Search	76
	4.3.2. Network Search	77
	4.3.3. Definition Search	79
5.	***APPLICATIONS***	***81***
5.1.	Speeding up Knowledge Retrieval	81
5.2.	A Literature Based Model for Parkinsonism	83
5.3.	Coverage Analysis I: Substances Affecting Parkinsonism	87
5.4.	Coverage Analysis II: Diseases Caused by Borrelia	98
6.	***DISCUSSION***	***99***
6.1.	Accuracy Evaluation	99
6.2.	Literature Based Model Generation with EXCERBT	101
6.3.	Knowledge integration	102
6.4.	Summary	103
7.	**CONCLUSION**	**105**
List of Abbreviations		*109*
List of Figures		*111*
List of Tables		*115*
References		*117*
Appendix A		*127*
Appendix B		*155*
Publication Record		*157*

1. INTRODUCTION

"The monkey that had no realistic perception of the branch he was jumping for was soon a dead monkey - and did not belong to our ancestors"

G.G. Simpson 1963: *"Biology and the nature of science"*

1.1. From Data to Knowledge

The question, how a system (a human mind or, nowadays, a computer) can introduce a semantic structure ("meaning") into an amorphous, unstructured amount of data (the world of "phenomena" or "singular observations"), has a very old history in philosophy. For Plato (428/427 - 348/347 B.C.E.), an independent, immutable and eternal transcendent world of "concept objects" existed. This world of "general ideas" or "concepts" e.g. "justice", "red color", "power" or "equality" had, according to Plato, a "higher level" of existence than the inferior world of the human life filled only with concrete entities like singular persons, stones, flowers or other objects. Only by imperfect contacts of the human mind with this superior world, a conceptual, albeit error-prone understanding of the world of the ideas could be achieved. The mathematician, literature Nobel Prize laureate and philosopher Bertrand Russell (1872-1970) subsumed the voice of many critics of Plato in his book "The History of Western Philosophy": "*Plato's doctrine of ideas [forms] contains a number of obvious errors. But in spite of these it marks a very important advance in philosophy, since it is the first theory to emphasize the problem of universals, which, in varying forms, has persisted to the present day. Beginnings are apt to be crude, but their originality should not be overlooked on this account. Something remains of what Plato had to say, even after all necessary corrections have been made. The absolute minimum of what remains, even in the view of those most hostile to Plato, is this: that we cannot express ourselves in a language composed wholly of proper names, but must have also general words such as 'man', 'dog', 'cat'; or, if not these, then relational words such as 'similar', 'before', and so on. Such words are not meaningless noises, and it is difficult to see how they can have meaning if the world consists entirely of particular things, such as are designated by proper names.*" Indeed, such *universals* or *categories* are prerequisites for understanding and describing the world we perceive. By using universals, it is not any more necessary to remember all possible relations a concrete object can have. It is enough to know that a concrete object is a member of a certain category, e.g. the category "stone" or "human being", to know that some forms of interactions are possible for this object while others aren't. Without a shared common ontology of the world we live in, without a shared understanding of concepts like "equality", "larger than", "human", "death" or "child", communication between human beings would be impossible as well as any abstract, conceptual understanding of the world. Leo Obrst and Howard Liu (*Jack Par et al., 2002*) explained the necessity of an internal conceptual model or "ontology" by an example of an average person trying to understand a scientific publication in particle physics on interacting bosons. A person lacking a sound background on particle physics will not be able to decipher the meaning of the glyphs contained in the publication because an average person does not have the background knowledge, an internal ontological model of the concepts of that research field, which is essential for understanding and interpreting the presented data. For such a person, the publication will be an unstructured, meaningless agglomeration of words. This example also elucidates the connection between "data" and "knowledge": Only if an interpretation of the data (here: the agglomeration of words in a publication on bosons) can be achieved by the human reader ("the interpreter"), the reader will be able to gain knowledge by this publication (*Figure 1-1 A*). Interpretation (*Figure 1-1 B*), according to Obrst and Liu, is the mapping between notations (pure data, glyphs) and what those notations are intended to mean in a human-defined universe of discourse (the internal ontology of the world the interpreter has in mind). It shall be stressed here there that the equation of *Figure 1-1* does not only hold true for humans but for any data-interpreting system. Computer systems described in various science fiction novels and films being able to answer semantic queries like "give me all planets lying within a radius of 17.000 light years from Andromeda nebula" requires not only that the computer has an internal concept of what the Andromeda nebula is and where it is located, it also needs to have an ontology for the concepts "distance" and "planet". The difference between a human interpreter and a computer is, besides different "hardware infrastructure", the way by which this internal ontological knowledge was introduced into the system.

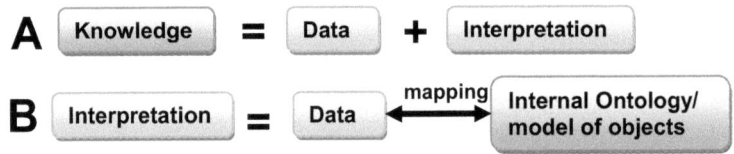

Figure 1-1: A: *Equation expressing the relationship between knowledge and data;* B: *Definition of "Interpretation" (derived from (Jack Par et al., 2002)*

1.2. Evolutionary Roots of Human Mental Ontologies

Today, an interdisciplinary approach settled in analytical philosophy as well as evolutionary theory tries to reveal the evolutionary background of the core semantic concepts and ontologies of human beings formed by millennia of natural selection in our minds (*Gerhard Vollmer, 2002; Gerhard Vollmer, 2003*). One sentence expressed by G. G. Simpson (1963) very well elucidates the core of this recently emerged evolutionary based theory of cognition: "The monkey that had no realistic perception of the branch he was jumping for was soon a dead monkey - and did not belong to our ancestors." In this view, the ultimate reason for the intersubjectivity of the core ontologies shared by all humans is their common evolutionary origin. Those ontologies also had to resemble the external, "real" world at least to an extent that vital interactions between the organism and its environment were possible (e.g. hunting, flight, social interactions and others). The evolutionary based theory of cognition also implies that we should not expect human mind mental concepts of the world to be perfect or exactly resemble reality. Human mind models of the world, as any other feature of human beings, are a product of evolutionary development overformed by environmental influences. They had to be good enough for the organism to pass its genetic information to the next generation, but they may be insufficient to comprehend every aspect of theoretical physics. Also here, George Box's famous statement holds true: "All models are wrong, some are useful" (*Box, 1979*).

1. INTRODUCTION

<u>Ontological Sources for Computational Data Interpretation in Biology</u>

A large and growing number of biological primary databases make a lot of the experimentally gathered information freely available for the public. Secondary databases containing curated or computationally processed data also contribute to the globally available biomedical data space. Some of the most important databases for biologist are, for example, Entrez Gene (*Maglott et al., 2005*), SwissProt (*Bairoch and Apweiler, 1999*), KEGG (*Ogata et al., 1999*), PubChem (*Shang and Tan, 2005*) or OMIM, but the list of publicly available databases is much longer. The 2007 version of the "Database of Databases" DoD2007 (*Babu et al., 2007*), an online resource listing many of the existing data repositories for biology, included 1082 databases. Data contained in those databases is well structured as the development of a performant and maintainable database requires the appropriate organization of data entries and associated information in the form of tables and the elimination of redundancies. A database may implicitly represent a semantic domain model, but performance or other considerations also play a role in the development of database schemas. The data organization within those databases is therefore semantically weak. Nevertheless, databases are a valuable ontological source assigning the entity names contained in them to an ontological category, e.g. "protein" or "tissue". In many cases, databases map concepts to multiple terms representing the same concept, so called synonyms, e.g. "PD", "Parkinson diseases" and "Parkinsonism". In addition to classical databases, a large amount of ontologies containing also a variety of relation types other than "is a" or "is synonym of" are available for the biological domain[1]. The ontological models of those resources often are of high complexity. A computer system designed to (phenotypically) "understand" the world or a part of it semantically must be able to map data given as input to one or several of these internal ontological models of the world.

1.3. Systems Biology – the Science of Integrating Biological Data

According to Denis Noble, living beings are multi-scalar systems with feedback and feed forward loops between multiple scale levels (*Noble, 2008*). Levels in biological systems are, for example, the level of molecular structure and interaction, of gene-regulatory networks, gene-phenotype relationships or regulatory interrelations between tissues or organ systems. Noble, rejecting the term of "emerging properties" in favor of "system properties", emphasized, that these properties were properties of the whole system, not of the singular components, and required integrative analysis and a systems approach (*Noble, 2008*).

Systems biology is an integrative science that aims at the global characterization of biological systems (*Teixeira et al., 2007*). It relies heavily on the gathering and computational processing of high throughput data, data integration and network generation.

Biomedical research in the late 1980ies and 90ies was focused on detailed examination of single genes or gene products by means of PCR, Immuno Assays and other experimental techniques which still represent the fundamental tool set of a molecular biology wet lab. These approaches are of crucial importance to molecular biology as they deliver fine-grained knowledge on the molecular level supported by detailed, empirical examination, e.g. on physical interactions between two proteins. At the beginning of the 21th century, the 'omics' era expanded the focus of research to the

---

[1] <u>www.obofoundry.org</u>

1. INTRODUCTION

examination of related biological entities to the system level. The list of 'omics' disciplines has been growing continuously over the last years: Genomics, the oldest 'omics' discipline, takes into account the entire human genome and involves not only studying the actions of single genes but also the interactions of multiple genes with each other and with the environment (*Newell et al., 2007*). Metabolomics examines the dynamics of metabolite concentration of a system (a cell or tissue) and the influence of those metabolites on gene regulation networks or phenotypic traits. Proteomics systematically analyzes proteins as well as their interactions, modifications, localization and functions (*Coiras et al., 2008*). The emergence of the new 'omics' fields was made possible by the availability of high throughput (HT) methods such as DNA micro-arrays or MALDI and had several technological as well as conceptual implications on Systems biology. A multitude of biological subdisciplines concertedly examine biological systems with a broad methodological arsenal in order to understand the function of living systems on all scales of complexity.

In Systems Biology, the "classical" component properties such as the sequences of genes or the structures of proteins as well as the "system properties" are gathered and interlinked with each other in order to generate qualitative and quantitative models of biological systems. The data generated by examining biological systems on a variety of system levels by a multitude of methods and subdiscipline is both a blessing and a curse. It is a blessing, as this data is the fundamental basis and prerequisite for modeling and understanding biological systems in their actual complexity. It is also a technical and conceptional curse. In technical hindsight, the sheer amount, heterogeneity and scattered distribution of data is a challenge. Computational solutions for collecting, managing and preparing the tremendous and constantly increasing heap of data emitted by a multitude of research groups in a multitude of formats are urgently required. Closely connected to this technical challenge is the conceptional problem how to connect those distributed data resources semantically.

1.4. GeKnowME

For Systems Biology, the semantic representation and integration of the scattered information is a prerequisite in order to reveal the interdependencies of different entity types, functional modules and cellular organization levels hidden in those independently maintained, heterogeneous resources.

A variety of Information Integration Systems (IIS) exist integrating data resources in the biomedical domain based on data warehousing and federated/peer data management systems. They differ from each other regarding the place where the data of the different resources is maintained, regarding the existence of a unifying integration schema and regarding the applied mapping approach between the integrated data sources. Nenova K. (2009) discussed in her doctoral thesis the pros and cons of these approaches for information integration in biology and introduced a novel, semantic and subject centric information integration approach. The implementation of this new approach, GeKnowME (Generic Knowledge Modeling Environment), is based on the TopicMap standard and allows the semantic integration of heterogeneous, locally maintained data resources in combination with a very flexible, semantic knowledge modeling and retrieval schema. A detailed description of the core principles of the system can be found in *Nenova K., 2009*. One core advantage of this new approach is that the data integration instance is not obliged to care for regular updates of the integrated resources nor does this instance has to create a universal data integration schema meeting the demands of any possible user. Rather, a client-system can individually select which of the integrated resources, topic- and association types are of interest and shall be considered in each query. GeKnowME is therefore a highly flexible system regarding the integration of new resources and knowledge domains, topics and relation types but also regarding the question which fraction of the huge knowledge space shall be presented to each client. An overwhelming amount of data can be as detrimental for knowledge generation in research as a lack of data. GeKnowME has shown in several use cases in the context of genetically caused human diseases that it can efficiently integrate heterogeneous data resources in a subject centric, semantic way suiting to the requirements of researchers coming from different fields of research.

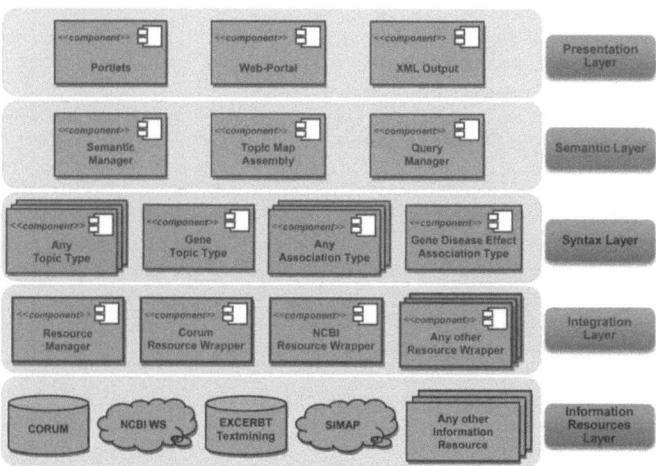

Figure 1-2: *GeKnowME five tier system architecture (Figure taken from Nenova K., 2009).*

1.5. Literature Mining: Mapping Textual Data to Ontological Models

The number of biological databases and the amount of data stored therein is enormous. Although these databases make much of the generated data publicly available, the largest fraction of theoretically available biomedical knowledge is described in a tremendous, exponentially increasing amount of scientific literature. Today, it is no longer possible for a researcher to keep up-to-date with all the relevant literature manually *(Jensen et al., 2006)*, and automated text mining (TM) approaches for speeding up the process of information retrieval (IR) and relation extraction (RE) from natural language texts are essential for annotators, experimentalists and medical practitioners. The key function of text mining for systems biology is to efficiently retrieve and structure the information hidden in millions of scientific publications in a way that it can be connected semantically to other knowledge resources. This is a technically challenging task, not only due to the amount of data, but also due to the amorphous, unstructured way knowledge is represented in natural language texts.

The data stored in biological databases usually is already structured in a non-redundant, subject-centric way. The core challenge in the semantic integration of those

1. INTRODUCTION

resources therefore is the creation of a flexible, semantically strong data integration and mapping procedure. In order to integrate knowledge contained in unstructured text, the semantic structure of a text has to be revealed at first by automated recognition of semantic concepts and their interrelations. In addition, a transformation of the document-centric information representation in freetext into a subject-centric representation schema has to be accomplished.

In order to support hypothesis generation and knowledge retrieval for systems biology, a text mining system should be able to address the following four core requirements:

- **Broad coverage of concept types**: Systems Biology tries to generate qualitative models for highly complex, dynamic and diverse systems. Text mining systems assisting in this task therefore have to cover a broad number of concept types such as proteins, phenotypes, tissues, metabolites, miRNAs and many more.

- **Broad coverage of relation types**: the diversity of supported concept types results in the requirement for a TM system to support a diversity of possible relation types. General relation types such as "regulation" or "activation" as well as highly domain specific relation types like "phosphorylation" are required to describe the biochemical processes taking place in living cells. Those semantic relations stated in text are recognized by applying more advanced natural language processing (NLP) methods. Merely cooccurrence-based approaches are too unspecific and tend to overload the user with too much irrelevant information, especially for hub terms.

- **Scalability**: the existing approaches for detecting instances of biomedical concepts and their interrelations in natural language text are highly demanding regarding processing times. This is a notable technical challenge, as the available amount of textual data, e.g. the MEDLINE database, is very large. Approaches for detecting entities and relations in text therefore have to be highly efficient if they are to be applied on the textual resources currently available for information retrieval in Systems Biology.

- **Subject-centric representation**: the TM system should support the transformation of the document-centric representation of information in natural language text to a subject-centric representation. This transformation is essential for network generation and data integration.

To my knowledge, currently no publicly available text mining system exists covering all those requirements. Many systems support only a very limited set of entity and relation types, usually genes. The main reason for this observation is probably the considerable amount of time necessary to collect and maintain comprehensive term lists and dictionaries for a multitude of biological entity classes and the necessity to specifically adapt the applied detection strategy for terms within free text for each integrated ontological class.

The Chilibot system (*Chen and Sharp, 2004*), for example, is a text mining system for the identification of relationships (activation, inhibition, regulation) between genes or between any submitted keywords. Chilibot can be imagined as a text mining system having a kind of "internal knowledge" or "internal ontology" for the entity type *gene*, as

1. INTRODUCTION

it comprises a gene term dictionary compiled from six different gene and protein databases. This knowledge allows semantically "open" queries, e.g. queries revealing the genetic context of an arbitrary submitted term. A list of instances of the concept *gene* standing in regulatory/activating/inhibiting relation to the submitted term, e.g., "t cell proliferation", can be returned. One downside of dictionary based ontological "knowledge" is, that it is never complete and, especially in the life science domain, difficult and time-consuming to keep up to date (there does not exist one universal and comprehensive ontology containing all names and synonyms of all known genes; the only possibility to get a good coverage on that concept is to integrate the names derived from several gene-related databases). Especially for Systems Biology, however, a broad coverage of many biological ontological concepts is required. Chilibot is not completely constrained to *genes*. In addition to the gene context search, the system offers the possibility to submit lists of arbitrary terms. Chilibot automatically extracts relations between these terms from the biomedical literature without assigning these terms an ontological category. This feature allows the submission and processing of terms belonging to other categories, e.g. *metabolites, phenotypes, tissues* and many more. However, this permissiveness regarding the submitted terms is coupled to a semantic weakness: Chilibot can search for connections between any element of the submitted term list, but it can not find relevant relations to entities of a certain category (other than *gene*) *not* contained in this list. It does not have an internal ontology for categories like *metabolite*, which is the prerequisite for processing semantically "open" queries like "give me all instances of category *metabolite*, being related to the submitted instance *smooth muscle* of category *tissue*". Semantically "open" queries determine only the category the returned results have to belong to, they do not determine the instances of this category. This information is to be delivered by the system. Chilibot supports this kind of queries only for the gene category. As it has no concept of metabolites or phenotypes, it can not "answer" semantically open questions for any *non-gene* context of a submitted term. For concepts other than *gene*, only semantically "closed" queries can be submitted to Chilibot in the form of a pair wise search for connected elements contained in submitted term lists. A semantically "closed" question is of the kind "find relations between term A and term B stated in literature". Here, the user already provides the system with a kind of hypothesis. He implicitly assumes that the members of the submitted list could be related, and the system tries to find evidences for this user provided hypothesis.

Semantically "open" queries are of particular relevance for the retrieval of "new" knowledge as the user does not have to submit relations he already knows or speculates about. The syntax of these "open" queries requires as input only the submitted term and some ontological constraints regarding the relation type and the type of entity the user is interested in. In analogy to the "open questioning" strategy in Rhetoric, "open" questions like "Which *persons* did you meet at your last trip to Sweden?" leave it to the questioned system to tell the story. Semantically closed questions in Rhetoric ("Did you meet Peter at your last trip to Sweden?") only allow an informationally poor, binary "yes" or "no" answer, optionally enriched with some additional information ("Yes, in Stockholm at the airport" or, in the case of text mining, a list of supporting sentences in case a relation was found). A prerequisite for any text mining system being able to cope with semantically open queries is, however, the existence of a core, system-inherent ontological knowledge on what a *gene*, a *phenotype* or a *tissue* actually *is* and what kind of relations they may support. Correspondingly, Chilibot is able to generate hypothesis automatically from free text but this feature is confined to *gene*-regulatory networks, because genes are the only objects mapped to a system-inherent ontological framework.

1. INTRODUCTION

For all other terms not mapped to such a semantic framework, Chilibot can search the literature for possible interconnections merely between the submitted terms. An expansion of the knowledge space by means of semantically open queries is not possible for any other category than the genes. A further limitation of Chilibot is the fact that it considers only the text content of the first 500 abstracts returned by PubMed for the submitted search terms. Much information stored in the whole MEDLINE corpus and other text resources is not considered.

Another well known text mining system in the life science domain is MEDIE (*Ohta et al., 2006*), a semantic search engine retrieving biomedical relations based on the whole MEDLINE corpus. MEDIE has the benefit of covering a tremendous amount of literature that was semantically structured by assigning different semantic roles (subject, verb, argument) to sentence parts. It also comprises a *gene-* and *disease* term dictionary. Although it is not possible to submit semantically open queries in the form presented beforehand, it is possible to retrieve sentences where subject, verb and argument parts contain the keywords provided by the user for those three semantic 'slots'. Thus, it is possible to retrieve all sentences where the subject part mentions a certain term, e.g. "p53", and the verb is 'activates'. The semantic framework used for sentence retrieval does not make use of a biomedical ontology, but genes and phenotypes mentioned within the returned sentences are highlighted with the help of the dictionary. The output is not subject-centric, but sentence-centric. It is therefore not possible to generate literature based networks based on real biomedical entity types like *genes*, *phenotypes* or *tissues* with MEDIE. It is also not possible to constrain the search results to sentences where the biological entities mentioned in the arguments part are, for example, of the type *metabolite* as this ontological category is not applied during sentence retrieval.

The Info-PubMed System[2], a text mining based browser for protein interactions developed also by the Tsujii group is an example of a text mining system covering many of those features necessary for literature based knowledge extraction for systems biology: it covers a sufficiently large text corpus (MEDLINE abstracts); it supports a subject-centric representation of relations in the form of related gene pairs each connected to at least one supporting "evidence sentence", a prerequisite for the construction of subject-centric networks; it supports the submission of semantically open queries for all genes interacting with a gene of interest; the supported relation type ("interaction") is semantically meaningful and directed. In addition, a semantically weak, cooccurrence based relation type is supported. The drawbacks of this system are, however, that only one single ontological category for biomedical entities (gene/protein) and two relation types (cooccurrence, interaction) are supported.

Polysearch (*Cheng et al., 2008*) currently appears to fulfill the highest fraction of requirements for a text mining system for Systems Biology: it covers the whole MEDLINE database and several additional text sources, several entity types like gene/proteins, metabolites, diseases and others and presents the results in a subject centric way. The drawbacks of the system are that it does only support one comparatively unspecific relation type "associated with" and has very long response time (a query for genes associated with the disease Parkinson: > 10 minuses, disease synonyms not considered). Due to the long response times, an interactive usage and fast information retrieval is therefore in many cases not feasible.

---

[2] www-tsujii.is.s.u-tokyo.ac.jp/info-pubmed/

1. INTRODUCTION

1.6. Motivation

Over the last years, a broad set of different machine-learning- or rule based approaches mainly for the detection of gene- or protein names in text as well as for the extraction of protein-protein interactions (RE) has been developed and compared to each other regarding sensitivity and specificity in competitions like the BioCreAtIvE task (*Hirschman et al., 2005*). Currently, those BioCreAtIvE-style competitions are important for the consolidation and improvement in biological information extraction (*Altman et al., 2008*). However, given the number of publications presenting new approaches in various biomedical text mining sub-disciplines, the amount of publicly available text mining systems integrating all the required tasks from entity recognition to relation extraction and additionally being able to cover large literature resources such as MEDLINE and represent the gathered facts subject-centrically in a user-friendly (web)-interface is still very limited (*Meystre et al., 2008*). As it seems, the move of biomedical text mining from research to practice has not fully been accomplished jet. None of the three described, well known TM system and, to my knowledge, no other publicly available system, meets all the four demands of System Biology to a TM system. Either the number of supported ontological categories, prerequisite for semantically powerful, "open" queries, is too small, the coverage of the available biomedical literature is insufficient or the results are not returned in a subject-centric representation and is therefore not suited for data integration.

In this thesis, a novel text mining system, EXCERBT (Extraction of classified entities and relations from biomedical text), is presented. The idea behind EXCERBT is the observation that the best NER or RE algorithm is in practice of limited value if it does not scale to text corpora being as big as MEDLINE and that the confinement of existing TM solutions to only one or two relation types and only a few ontological categories of biomedical entities is not sufficient to address complex biological questions like the genesis of multifactorial disorders or the detection of potential drug candidates for their treatment. In order to automatically extract knowledge from biomedical literature for systems biology, a multitude of ontological entity classes has to be integrated in a text mining system to constitute a kind of system-immanent, ontological basic knowledge. EXCERBT aims at providing the user with an intuitive interface for submitting "open" semantic queries on a wide set of relation- and entity types being of relevance for practical, biomedical research.

An important design principle of EXCERBT is its extensibility regarding text sources, entity types and relation types and a subject centric way of representing the extracted relations. The modularity of the system architecture ensures the possibility to exchange the underlying algorithms for Named Entity Recognition or Relation Extraction without any alteration to the database schema or the core system architecture.

In addition, EXCERBT is capable of automatically generating a lexicon from any sufficiently large text corpus such as MEDLINE that can be used for automated annotation or manual lookup of any term relevant in the biomedical context.

1. INTRODUCTION

2. TEXT MINING FOR LIFE SCIENCE

> *"**Text mining** is the application of techniques from machine learning, natural language processing (NLP), information extraction and statistical/mathematical approaches to automated extraction of useful knowledge from text [Krallinger M. et al., 2005]."*
>
> Jeyakumar Natarajan et al., 2007, citation retrieved by the definition search module of the EXCERBT text mining system for the term "text mining".

2.1. Why Text Mining

No current text mining tool reaches the accuracy and comprehensiveness of textual understanding of a human reader. The power of text mining lies in the possibility for automated, machine based processing of large text corpora to preprocess and structure the literature and help human readers extract relevant knowledge from text more efficiently. Increasing the efficiency regarding working time and costs spent on gathering relevant information from literature is therefore the major drive for text mining, although there exist additional beneficial aspects that will be illustrated in this chapter.

2.1.1. THE FLOOD OF PUBLICATIONS

The biomedical literature is growing at a exponential pace *(Hunter and Cohen, 2006)*. In 2007, more than 713.000 entries were added to MEDLINE (~ 2.000 per day). *Figure 2-1* depicts the numbers of new MEDLINE citations published per year from 1960 to 2008.

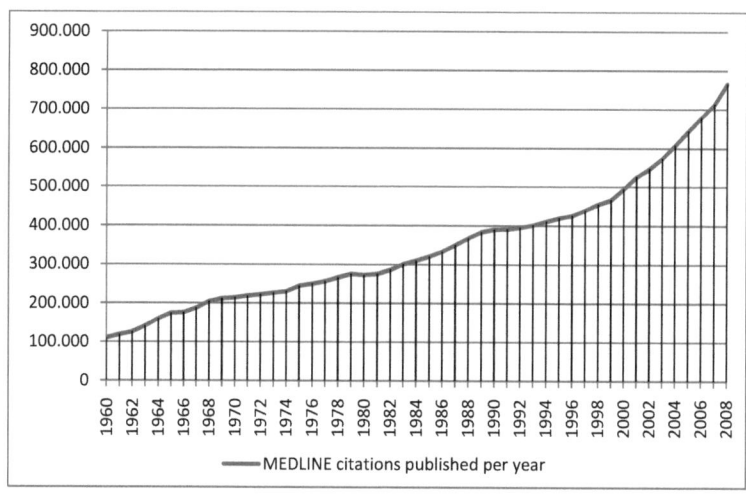

Figure 2-1: Growth of MEDLINE: Number of new MEDLINE citations published per year (1960 - 2008)

2. TEXT MINING FOR LIFE SCIENCE

Meanwhile, keeping up with the flood of published papers manually is impossible for most fields of research. The data flood problem is tightened by the fact that in many research areas, the knowledge published in one field of study is not sufficient for a comprehensive understanding of the relevant processes. Scientists searching for dietary components relevant for the development of a phenotypic trait also need information on environmental or genetic factors which may influence the development of the examined trait in order to correctly interpret their results and integrate them into existing models for the genesis of the phenotype. For medicinal practitioners, there is the need to integrate information on many different subdisciplines to find possible causes for a disease and to prohibit interfering effects of prescribed pharmaceuticals. For the development of myopia, for example, genetic factors are known to have a substantial impact on the development of the disease *(Goss and Jackson, 1996; Zhang et al., 2007; Zhao et al., 2001; Chiou, 2001)*, but also environmental factors, especially the amount of time spent on reading and other near work *(Goss et al., 1996; Ip et al., 2008; Peckham et al., 1977)*, education *(Angle and Wissmann, 1978; Richler and Bear, 1980)*, substances such as sulfonamides *(Bovino and Marcus, 1982)*, nicotine antagonists *(Markgraf and Langer, 1975)* and some pesticides *(Tokoro et al., 1976)* play a role in disease development. Clearly, it is not possible to manually read all the papers of disciplines as diverse as toxicology, molecular genetics, linkage analysis, nutrition science, developmental biology, pharmacy and surgery which all contribute to the knowledge that is theoretically available on myopia. In addition, not only the number of journals and papers increases every year, the number of biomedical disciplines also increases with the growing knowledge on bio-molecular networks (the detection of the impact of miRNAs on gene regulation lies back only a couple of years from now *(Ambros, 2008)* but is now subject of wide scientific attention). While the sparse knowledge available for an uncharacterized disease may be obtained by entering the disease name to the PubMed search interface, this strategy is not possible for myopia returning almost 13.000 abstracts. The problem here is that the key word myopia is too loose while entering additional key words like "near work" requires the user to already know what he is looking for. Text Mining methods can help to group abstracts dealing with similar subjects (document clustering) and to provide means to search text semantically for genes, metabolites and other factors having an influence on myopia which is not possible by the Boolean search operators "AND" and "OR" alone. Given the loss of relevant information due to the limited time a human can spend on literature search, those text mining tools need not be perfect to significantly speed up the process of information retrieval and extraction.

2.1.2. LINKING TEXT TO PRIMARY DATABASES AND ONTOLOGIES

The availability of a multitude of ontologies of different research fields is a convenient peculiarity of text mining in the biomedical domain. Relations extracted from literature can easily be integrated into complex, hierarchical semantic frameworks provided by the integrated ontologies. In addition, a lot of primary databases like Entrez Gene *(Maglott et al., 2005)*, KEGG *(Ogata et al., 1999)* or SwissProt *(Bairoch et al., 1999)* exist containing experimentally verified and manually curated information on genes, metabolites and phenotypes and on the relations interconnecting them. The Entrez Gene database, for example, stores gene-specific information on sequenced genomes of a selected set of organisms *(Maglott et al., 2005)*. The unique and stable Entrez Gene identifiers are linked to several other NCBI resources covering map location, gene products and expression data, phenotypes (OMIM), homologs, protein domains as well as information contained in non-NCBI databases and the GO ontology *(Ashburner et al., 2000)*. Links are introduced to Entrez Gene by applying automated analysis methods and by manual inspection of the corresponding literature. The relations stored in Entrez Gene can therefore be considered as a comparatively reliable informational backbone of biological knowledge but they certainly do not represent all the relations which are theoretically available by a comprehensive evaluation of all the published literature. By identifying gene- and metabolite names in texts (NER) and by extracting the relations between those entities proclaimed by the authors (RE), text mining can help to extend this knowledge backbone to a multitude of additional relations and entities. TM systems can also help to interlink completely independent databases for genes, metabolites or miRNAs by connecting those entities if they are mentioned together within one sentence or document or if a semantic relation between those entities was detected. As scientific publications are the canonical way in which new experimental results are presented to the public in almost all biomedical subdisciplines, text mining approaches are obvious candidates for the task connecting the steadily increasing amount of data generated by researchers from different scientific areas.

2.1.3. ACCURRACY AUGMENTATION BY SUPERPOSING 'OMICS' DATA

„Literaturomics" is currently (January 27th 2009) a term "in statu nascendi": a search for this term in Google returns only four independent hits. The term is listed, for example, in the "alphabetical list of omes and omics" of Omics.org[3]. According to a conclusion by analogy, "Literaturomics" is the automated extraction of knowledge from the literature considering large text corpora such as MEDLINE. It is the 'omics' approach to literature mining.

By the nature of the approach it is not possible to extract "new" information by literature mining in the strict sense of the word although this criterion has often been considered as a necessary as well as characteristic feature of a text mining system. The relations directly connecting two entities described in a scientific publication have actually been generated by various forms of empirical experimentation. TM approaches detect those described relations a second time, not within a cell, but within a piece of text. The detection of indirect relations, again, does not extract "new information" due to formal logic considerations: if one paper conclusively describes that "A" regulates "B" and a second paper gives reasonable evidence that "B" regulates "C", the conclusion that "A" has an influence on "C" is, according to logics, not "new", as this information is implicitly contained in the two observations (here functioning as premises) provided that the relation type is transitive. Actually, the "detected" indirect relation is a tautology given both premises. From a practical point of view, however, relations which are implicitly contained in literature but which are not mentally present to the researchers because those are overwhelmed by the amount of literature, are factually not existent (for mankind, for research). Finding "new" information in literaturomics actually means extracting all relevant relations efficiently and presenting it in a way that a human reader can easily detect the direct as well as the indirect links. In this sense, literaturomics can – as other 'omics' disciplines have always done, really generate "new" knowledge.

The data generated by text mining usually is of low accuracy compared to data generated by manual literature inspection, but the problem of reduced accuracy is common to many high throughput technologies: the genes with an increased expression profile detected by a micro array experiment are not all necessarily affected by the

---

[3] Omics.org: http://omics.org/index.php

environmental condition examined. However, by a super-positioning of multiple knowledge networks extracted by several independent high throughput technologies of different 'omics' fields, the accuracy of a detected relation can be raised. A relation is more trustworthy if it has independently been detected by several different methods. Network-superposition can help to increase the reliability of the results obtained from two data sources of low accuracy. For example, an expression profile indicating a regulatory relation between an applied protein "A" and a potential target gene "B" can be considered as more reliable if a text mining method was able to extract indirect relations suggesting that " A" acts on gene "C" and "C" has an impact on gene "B".

As indicated in the previous chapter, a superposition of text mining results with highly reliable curated data is also a possible option. Here, the focus lies not in increasing accuracy but in reducing the amount of trivial and commonly known relations (*Jensen et al., 2006*) which can make up a significant fraction of knowledge extracted from literature.

2.2. Peculiarities of Biomedical Literature

Although the principal challenges associated with automatically extracting knowledge from natural language texts are the same for newspaper text as for biomedical publications, there exist some domain specific peculiarities of the biomedical sublanguage. For example, the distribution of POS tags in the biomedical literature slightly differs from that observed in general English newspaper texts and the fraction of technical terms is higher (*Krallinger et al., 2008*).

Many authors of scientific publication are not native English speakers. Therefore, the variability of their texts regarding writing style, including sentence length and word usage (*Figure 2-2*), is higher than that of native English speakers (*Netzel et al., 2003; Grishman, 2001*).

2. TEXT MINING FOR LIFE SCIENCE

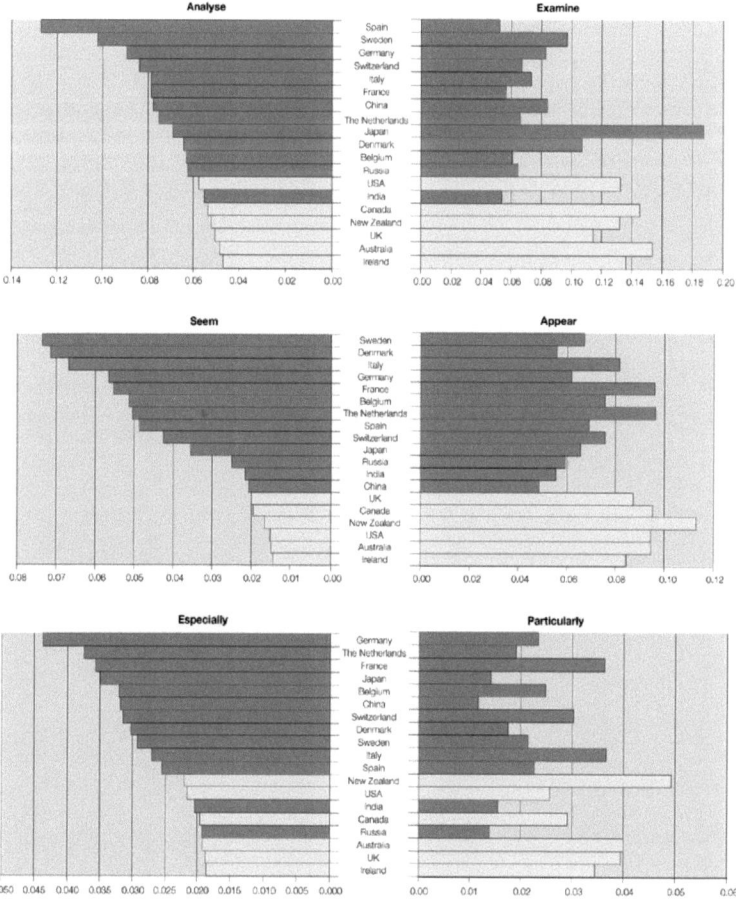

Figure 2-2: Word usage per abstract for 13 countries. Dark blue bars: countries in which English is not the main language. Light blue bars: 6 countries in which English is the main language. The image lists two words not generally used in English-speaking countries (left side) and their equivalent words commonly used by native English speakers (right side) - (Netzel et al., 2003).

Many TM applications such as sentence splitters, syntactical parsers or POS taggers used in the general as well as biomedical domain have been developed and trained on newspaper texts. A frequently used corpus is the Penn Treebank corpus (*Marcus et al., 1994*). Due to the depicted deviations of the scientific sublanguage from newspaper text, a gain in accuracy can be expected by training TM algorithm on a biomedical text corpus like GENIA (*Kim et al., 2003*). However, the size of the available biomedical text corpora is often remarkably smaller than that of the general English domain and there may not exist a corpus for every subtask. The construction of such a sublanguage specific corpus is a time demanding work and updating it from time to time may be necessary due to the continuous evolution of the sublanguage (*Krallinger 2008*). Many adaptations of TM algorithms to the sublanguage exist, e.g. MedPost (*Smith et al., 2004*), dTagger (*Divita et al., 2006*) for POS tagging, Enju (*Miyao and Tsujii, 2005*) for syntactical parsing and BIOSMILE (*Tsai et al., 2007*) for Semantic Role Labeling. However, the gain in accuracy has to be traded off against the time for corpus construction and adaptation of the TM tool in every individual case.

As mentioned in chapter 2.1.2, a further peculiarity of mining biomedical texts is the availability of a large number of ontologies. Early in the development of biomedical research the diversity of methods, model organisms and biological processes examined on a molecular as well as macroscopic scale triggered the development of ontologies and controlled vocabularies to link those research fields with each other. The basic components of an ontology are terms or symbols (usually words) that represent concepts and the links or relationships between these terms (*Baldock and Burger, 2005*). Ontologies which can be interpreted by humans as well as machines are required to ensure that the generated data can conceptually be integrated in a coherent knowledge model. Gene Ontology (*Ashburner et al., 2000*) focuses on biomolecular functions, processes and cellular components and is probably the most prominent example. A list of more than 70 ontologies (January 2009) covering a multitude of biologic domains can be retrieved from the web page of the Open Biological Ontologies (OBO) consortium[4]. The comparatively highly developed standard of ontologies in the biological domain facilitates the integration and interpretation of data extracted from the literature provided that a linking of text and ontological entry is possible.

2.3. Three Levels of Textual Analysis

The task of automatically exploiting and managing the knowledge hidden in text involves several independent steps, e.g. finding the documents of relevance for a given subject (information retrieval (IR) e.g. by means of document clustering), detecting biomedical terms and entities within the retrieved texts (NER, optionally comprising also disambiguation and acronym resolution) as well as detecting the semantic relations connecting those entities (RE). Finally, the gathered information has to be integrated and presented in a user friendly way. Text mining systems usually consider several different aspects or "layers" of human natural language (*Figure 2-3*).

---

[4] The OBO Foundry: www.obofoundry.org

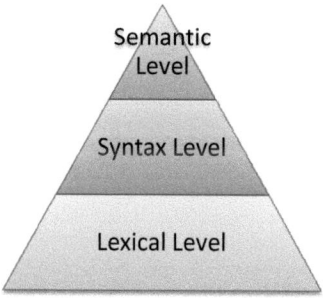

Figure 2-3: The three main levels of natural language text

The Lexical Level

At the bottom level of the pyramid, the lexical level, are the simple words, also called "lexemes". A word (except in the case of ambiguity) stands for a distinct concept and relates to one or more morphemes. For example, the verb "extract" corresponds to its morphemes "extracted" or "extracting". For the NER task, the correct word boundaries have to be determined in the tokenization step and all the different morphemes caused by variations in tense, singular and plural forms have to be linked to the underlying lexeme. This linking is usually accomplished by applying the PorterStemmer algorithm (*Ananiadou and McNaught, 2006*). The NER task in many TM systems deals largely, but not exclusively, with the lexical level of language.

The Syntax Level

The "grammar" or "syntax" of a language consists of a set of rules defining the correct usage and positioning of words of different lexical categories like nouns, verbs, adjectives or adverbs in a phrase or sentence. The first step of syntactic analysis of a sentence is usually the categorization of words into different lexical categories like verb, adjective, noun or adverb, the so called "part of speech (POS) tagging". Usually, hidden Markov Models trained on corpora manually labeled with POS tags come into operation here.

The Semantic Level

The semantic information expressed within a sentence actually makes up what text mining is all about. The semantic level of a text contains the meaning and the semantic relations between entities an author wants to tell his readers. Relations between concepts are linguistically mediated through verbal expressions (including nominal or adjectival forms) which can semantically be subsumed to one corresponding argument frame (*Ananiadou et al., 2006*). For example, the three syntactical variants "protein A activates B", "activation of B by protein A" and "B-activating A protein" on the semantic level all represent the same relation *activation (protein A, protein B)*. In order to extract the semantics from a sentence, it is necessary at first to know at what position in the text a certain semantic concept, e.g. a certain protein or phenotype, is mentioned (NER). In the second step, the existence and type of semantic relations between those entities can be extracted (RE).

<u>Shortcomings of the Three Level Model:</u>

Although the presented three level model of text is commonly used to depict the main levels of textual analysis, the differentiation between the lexical and syntactical level is not as simple as suggested beforehand. The rules how to construct a sentence correctly and the rules for creating morphological variants of words can in practice not be strictly separated. Both tasks are often subsumed by linguists under the term "morphosyntax". The function of grammar is to express, support and specify relations between entities. However, this function can also be fulfilled by some words belonging to the lexical level. The following examples are all derived from *Berger, 2008* in order to explain the complex interrelation between grammar and semantics: In English, German or French, for example, expressing the tense of an action is done by grammatical rules defining the morphological form of the relevant verb. Additional words/lexemes like "yesterday" are not necessary to express that the sentence "he missed the bus" happened in the past. In this case, "yesterday" has a purely lexical function. In other languages like Chinese, it is not possible to denote the time or the person by verb inflection. Here, words like "yesterday" are mandatory in order to indicate the tense. In Chinese, therefore, "yesterday" has a kind of "grammatical" function. The relation expressed in the English sentence "If Sabine comes I will not come." is expressed in Turkish by the sentence "Sabine gelirse, bin gelmem". The conditional word "if" is not necessary in the Turkish sentence as this condition is expressed by grammar, namely the word endings which are attached to the word stem and indicate the condition. To sum it up, the distinction of three distinct textual levels, although commonly used, is only a rough simplification of reality. In fact, some languages, like Turkish or Finnish, mainly use grammar, while others, like English or Chinese, are strongly based on the lexical level in order to express and specify semantic relations between entities. Most languages are somewhere in-between. A TM approach working well on English texts might therefore fail when applied on a different language due to different relevance of syntactical rules for expressing semantics. Today, most linguists therefore draw a completely different border. They do not consider grammatical rules on the one hand and the words of the lexical level on the other hand but distinguish between "function words" and "content words". "Function words", like "he" or "she", are highly general and therefore considered as fulfilling a "grammatical function" while nouns, especially proper nouns, are considered as being not generic but to represent only a certain concept. The distinction is, however, not easy to draw either.

While a human reader who is not skilled in linguistics is usually not able to explain the formal grammar rules that define the syntactic structure of a sentence, he usually has no difficulties in understanding the meaning and semantic relations expressed within a piece of literature. Unconsciously, a human reader detects the appropriate word boundaries and links the words to the corresponding semantic concept. For a human, it is no problem to intuitively know if the term "bank" in a text corresponds to a banking institution or an earth dam as he is aware of the context. Although there exist a huge and theoretically infinite number of ways to state that A activates B in a syntactically correct way, a human will usually have no difficulties to detect the semantic roles of terms in a sentence correctly. For a computer, the correct identification of concepts within texts, context dependent term disambiguation, and the correct identification of the semantic relations between the concepts are anything but trivial. For the automated, computer-based extraction of semantic concepts and relations from text, a text mining system usually has to consider the information contained in all or at least most of the pyramid levels. For each level, several processing steps have to be applied which are all possible sources of error. Even the step of splitting text to sentences at the beginning of the analysis can produce errors, often due to punctuation errors introduced by the authors or the publisher. The complexity of the task and the multitude of interdependent subtask are severe obstacles in the development of text mining systems being able to reliably and comprehensively extract knowledge from natural language texts.

2.4. Evolutionary View on Human Grammar

Although the aim of this work is of technical nature, namely to find technically adequate means to automatically extract semantic relations from biomedical texts on a large scale basis, an evolutionary view on language helps to understand the interrelation of the lexical, syntactical and semantic level of human language. Therefore, a short glimpse on some biological aspects of human language shall be given here.

The case of the Pax6 gene is a highly interesting subject for evolutionary biologists. Pax6 is a highly conserved transcription factor among vertebrates and is important in various developmental processes in the central nervous system *(Osumi et al., 2008)*. Pax6 is a master gene in eye development in both vertebrates and Drosophila *(Aruga et al., 2007)*. This is remarkable, as the "construction plan" of a vertebrate eye is completely different from that of an insect eye composed of dozens of ommatidia. This example stands for the phenomenon that in biology recycling is preferred to reinvention. It is much easier (in the sense of occurring with higher probability) that an adaptation to environmental changes or altered anatomical requirements is reached by gradually changing existing structures due to means of natural selection over several generations than by the creation of completely new proteins or anatomical traits.

For human language, a similar case appears to exist regarding the Foxp2 protein. Like in the case of Pax6, no single gene exists being solely responsible for such a complex organ like the eye or such a complex anatomical and behavioral phenomenon like human language. However, Foxp2, like Pax6, is a highly conserved protein detected in reptiles as well as man *(Scharff and Haesler, 2005)*. In all singing birds which have to learn their species- or region specific dialect of singing, this gene is highly expressed specifically in that period of time when fledglings learn to sing. The gene is expressed in a region of the bird brain which anatomically resembles the Nucleus caudatus in humans – a region which is known to be essential for the creation of grammatically correct sentences *(Haesler et al., 2007; Haesler, 2007)*. Humans with mutations in this 'language gene' show severe speech and language disorders *(Takahashi, 2006; Ferland et al., 2003) (Enard et al., 2002)*, especially regarding the ability to recognize and apply basic grammatical patterns *(Gopnik, 1999)* like plural generation but also show reduced motor control of mouth and face musculature *(Berger, 2008)*. The defects in grammatical understanding and power of facial expression were not accompanied with reduced intellectual capacities or defects in the facial musculature. Mice with a disruption of one Foxp2 copy showed a significant alteration in ultrasonic vocalization while the disruption of both copies caused severe motor impairment and complete absence of ultrasonic vocalizations *(Shu et al., 2005)*. This connection of motor control and impaired language abilities have led to the speculation that the neural processing of complex human grammar rules can evolutionary be lead back to the control of mimics and facial expression *(Ackermann, 2008)*, a complex task of crucial role for the fitness of an ape living in large social communities. Foxp2 is also subject of intensive studies of Paleogenetics regarding the question when such human-specific traits as a complex, symbolic language, came into existence *(Coop et al., 2008; Krause et al., 2007)*.

Several observations support the view that great apes, like humans, are able to use symbolic codes comprising of 100 to 300 symbols to communicate (Berger, 2008). Chimpanzees tought to use symbolic codes on a keyboard are able to generate sequences of two to four words and are able to understand the syntax of complex sentences like "pick up the ball which is inside the corn flakes box". Even a creative and metaphorical usage of symbols by apes has been observed, e.g. "straw" in order to refer to a sparkler. Due to anatomical constraints (control of larynx and mouth) the abilities of apes to apply symbolic language in the form of speech is, however, very limited (Enard et al., 2002). Although the difference of human and ape symbolic language appears to be more of quantitative than of qualitative nature, the complexity and size of the human language code as well as the elaborateness of the grammatical rules are unique to human beings and the question of the evolutionary benefit of such a complex phenomenon arises.

One common thesis is that a complex language was necessary in human development in order to communicate hunting strategies or the handling and manufacturing of a growing number of tools. On the lexical level, this explanation appears very sound. A single lexeme for 'predator' may have been sufficient under ancient environmental conditions where the fight-or-flight reaction of the human ancestor was the same irrespective of the type of the predator. From that point of time on where human ancestors developed the possibility to react specifically to a certain threat, e.g. a snake or a lion, a more elaborated lexicon had to be developed in the form of distinct mental concepts but also regarding the symbolic code used to communicate the threat to fellow members of the social group. The lexical space of current English is huge and resembles the complexity of human life today: The second edition of the Oxford English Dictionary (OED2) contains more than 600.000 definitions, several 10.000 technical or sublanguage typical terms not considered.

The large diversity of grammar rules found in different languages, however, cannot be explained thus easily. At first, grammar is often not necessary in order to communicate semantic content. Given the appropriate context, the call "lion" will be much more efficient in communicating the semantics, in this case a warning, than the grammatically correct version "I have just recognized a lion down the hill and assume he could be a threat to our community". Interjections like "Ah!", "Boah!" or "Iii!" communicate a lot of semantic information but lack any grammatical structure. If a human intends to learn a trade like pottery or weaving or wants to build up a furniture from a construction kit, learning by observing and copying others or looking at a constructional drawing will in most cases be much more efficient than reading a grammatically elaborate but purely text-based handbook on pottery or furniture assembly. In addition, the grammar of many languages is unnecessarily complex. English, like Turkish or Japan does only know one grammatical sex while German and French makes use of three different grammatical sexes which are attributed more or less arbitrarily ("der Baum", "die Eiche", "das Holz"). In English, the word order in subordinate clauses is the same as in the main clause: "Some people say that it will rain tomorrow" does not differ from "It will rain tomorrow" regarding word order. In German, "Manche Leute sagen, dass es morgen regnen wird" differs from "Morgen wird es regnen", one out of many aspects making it difficult for non-German speakers to learn this language (Berger, 2008). Using sentences following abstract grammar rules often implies extending the length of a sentence without adding any additional meaning. For example, the sentence "it rains" formally contains a subject but the subject "it" is not associated to any semantically meaningful concept. To sum it up, almost any highly complex relation can be expressed in a grammatically simple way, e.g. in the form of a sequence of short main clauses. At the same time it is possible to express a small set of simple semantic relations in a grammatically correct but overwhelmingly complicated way so that it is almost impossible to understand the meaning. In fact, several postmodern authors appear to use the grammatical possibilities of language more for the purpose of hiding than revealing the semantic content of their argumentation *(Sokal et al., 1999)*. For all this reasons it appears questionable if the correct communication of semantics was the only evolutionary reason for the development of grammar. The expression and assertion of social hierarchies as well as the membership to a distinct social group or stratum probably also have played significant roles *(Berger, 2008)*. In many cases, usage of an elaborated and complex grammar seems to fulfill an evolutionary function similar to that of a peacock's fan: By making long, syntactically complex sentences, authors or speakers show intellectual and sexual fitness to potential competitors, friends and mates *(Berger, 2008)*. The longer and syntactically complex a sentence is, the higher are the mental capabilities required to remember the content of all the main- and conditional clauses and to finish the sentence in a grammatically correct way.

Although it can be assumed that the intention to communicate semantically meaningful relations between biomedical entities is the main motivation behind the submission of scientific publications, those merely social aspects should not be neglected. It has been discussed if an annotation of entities and relations by the authors or publishers could lead the way to facilitate text mining applications in the biological domain (Gerstein *et al.*, 2007; Hahn *et al.*, 2007). It appears questionable if the benefits of author-sided annotation for TM will be able to motivate authors to do the tedious work of semantically annotating their abstracts, not to speak of the rest of their articles. In many cases, it would already be a tremendous help for existing TM approaches if authors would restrain themselves to the usage of grammatically simple main clauses and use as few propositions as possible. However, due to the social function of human language and grammar usage, already this hope is probably illusory. For reasons explained beforehand, a simplification of publication style on the author's side appears out of scope and it remains a challenge for the developers of TM systems to cope with the complexity of human language.

2.5. Key Steps in Literature Mining

Figure 2-5 shows the core steps usually applied in literature mining (IR, NER and RE). In addition, the step "system integration" is mentioned, as the integration of a multitude of heterogeneous data structures required for NER and RE and the integration of the generated positional data is mandatory to make the data accessible to the public in a convenient way.

Figure 2-4: Key steps in literature mining

2. TEXT MINING FOR LIFE SCIENCE

2.5.1. INFORMATION RETRIEVAL

According to the definition of (Nadkarni, 2002), Information retrieval (IR) is the field of computer science that deals with the processing of documents containing free text, so that they can be rapidly retrieved based on keywords specified in a user's query. PubMed – the most widely used document retrieval engine in biology – provides the well known Boolean keyword search model as well as a vector based document classification schema for suggesting "Related Articles". In addition to those two document retrieval approaches offered by NCBI, additional information retrieval and document clustering approaches have been developed which offer further search possibilities.

Probably the most well known MEDLINE abstract retrieval system besides PubMed is GOPubmed (*Doms and Schroeder, 2005*). GOPubmed forwards a conventional PubMed-style query to PubMed and detects the position of GO terms within the returned set of abstracts. The abstracts are grouped according to the GO terms mentioned in them and integrated into the GO tree. The user has the possibility to selectively consider only those abstract containing his search terms as well as, for example, a certain molecular process represented as a separate branch in the GO tree. Information retrieval is sometimes used as a filter for some TM systems in order to consider only those abstracts matching certain conditions before applying the time demanding NER and RE steps. The Texpresso system, for example (*Muller et al., 2004*) comes in various sub-systems based on different text corpora dealing only with one distinct topic such as C. elegans, Arabidopsis, D. melanogaster, neuroscience or Alzheimer's disease. Information retrieval and document clustering systems may therefore, like GOPubmed, function as independent systems but they may also function as preprocessing and filtering procedures in text mining systems developed for relation extraction.

2.5.2. NAMED ENTITY RECOGNITION

Named entity recognition (NER) is the task of identifying substrings in a document that correspond to particular entities (*Cohen and Minkov, 2006*). NER is the first step in relation extraction: in order to extract relations between entities, the involved entities have to be identified in the text. Two types of NER can be distinguished, although a mixture of both approaches is possible: rule or machine-learning based entity recognition approaches search for/learn textual patterns which are characteristic for a given type of entity and label matching words with the corresponding biomedical type. For example, words ending on 'ases' can be assumed as belonging to the family of enzymes while 'osis' or 'elitis' often terminate disease terms. Dictionary-based approaches, on the other hand, use lists of names compiled from primary databases and ontologies (for gene names e.g. Entrez Gene, for phenotype names OMIM or SNOMED) and search for these names in the text. The second approach has the advantage that the detected entities are automatically linked to the database or ontology used to compile the name list but the detected names are limited strictly to the terms contained in the compiled list. Rule- or machine-learning based methods have the advantage of general applicability as they detect patterns which will in many cases match also to newly introduced gene and disease names hitherto not contained in any database or lexicon. However, linking the detected entities directly to the original identifiers in the database is not possible for entity recognition algorithms that are not dictionary based. In order to have the best of both worlds, dictionary-based NER approaches are sometimes combined with hand-crafted rules or statistical methods in order to improve the accuracy of the entity recognition process (*Chun et al., 2006*).

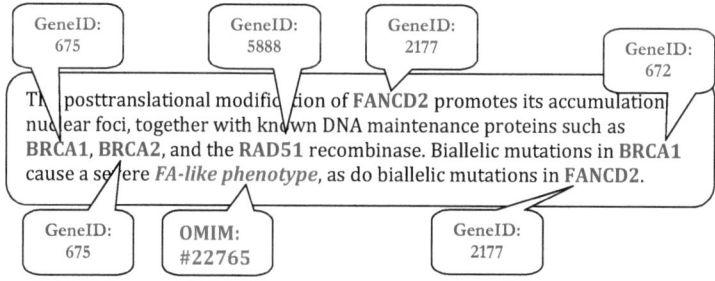

Figure 2-5: Applying NER on a piece of biomedical text. Words resembling genes (blue) and phenotypes (red) have been detected, labeled and linked to the identifiers of Entrez Gene and OMIM.

Technical Challenges

Although appearing trivial at first glance, NER is a highly complex task. The correct detection of the starting and ending point of a word is already a challenge: A dictionary based approach using the Entrez Genes database as the source of gene names probably will be able to categorize only the term "RAD51" correctly as gene and link it to Gene ID 5888 (organism=human), while a human reader would probably consider both words "RAD51 recombinase" as word representing this gene or gene product. This problem is of major relevance if very complex names consisting of several words, so called "compound names", have to be detected as it is often the case for metabolite names. For example, every mentioning of the term "glucose-6-phosphate" is recognized, using only dictionary lookup, as three independent substances: "glucose", "phosphate" and "glucose-6-phosphate". The question, whether tokenization should take effect on dashes, hyphens and brackets, has also to be decided. For example, if tokens are split after the occurrence of blanks but not after the occurrence of hyphens, the two words "glucose-6 phosphate" and "glucose-6-phosphate" are recognized by the text mining system as completely different words. This is a benefit if both expressions really refer to different concepts, but it is an obstacle to NER if the use of a hyphen in place of a blank and vice versa merely results from spelling variants used by different authors or from spelling errors.

A related problem concerning the correct boundaries of a word is the problem of fuzzy names commonly used to describe phenotypic traits. The expression "the glucose level increased", "an increased glucose level", "a substantially increased glucose level" and "an increased level of glucose" all resemble the same phenotypic property, but the order of words is different. The existence of word insertions ("substantially") in addition to the variability in word order renders a search strategy based on simple dictionary based term matching inappropriate, at least for detecting phenotypes and descriptive names.

An additional challenge for NER is the multitude of morphemes resembling the same entity. Authors may use the plural form "steroids" as well as the singular "steroid" to refer to the same concept. One possible solution is the extension of the used lexicon. Due to the size of most databases used as terminological resources for text mining, it is not feasible to do this extension by hand. Automatically adding missing plural or singular forms is in itself a complex task and not free of errors. Another way to solve the problem of morphological variability of names is stemming. Stemming reduces all morphologic variants to the word stem. However, this reduction can also introduce errors, especially regarding gene names and acronyms ending with "s". An "s" at the end of a gene name or acronym, contrary to most metabolite or phenotype names, does not indicate a plural form. By removing the terminal s in the process of stemming, different genes could wrongly be mapped to the same word stem and cannot be distinguished any more by the depicted stemming-based NER approach.

An additional obstacle is the fact that most primary databases for genes, metabolites and other entity types have not been constructed for text mining purposes and are often not confined to solely one central type of entity. KEGG compound, for example, contains many names which are actually no metabolite but enzyme or protein names (e.g. "beta adrenergic receptor" entry C01141) while many disease names in OMIM are actually gene names (e.g. OMIM *605882). In many cases, hereditary diseases were described long before their genetic background was elucidated. After identifying a gene causatively involved in the genesis of the disease, the acronym form of the disease name was often used to build the gene name. Therefore, not every term labeled as "disease" by a NER algorithm using a disease database like OMIM as dictionary necessarily is indeed of the type "disease".

Processing speed is also an important aspect in NER although many papers introducing new approaches for detecting names of genes and metabolites mention only precision and recall values for the NER and/or RE step. If a NER algorithm or heuristics is to be applied in practice on text corpora such as MEDLINE, it must be able to detect many hundred thousand terms within millions of abstracts in a reasonable time. Due to the common absence of information on processing speed and the fact that an NER algorithm performing well for gene names may fail in the detection of phenotypic traits, a comparison of the usability of different NER approaches in biology is a tedious work and the integration of the multitude of NER approaches for different entity types into one uniform text mining platform is a technical challenge. For example, a dictionary based NER algorithm for detecting gene names may require indexing procedures that do not apply stemming and are case sensitive while a NER approach for detecting phenotypes may rely on indices generated by case-insensitive tokenization in combination with stemming. The technical problems connected with managing a multitude of data structures and indices optimized for NER for a multitude of different entity types is probably one of many reasons for the fact that most TM applications for biology are highly specialized for one specific NER and relation extraction task with a very limited number of integrated entity types.

Even NER approaches reaching excellent recall values in detecting entities in sentences like those depicted in *Figure 2-5* will currently, however, fail to detect all mentioned entities and relations in natural language text. One important reason for this is the reference problem arising from the usage of pronouns: if an author describes some functional aspects of a certain gene, for example, Brca1, in a paragraph of text, he will not constantly use the term "Brca1" to refer to the described entity. Usually, he will start his explanations by using the original name "Brca1" in the first sentences and will later on refer to the gene by using the pronoun "it" or the expression "this gene" in the following sentences. For a human reader, resolving the reference is usually a trivial task, but for sentence based NER, the resolution of a reference within sentences or, even worse, crossing sentence borders, is a considerable challenge.

A further challenge of crucial relevance for NER in biology is term ambiguity. While words resembling one semantic concept are called "synonyms", words which stand for multiple distinct semantic concepts are called "homonyms". Homonyms are ambiguous because by only considering the lexical information of those terms it is not possible to decipher the semantic concept represented by the word. For disambiguation, the word context has to be taken into account. The ambiguity problem is especially relevant for biomedical TM approaches as a high fraction/~12 % of the words in biochemical abstracts are technical terms of this discipline (*Krallinger et al., 2008*). Those technical terms often are acronyms derived from compound names. Due to their shortness, these acronyms are particularly affected by the ambiguity problem. Two examples:

- AIP: "acute intermittent porphyria, OMIM #176000" but also "AH receptor interacting protein" – SwissProt entry O00170

- PDS: "Pendred syndrome" – OMIM #274600 but also "Phytuene desaturase" – SwissProt entry P80093

And the number of acronyms and abbreviations in biomedical texts is rising (*Ananiadou et al., 2006*). In addition, several gene names are homonyms to common English terms like 'blue', 'red', or 'eyeless'. The ambiguity regarding the entity type (gene or phenotype) is therefore accompanied by ambiguity regarding the question whether a term belongs to the technical terminology of biomedical research or the common English vocabulary.

For gene names, a further complication is introduced by the fact that genes are usually occurring in several distinct taxa. They may have the same or distinct gene names irrespective of the biochemical function these genes fulfill in different species.

While the aforementioned challenges are usually addressed by considering information of the lexical and syntactical level of text analysis, disambiguation requires the consideration of semantic information. It has been discussed if an annotation of words by authors or publishers could lead the way to resolve the disambiguation problem in biology but the success of the suggested approach is questionable (*Hahn et al., 2007*). NER ideally covers all levels of textual analysis and resembles the first step in the process of automated relation extraction from text.

2.5.3. RELATION EXTRACTION

Relation extraction (RE), also sometimes referred to as information extraction (IE), is the task of detecting whether a relation exists between entities detected in the NER step in a piece of literature. The ultimate goal of RE is the detection of the type and direction of such a relation. The accuracy of RE heavily depends of the quality of the anteceding NER step (*Chun et al., 2006*).

The simplest approach of extracting relations between biomedical entities is cooccurrence. Cooccurrence-based approaches, often referred to as 'bag of words' approaches, do not consider any syntactical information of a sentence. Instead, this approach considers the probability that two terms are mentioned together in one abstract or sentence (document- or sentence based cooccurrence) given the frequency of occurrence of each single word within the examined text corpus. As cooccurrence is merely based on NER and statistical calculations, this method has been sometimes criticized as not being a text mining approach at all. The limitation of cooccurrence clearly is the complete lack of information of the type of relation and a large number of false positive results as the co-mentioning of two terms does not always imply a direct relationship between those entities. On the other hand, cooccurrence is a straight forward approach characterized by excellent recall values (depending only on the quality of the NER step) and comparatively easy implementation as it requires only basic skills in statistics which are, contrary to linguistic skills, common among biologists and bioinformaticians developing TM systems for biology. Furthermore, cooccurrence can be applied to connect any type of entity while extracting semantically typed relations usually requires the development of rules or machine learning approaches for each single relation type. As cooccurrence-based TM systems abstain from the time-demanding analysis of syntactical information, the scalability of those systems is comparatively high rendering them as good candidates for large scale text mining applications processing text corpora as big as MEDLINE. Well known and in practice very useful systems like iHop (*Hoffmann and Valencia, 2004*) and Texpresso (*Muller et al., 2004*) are based on cooccurrence and are a valuable aid in speeding up the process of finding related biomedical entities.

A commonly used approach in biomedical literature mining applies rules and regular expressions in order to extract semantic relations from text. In principle, these rules can be applied to raw text. Due to the (in theory) infinite number of ways in which a certain relation type between two entities can be stated (passive or active voice, variations due to tense, presence and position of adjectives or adverbials), most of the current rule-based RE systems try to increase the abstraction level by considering the POS tags instead of or in addition to the lexemes (*Zweigenbaum et al., 2007*). Syntax trees represent an even higher level of abstractions. Rules and regular expressions developed to match against syntax trees therefore have an increased coverage compared to rules and regular expressions matching against raw text. Syntax trees encode semantic relations between sentence constituents, e.g. subject, verbal phrases and object phrase (*Figure 2-6*).

2. TEXT MINING FOR LIFE SCIENCE

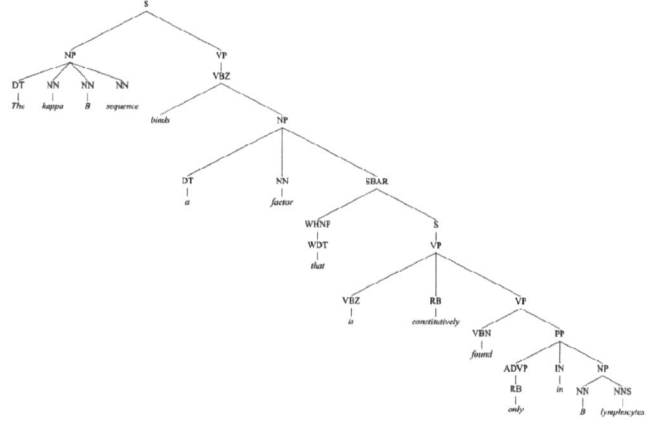

Parser. Figure

Rules developed to extract relations from syntax trees have been shown to reach high precision and recall values in the task of relation extraction. The RelEx system (*Fundel et al., 2007*) applies rules to extract protein protein interactions from dependency trees generated by the Stanford Parser (*Klein and Manning, 2003*). On the LLL challenge test set, the system achieved recall/precision values of 85/79% outperforming all concurring approaches. Due to the fact that most of the syntax parsers used for BioNLP had processing times of one to several seconds per sentence, the extraction of syntax trees for large text corpora such as MEDLINE currently containing more than 100 million sentences was not an option for many groups working on semantic RE. Some TM systems, e.g. the RelEx (*Fundel et al., 2007*) or MEDIE (*Ohta et al., 2006*) system, have managed to process text corpora as big as MEDLINE with the help of a powerful cluster infrastructure. Most RE systems for biology applying shallow or full parsing work on a limited set of MEDLINE abstracts only. The RLIMS-P system (*Yuan et al., 2006*), for example, applies shallow parsing (identifying syntactical coherent noun- or verb groups but not the hierarchical dependencies between those groups or sentence constituents) on phosphorylation-related abstracts only. Chilibot (*Chen et al., 2004*), applying POS tagging in combination with shallow parsing, processes the first 500 abstracts returned by PubMed for a submitted set of search terms. However, the speed of syntax parsers has been increasing significantly over the last years. The "mogura" variant of the 2.3v Enju parser (*Miyao and Tsujii, 2008*) designed for biomedical literature mining released July 2008 reaches processing times of fifty ms per sentence (*Figure 3-2*). Due to the notable improvement in parsing speed over the last years, the fraction of biomedical TM systems making use of syntactical parsers also on large text corpora will probably further increase in the future.

Machine-learning based RE systems like that of (*Craven and Kumlien, 1999*) can be trained on lexical as well as syntactical text level features like special lexemes, POS tags or syntactic roles. Depending on the feature set, a sufficiently large text corpus has to be created for training, often involving time consuming manual annotation of the features to be considered. While machine-learning based approaches require a time-consuming annotation of text corpora, rule based methods require the compilation of hand-crafted rules. Therefore, it is not possible to render either the rule- or machine based approach as generally faster to accomplish.

The fine grained information contained in syntax trees can not only be used for developing rules for relation extraction but also to train support vector machines or other machine-learning software systems to assign semantic roles like subject, predicate, argument, location or time to sentence constituents. In order to connect the syntax trees with semantic relations with the help of machine learning, at first a corpus of syntax trees annotated with semantic roles has to be (manually) created which can be used as training set. This approach to extract sentence constituents representing a certain semantic role is called "Semantic Role Labeling" (SRL). In the general English domain, the ASSERT system *(Pradhan et al., 2004)* based on syntax trees generated by the Charniak-Lease parser *(Lease and Charniak, 2005)* resembled for several years the state-of-the art approach to SRL. Recently, Semantic Role Labeling programs specially adapted to the biomedical domain have been developed, e.g. BIOSMILE *(Tsai et al., 2007)*. The current version of the Enju syntactic parser (2.3v, 2008) also comes with some SRL functionality although not all PropBank roles are supported. In the depicted, conventional SRL approach, the syntax tree is only a means of extracting the semantic roles of a sentence, not an aim in itself.

SRL in itself is not an RE method in the strict sense as it detects relations between sentence constituents, not entities. However, the semantic components and predicate-argument structures (PAS) can be a valuable help in this task. The semantic labels generated by SRL directly reveal semantic information contained in a sentence and hide the complexity of the syntactical level which is usually only a means in literature mining to retrieve the semantic content. The easy interpretability of the output generated by SRL programs compared to syntax tree generation is also advantageous, as "all or most of the demonstrably useful biomedical text mining systems have been built not by text mining specialists, but by computational biologists" *(Cohen and Hunter, 2008)*.

2.5.4. SYSTEM INTEGRATION

The automated extraction of knowledge from natural language text is a highly complex task connected with a multitude of interdependent processing steps. The name list used in NER by dictionary based approaches has to harmonize with the tokenization and stemming schema used in the preprocessing steps where the index structures are generated. Search strategies adapted to a variety of biomedical entity types have to be developed which may require different indices for different concept types (e.g. case-insensitive indices for phenotypes and case-sensitive indices for short gene-names and acronyms). If not only MEDLINE but also other text resources, namely full text articles, are to be considered, the relation extraction schema has to take into account that the length of an abstract is only a fraction of that of a full scientific paper and that the length of an average PubMed Central sentence also exceeds that contained in an abstract. These differences may affect the applicability of a specific RE strategy. Last but not least, for a TM system that is of use in practice, it is not enough to develop a set of NER an RE algorithms with good accuracy. Both steps in addition have to be able to cope with the size of the integrated text resources and positional information in a reasonable time. If relation extraction is done not only for singular queries but for hundred-thousands of gene or phenotype names, this task usually is done on a cluster and the retrieved data is stored to a database. The extracted data is typically of immense size and requires the development of a database or software schema specially adapted to handle this large amount of data efficiently. For the generation of literature-based knowledge networks, a transformation has to be accomplished from the positional, document-centric information retrieved during NER to a subject-relational representation of knowledge. Subject-relational knowledge graphs derived from literature are often scale free *(Chen et al., 2004; Palakal et al., 2007, personal observation)*. This means, that entities exist, e.g. frequently mentioned tissues or phenotypes, which can be connected to more than 2 million (EXCERBT: "blood": 2.1 million) pieces of positional information and to several thousand co-occurring entities. Such "hub terms" are serious challenges for the development of a text mining database showing short response times.

In order to built up a TM system providing the possibility to search for a broad and easily extendable set of relation- and concept types, a multitude of software modules (dictionary generation, index generation, ER, RE and others) and data structures (indices, databases, flat files) have to be integrated into one methodological and conceptional coherent software framework. The amount of time spent for improving the accuracy of each NER and RE subtask has to be carefully weighted against the time necessary for maintaining the system and for generating and updating the integrated data. Although currently the majority of the publications in the field of BioNLP focuses on comparison and improvement of algorithms and methods for syntactical parsing, NER and RE, a fundamental challenge in the construction of a broad scale text mining system is the question on how to integrate the multitude of modules, algorithms and data structures fulfilling all the necessary processing steps in a way that the final system is marked by good accuracy and response times, maintainability and extensibility.

3. RELATION EXTRACTION BASED ON SEMANTIC ROLE LABELING

"The art and science of asking questions is the source of all knowledge"

Thomas Berger

The semantic relation extraction in the EXCERBT TM system is based on Semantic Role Labeling. In the following chapters, an introduction to the core concepts of this technique will be given and the applicability of SRL to relation extraction will be evaluated and discussed.

3.1. Introduction to SRL

Semantic Role Labeling (SRL) determines the semantic roles syntactic constituents of a sentence play in relation to a certain predicate. Typical semantic roles according to the annotation system of the PropBank corpus (*Palmer et al., 2005*), a newspaper corpus many of the existing SRL systems are based on, are the actor in the verb (labeled with "ARG0") and the thing acted on (typically "ARG1"). In addition to this core set of roles, all verbs can also have so-called "modifier" (ARGM) arguments such as location ("ARGM_LOC"), time, cause and others. A simplified list of semantic roles and modifying arguments according to the PropBank annotation schema is given in *Table 3-1*. A set of a verb and its corresponding semantic arguments is called "predicate-argument-structure" (PAS).

Sentence:
Thus, the leverage has amplified the fund's portfolio losses.

PAS:
[ARGM-DIS Thus] [ARG0 the leverage] has [rel amplified] [ARG1 the fund's portfolio losses].

Figure 3-1: PropBank sentence with annotated semantic roles

3. RELATION EXTRACTION BASED ON SEMANTIC ROLE LABELING

Table 3-1: Core set of PropBank Semantic Role Labels

LABEL	SEMANTIC ROLE
ARG0	in general the subject
ARG1	in general the argument
ARG2	depending on the frame
ARG3	depending on the frame
ARG4	depending on the frame
ARG5	depending on the frame
ARGM_LOC	location
ARGM_CAU	cause
ARGM_TMP	time
ARGM_DIS	discourse connectives
ARGM_ADV	general-purpose
ARGM_PNC	purpose
ARGM_MNR	manner
ARGM_DIR	direction
ARGM_NEG	negation marker
ARGM_MOD	modal verb

Most role sets, according to *Palmer M. et al. (2005)*, have only two to four numbered roles (labeled with ARG0 to ARG3), but particular for certain verbs of motion, up to six roles (labeled with ARG0 to ARG5) are possible. For the verb "move slightly", one possible role set is listed in Table 3-2.

Table 3-2: Three exemplary frames and associated semantic roles of the core arguments (Palmer et al., 2005).

FRAME FOR „SELL"		FRAME FOR „BUY"		FRAME FOR „MOVE SLIGHTLY"	
LABEL	SEMANTIC ROLE	LABEL	SEMANTIC ROLE	LABEL	SEMANTIC ROLE
ARG0	seller	ARG0	buyer	ARG0	causer of motion
ARG1	thing sold	ARG1	thing bought	ARG1	thing in motion
ARG2	buyer	ARG2	seller	ARG2	distance moved
ARG3	price paid	ARG3	price paid	ARG3	start point
ARG4	benefactive	ARG4	benefactive	ARG4	end point
				ARG5	direction

It is important to note that the same set of roles can be expressed by more than one distinct syntactical expression, so called "syntactical frames". The set of a semantic role set and its corresponding syntactical frame is called "frame set". A verb can be connected to more than one frame set, if the verb has multiple different meanings (polysemous verb), like it is the case with the verb "decline" (*Palmer et al., 2005*). Framesets, like lexemes, show a Zipfian distribution (*Palmer et al., 2005*): only a small number of verbs is connected to many framesets while the majority of verbs is connected to one single frame set only.

Table 3-3: Multiple frame sets for the polysemous verb "decline" (Palmer et al., 2005)

FRAME SET „GO DOWN INCREMENTALLY"		FRAME SET „DEMURE, REJECT"	
LABEL	SEMANTIC ROLE	LABEL	SEMANTIC ROLE
ARG0	-	ARG0	agent
ARG1	entity going down	ARG1	rejected thing
ARG2	amount gone down by	ARG2	seller
ARG3	start point	ARG3	price paid
ARG4	end point	ARG4	benefactive
EXAMPLE	...[Arg1 its net income] declining [Arg2-EXT 42%] [Arg4 to $121 million] [ArgM-TMP in the first 9 months of 1989]	EXAMPLE	[Arg0 A spokesman] declined [Arg1 *trace* to elaborate]

3.2. Biomedical SRL systems

The application of Semantic Role Labeling in the biomedical domain was conceptually introduced as a promising approach by Kogan Y. et al. (*Kogan et al., 2005*), who showed that 76% of the verbs used in biomedical literature are also contained in the PropBank corpus. This observation implied that existing SRL systems developed on newspaper corpora should also be applicable for biomedical texts. During the last years, the number of SRL related TM systems and resources has been steadily increasing. PasBio (*Wattarujeekrit et al., 2004*), a collection of predicate-argument structures for event extraction in molecular biology, is a compilation of role sets and PASs for a set of biologically relevant verbs. Meanwhile, a biomedical text corpus (the BioProp corpus) annotated with semantic role labels according to the PropBank schema has been made available (*Tsai et al., 2007*) which is based on the GENIA Treebank, GTB and contains considerably fewer PASs (1.982) than the PropBank corpus. The SRL system BIOSMILE (*Tsai et al., 2007*) which is freely available as a web service has been developed and trained on the PropBank together with the BioProp corpus. The system exploits full parsing information to label semantic roles using a maximum entropy (ME) machine-learning model (*Tsai et al., 2007*). Due to the growing number of biomedical resources for SRL, the easy interpretability of the semantic labels generated by this approach and due to significant improvements regarding SRL labeling speed (*Pradhan et al., 2004; Collobert and Weston, 2007*), the impact of SRL on BioNLP can be expected to increase in the future.

3.3. SRL Based Relation Extraction

According to Kevin Kelly, founding executive editor of the Wired magazine, the idea behind the semantic web is the reduction of natural language text to a computer-readable noun, verb and predicate structure (*Buxton et al., 2008*). SRL, which attributes those semantic roles, among others, to words or phrases within sentences, therefore appears as promising approach in the field of automated semantic processing and evaluation of natural language text.

Relations between entities expressed in Predicate-Argument Structures in their simplest form (containing only the subject-verb-argument relation) can very easily be interpreted by humans as well as computers. They can be considered as a universal

3. RELATION EXTRACTION BASED ON SEMANTIC ROLE LABELING

representation of any kind of relation. The verb defines the type of the connection and connects the subject to the argument. As the aim of EXCERBT is the extraction and integration of a broad set of relation and entity types from literature, this subject-verb-argument structure was also considered as the core unit for data extraction and representation in EXCERBT. Clearly, many relation types relevant in biology are of a more complex structure. As has been explained before, especially verbs expressing locomotion or transport usually are connected to more semantic roles than only the mover and the thing moved. Such roles are, e.g., start- and end-point of movement. A system specifically developed for extracting that kind of relation would have to consider these semantic roles in addition to the subject and the argument. For a general purpose TM system, however, it is necessary to focus on semantic roles which are common to almost all relational expressions, namely the subject and the argument part. By considering only subject-verb-argument triples, almost all semantic relation types are covered at least regarding these two core aspects. The presented approach based on those information units allows an almost universal extraction and representation of the semantic relations stated in literature.

3.4. SENNA: A Neural Network Based SRL Program

Until recently, many SRL systems were based on the assumption that the accurate extraction of semantic roles contained in natural language texts requires the knowledge of the syntactical structure of its sentences. As neither the generation of the syntax tree nor the subsequent semantic classification of tree nodes is free of errors and syntax tree generation is a time demanding process, Weston J. and Collobert R. examined whether a direct extraction of semantic roles without the usage of syntax trees would be able to reach the accuracy of existing, syntax tree based SRL programs. They developed a Semantic Role Labeling program "SENNA" based on neural networks which semantically labeled sentences with state-of-the-art accuracy in only a fraction of the time required by comparable syntax tree based SRL systems.

3.5. Algorithm

SENNA *(Collobert and Weston, 2007; Collobert and Weston, 2008)* is a deep neural network architecture designed specifically for the task of semantic role labeling. Neural network architectures are software constructs mimicking the properties of biological neurons. They are widely used in bioinformatics as well as other disciplines like engineering for the task of supervised and unsupervised learning. The neural net of SENNA was trained on the PropBank corpus, a 45.000 sentence newspaper corpus derived from the Wall Street Journal (WSJ) corpus. In this corpus, the WSJ sentences were manually annotated with semantic roles according to the PropBank annotation schema *(Palmer et al., 2005)*. Corresponding to the PropBank formalism, each verb (and verb sense) has a human annotated frame which indicates the typical roles that should be assigned for this verb. SENNA's SRL algorithm at a conceptual level takes a sentence as input and outputs semantic roles for each word in the input sentence for every identified verb.

The first task of SENNA is to locate the verbs in the input sentence. This is achieved by training a part-of-speech tagger. SENNA then outputs a role for a chosen word in the input sentence given the verb of interest. Hence, the SENNA architecture is thus applied (number of verbs) * (sentence size) times. The internal structure of the neural network structure used in SENNA is as follows: words are first represented via a binary encoding as vectors of dimension (dictionary size), i.e. these vectors are all zeros apart from one 1, indicating the word's index into the dictionary. In the first layer of the network, these vectors are multiplied by a (dictionary size) x (50) dimensional weight matrix to yield 50-dimensional feature vector representations for each word (this is often called a "Lookup Table" layer). This weight matrix is learnt as part of the backpropagation step of the neural network, and embeds words in a low dimensional feature space that the network can use to represent syntactic and semantic features relevant for the task. Extra features are also added to encode for each word whether it is the verb of interest or the word to be tagged. The next layer applies a convolution, i.e. a sliding window with a window size of 3 words across the sentence that outputs 200 features for each position of the window to the next layer. This layer finds *local* features amongst neighboring words. The next layer applies a max operation across the sentence length to find *globally* relevant parts of the sentence for the classification task at hand. The final layers are classical linear layers, outputting for the word of interest which of the 23 classes of semantic roles it should be assigned (including the case of no role at all). Depending on the sentence length, the parsing speed of SENNA is between 25 and 390 ms/sentence. On the PropBank test set, SENNA has a per word error rate of approximately 14.5% which is state-of-the-art. The ASSERT parser/SVM-based method (*Pradhan et al., 2004*) obtains 16.54%. A detailed description of the algorithm and the evaluation process is given in *Collobert R. and Weston J., 2007, 2008*.

For this thesis, a variant of the algorithm described in (*Collobert et al., 2008*) was used employing some additional text pre-processing steps.

3.6. Evaluation of SRL processing times

Syntax tree based RE approaches try to label constituents of a parse tree according to a predefined set of semantic roles. This can be done by using a classifier, e.g. support vector machines (SVM), decision trees or log linear models. The generation of syntax trees and in many cases also the classification step are demanding, time consuming processes. Most SRL systems or full syntactical parsers used to derive semantic roles require on average 1 – 3 seconds to calculate the syntactical structure of a sentence, e.g. Lexicalized Stanford Parser (*Klein et al., 2003*) used by the RelEx system (*Fundel et al., 2007*): ~ 1 - 14 seconds/sentence, Charniak-Lease Parser (*Lease et al., 2005*), an adaptation of the Charniak Parser (*Charniak, 2000*) to biomedical text: 2.7 seconds (*Clegg et al., 2007*), BIOSMILE SRL system (*Tsai et al., 2005; Tsai et al., 2007*): 1,99 seconds/sentence (according to the authors) although meanwhile also faster alternatives exist (Enju 2.3 parser (*Miyao et al., 2005*): less than 50 – 500 ms/sentence (*Tsujii, 2006*)).

In order to assess the processing time of SENNA on biomedical sentences compared to existing general English as well as biomedical SRL programs and syntactic parsers, I compiled four sets of sentences. Each set contained 500 sentences derived from MEDLINE abstracts. The sentences of the test sets differed in length ranging from 65–75 characters for the shortest set to 235-245 characters in the longest set. Two SENNA variants were tested: The published SENNA version available on the NEC labs web site[5] ("SENNA-web") and a derivative version with slightly better accuracy regarding the semantic labeling of is-a relationships ("SENNA*"). The results are depicted in

---

[5] NEC labs: www.nec-labs.com/research/machine/ml_website/main/software.php?project=senna

3. RELATION EXTRACTION BASED ON SEMANTIC ROLE LABELING

Figure 3-2 where the processing times of all tested programs in relation to the SENNA-web version are plotted.

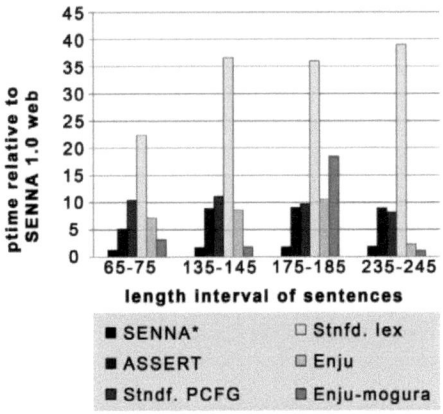

Figure 3-2: Performance comparison of SENNA with common SRL programs and syntactic parsers. Performance time (ptime) of SENNA* (a slightly slower variant of SENNA), ASSERT, two variants of the Enju HPSG parser and Stanford PCFG and lexicalized parser were measured relative to SENNA 1.0 web version on four test sets of 500 sentences each. The length interval of the sentences ranged from 65-75 characters for the first test set to 235-245 characters in the fourth test set.

As *Figure 3-2* shows, SENNA 1.0 web outperforms ASSERT by a factor of 5 – 10. For SENNA* the performance gain ranges between 4 and 8. The performance gain of SENNA 1.0 web compared to ASSERT is largest (factor 11) at a sentence length typical for biomedical sentences derived from MEDLINE abstracts (~140 characters) and even more impressing if compared to slower parsers such as the lexicalized Stanford- or Bikel parser. In absolute numbers, the processing speed of the SENNA 1.0 web/SENNA* versions ranged from 20 ms/25 ms per sentence from the shortest sentence set (65-75 characters) to about 220 ms/394 ms per sentence for the longest sentence test set. The processing time of the Bikel Parser was very long (612 – 42000 ms per sentence) and was therefore not included in the figure. The Enju-mogura parser appeared to have difficulties specifically with the 175 character test set that was used, processing times on other sentences of similar sentence length resulted in processing times comparable to the mogura results on the 65, 135 and 235 characters test sets.

3.7. Evaluation of SRL based RE accuracy

SRL by itself does not deliver agent – patient relationships between entities but delivers phrases and sentence fragments fulfilling a certain semantic role. In order to use SRL for relation extraction in the presented thesis, I made the following simplifying assumption: any entity mentioned in the ARG0 part was considered as subject and any

3. RELATION EXTRACTION BASED ON SEMANTIC ROLE LABELING

entity in the ARG1 part was considered as argument of the relation expressed by the connecting verb.

In order to assess the applicability of SRL for extracting relations between biomedical entities, the frequency of wrongly as well as correctly extracted relations based on this simplifying approach was determined on two test sets. This evaluation should reveal whether the proposed SRL based approach can be used with sufficient reliability to build up a large scale biomedical IE system.

Datasets

In order to evaluate the accuracy of the assumption that the relation between sentence parts labeled with "ARG0" and "ARG1" can be transferred upon the biological entities mentioned therein, two datasets were used:

- The first dataset (LLL'05) consisted of 77 sentences (genic_interaction_data.txt and genic_interaction_data_coref.txt) provided as training data set in the LLL 2005 Genic Interaction Extraction Challenge (*Nedellec, 2005*)[6]. Each sentence had been annotated with at least one interaction consisting of agent, target and the direction of the relation. The definite type of the relationship was not provided but was annotated manually for each sentence from the provided interaction information during the evaluation process. The data set did not contain any negative sentences.

- The second dataset (BC-PPI)[7] consisted of 173 sentences with at least one annotated relation and 743 negative example sentences. This set has been extracted by Jörg Hakenberg from the BioCreAtIvE 1A task (*Hirschman et al., 2005*) dataset by randomly selecting 1000 sentences and manually adding annotations on protein-protein interactions. Each annotated PPI consisted of an actor, a target and a specified relation connecting both entities.

As the chance of a falsely detected relation is assumed to rise with increasing length and complexity of a sentence and its syntactical components (e.g. by inclusion of one or more nominalizations or conditional phrases which may invert the meaning of the PAS structure), I checked whether the average length of the sentences in the test sets resembles the length of an average sentence taken from MEDLINE, OMIM or PubMed Central. As *Figure 3-3* shows, the average sentence length of both test data sets resemble the length of sentences contained in the most relevant biomedical literature sources. Thus it can be assumed that the accuracy obtained from the test data sets should be similar to the accuracy obtained when applying an SRL program to these literature sources.

---

[6] LLL 2005: data.jouy.inra.fr/unites/mig/text/LLLChalenge05/data/train/task1/
[7] BC-PPI: www2.informatik.hu-berlin.de/~hakenber/corpora/

3. RELATION EXTRACTION BASED ON SEMANTIC ROLE LABELING

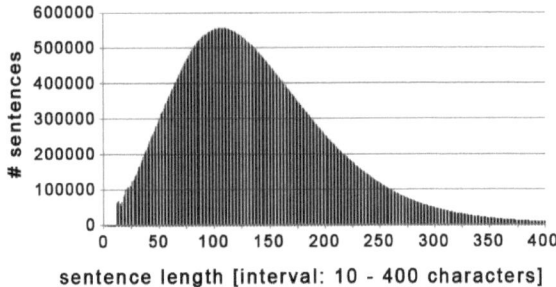

sentence length [interval: 10 - 400 characters]

Figure 3-3: Length distribution for 89 million biomedical sentences from PubMed abstracts (including the titles), the open access part of PMC full text articles and OMIM records with lengths between 10 and 400 characters. Extremely short or long sentences often result from errors in the sentence splitting step

Table 3-4: Evaluation of average sentence length in characters for the two test sets as well as for three sources of biomedical literature. *) including titles, **) excluding titles

SOURCE	NUM. EVALUATED SENTENCES	AVG. SENTENCE LENGTH*	AVG. SENTENCE LENGTH**
MEDLINE	84.930.500	137	152
PMC	3.523.463	207	208
OMIM	434.567	146	-
BC-PPI	1000	150	-
LLL'05	77	172	-

For each of the two datasets, all PAS's were calculated. As SENNA showed excellent processing times in combination with high SRL accuracy I chose SENNA for evaluating the accuracy of the proposed SRL based RE approach for biology.

Only those PAS's were considered in the evaluation which contained at least one ARG0 and one ARG1 label and a biological meaningful verb like "activates", "binds" or "inhibits". For example, PAS's like "[Analysis of the expression of a translational ywhE-lacZ fusion] (ARG0) [showed] (verb) [that ywhE expression is sporulation specific] (ARG1)" were ignored. Verbs like "suggest", "show" or "proved" occur frequently in biomedical text but usually do not contain relevant information (The ARG0 part of such PAS's in most cases lacks a biomedical entity). Those sentences were neither included in this evaluation nor do they contribute to any semantic relation in the TM system I created in this thesis.

For all annotated interactions in both test corpora, a detected relation was considered as true positive (TP) if the agent was mentioned within the ARG0 part, the target was mentioned within the ARG1 part and the verb of the corresponding PAS resembled the meaning of the annotated relation. If no such PAS existed for the sentence in which the interaction was annotated, this observation was considered as false negative (FN). If the actor was mentioned within the ARG1 part and the target in the ARG0 part or if any additional PAS existed for this sentence wrongly connecting the entities annotated within this sentence by a biological meaningful verb (e.g. "activates", "binds", "interacts" etc.), this observation was counted as false positive (FP). Some of the sentences of the BC-PPI dataset contained relations between proteins which had not been annotated in the corpus for not being a protein-protein interaction in the strict sense. Those relations were additionally taken into account in the evaluation. As the focus of this examination was the IE step, not Named Entity Recognition (NER), the problem of detecting protein and gene names in the test sentences was not addressed. Rather, the annotated gene- and protein names were used as provided by the LLL'05 and PPI datasets and precision and recall values therefore resemble only the accuracy of the relation extraction step.

Results

As *Table 3-5* shows, the precision of relation extraction in most cases delivered reliable results (78% on the LLL'05 and 68% on the BC-PPI data set) while the recall (38% and 45%) was comparatively low resulting in an F-measure of 0.51 and 0.55. It should be possible to raise the observed recall by retraining SENNA on an annotated text corpus containing also biomedical sentences. This positive effect on recall as well as precision has been observed for the BIOSMILE system (*Tsai et al., 2007*) after retraining the classifier on a biomedical text corpus. The effect is probably small because in most cases FN results were caused by relations expressed within nominalizations and complex syntactical expressions and not by errors in the semantic role labeling process. If only relations expressed in a verbal form ("A activate/d/s/ing B" or "B was/is/could be activated by A") had been considered, P/R values would have been considerably higher (78%/62% for the LLL'05 corpus).

Table 3-5: Evaluation of SENNA based RE on LLL'05 training- and BC-PPI corpus

TEST SET	TP	FP	FN	TN	PREC.	REC.	F-MEASURE
LLL'05	63	18	103	-	0.78	0.38	0.51
BC-PPI	133	62	159	799	0.68	0.45	0.55
Total	196	80	262	799	0.71	0.43	0.54

Figure 3-4 to *Figure 3-6* show biomedical sentences where the presented simplification is successfully applied to extract semantic relations between genes (TP), but also two cases where this approach leads to false positive results (FP).

3. RELATION EXTRACTION BASED ON SEMANTIC ROLE LABELING

Sentence: Yarden et al. (2002) showed that BRCA1 is essential for activating the Chk1 kinase.

⬇

PAS: [BRCA1 is essential for]ARG0 [activating]verb [the Chk1 kinase]ARG1.

⬇

True Positive RE: "BRCA1 activates Chk1"

Figure 3-4: True positive relation extraction based on SRL

Sentence: IL-1 receptor antagonist IL-1Ra regulates the progression of various inflammatory diseases.

⬇

PAS: [IL-1 receptor antagonist IL-1Ra]ARG0[regulates]verb [the progression of a vairety of inflammatory diseases]ARG1.

⬇

True Positive RE: "IL-1Ra regulates inflammatory diseases"
False Positive RE: "IL-1 regulates inflammatory diseases"

Figure 3-5: False positive relation extraction caused by errors in the NER step

Sentence: [...] partial loss of BRCA1 function activates the p53 protein.

⬇

PAS: [partial loss of BRCA1 function]ARG0 [activates]verb [the p53 protein]ARG1.

⬇

False Positive RE: BRCA1 activates p53"
Actual Meaning RE: "BRCA1 inhibits p53"

Figure 3-6: False positives caused by additional words reversing the meaning of the verb (here: "loss of")

3. RELATION EXTRACTION BASED ON SEMANTIC ROLE LABELING

Discussion

The comparison between the proposed approach and existing RE systems is difficult as only the RE step was measured while the values for precision and recall of existing systems often include losses caused by the NE step. In addition, the observed accuracies strongly depended on the test set of sentences the published text mining tools have been tested on: for PreBind P/R values for the detection and classification of interactions between 92%/92% (*Donaldson et al., 2003*) and 28%/52% (*Jose H, Vadivukarasi T, Devakumar J, 2007*) have been reported. PubMiner (*Eom J-H, Zhang B-T 2004*), an IE system for the extraction of gene, protein and enzyme relations using syntax analysis and event extraction, showed P/R values of 80.2%/73.9% for the relation extraction step. The RelEx system based on dependency parse trees and rules reaches P/R values including the NE step of 79%/85% on the LLL'05 test corpus (detection of instances of gene/protein pairs) and P/R values of 68%/83% on the LLL'05 test corpus if the entity position and direction of the relation had to be predicted in addition.

Precision of the presented approach (71%) is close to the values of current state-of-the-art IE approaches in the biomedical domain while the recall on the sentence level is comparatively low. However, due to high processing speed of SENNA compared to most existing syntax tree based approaches, very large text resources such as the whole MEDLINE database can be processed within only a few days time. Considering the fact that many relations between biomedical entities are described multiple times in MEDLINE abstracts, the recall of the presented approach at the interaction level can be expected to be significantly higher than the observed 43% on the sentence level.

Collobert R. et al (2007) have shown that for the task of SRL, the generation of a syntax tree is not necessary and that the speed of deriving semantic roles can be increased by about an order of magnitude by abstaining from syntax tree generation.

Although the current version of the biomedical syntactic parser Enju meanwhile reaches comparable processing times and provides some semantic role labels, it does not support modifying arguments of the PropBank annotation schema and can therefore currently not be considered as a standard conform SRL program. SENNA appeared as the most promising program for the task of SRL based RE regarding accuracy and processing time. Therefore I chose SENNA as basis for the semantic relation extraction. In case future versions of the biomedical Enju parser also support PropBank modifier arguments, the SRL engine can be exchanged without major changes to architecture of the text mining system I presented here.

4. THE EXCERBT TM SYSTEM

> *"Science is facts; just as houses are made of stone, so is science made of facts; but a pile of stones is not a house, and a collection of facts is not necessarily science"*
>
> Jules Henri Poincaré French mathematician

The EXCERBT TM system (Extraction of classified entities and relations from biomedical text) has been developed as a broad range text mining system covering a multitude of entity types, relation types and text sources. The aim of EXCERBT is to accelerate the retrieval of related entities from biomedical literature by providing universal, semantic and user friendly query interfaces for a broad set of semantic queries and by presenting the results in an intuitive, subject-relational form. The NER approach used in EXCERBT is based on a dictionary compiled from a variety of biological databases and ontologies. The relation extraction of EXCERBT is purely based on Semantic Role Labeling and, as an additional option for rarely mentioned concepts, cooccurrence. EXCERBT can be regarded as a showcase for the possibilities and constraints of a SRL based relation extraction system not considering any additional syntactical features.

In addition to relation extraction, EXCERBT introduces a new way to automatically generate domain specific lexica connecting terms with factual knowledge from any text corpus of sufficient size ("text2lexicon" functionality). Such a lexicon can be used for automated, large scale annotation of biomedical terms as well as for a manual lookup of individual unknown terms by a human.

The EXCERBT TM system can be functionally divided in a relation search[8] and a definition search[9] module. The system can also be partitioned regarding workflow considerations in a data generation task on the one hand and a data integration and representation task on the other.

---

[8] EXCERBT Relation Search: http://mips.helmholtz-muenchen.de/geknowme/web/excerbt/relation-search
[9] EXCERBT Definition Search: http://mips.helmholtz-muenchen.de/geknowme/web/textmining/definitionsearch

4. THE EXCERBT TM SYSTEM

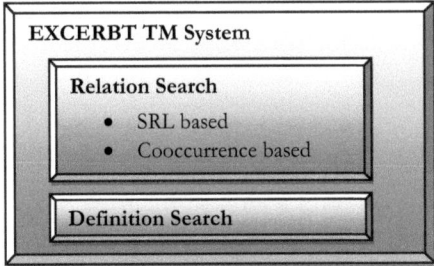

Figure 4-2: Two functional cores of EXCERBT

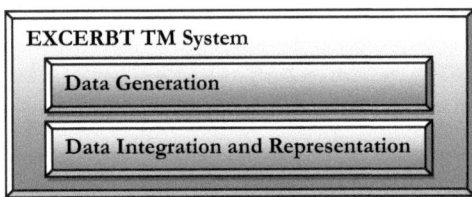

Figure 4-1: Two central data processing tasks in EXCERBT

In the following sections, the two main tasks of data generation and representation will be illustrated with the help of the "4+1 Architectural View Model" developed by Philippe Kruchten. This Model comprised five different views on a software system:

- <u>Use case view:</u> This view describes a set of possible scenarios of interactions between the user and the software system. Scenarios depend on the type and requirements of the user, on the data the user provides to the system as well as on the output he wants to receive.

- <u>Logical view:</u> This view describes how the different components of a system are functionally related to each other and which function is provided to the user.

- <u>Developmental view:</u> The bigger building blocks (modules) or system layers and their function are described here.

- <u>Process view:</u> Dynamic aspects of a system, e.g. threads, performance and sequence of system processes and user-system interactions are depicted in this view.

- <u>Physical view:</u> This view describes the type of software components and data repositories the system comprises. The physical distribution of those components on the hardware resources and the communication of the singular modules with each other and the user requests are illustrated.

As the physical distribution of the EXCERBT software modules are mainly the result of performance considerations, the process view and the physical view will be discussed together in the following chapters.

4. THE EXCERBT TM SYSTEM

4.1. Data Generation in EXCERBT

In order to detect biomedical entities and their relations in natural language texts, a large number of different working steps have to be applied. A description covering the technical procedures and tricks necessary to gather the required data from literature can be found in detail in the technical documentation of EXCERBT. Here, only the fundamental procedures and software modules as well as their interdependencies shall be depicted.

4.1.1. USECASE VIEW

Three main scenarios for data generation can be imagined:

- Setting up the EXCERBT system de novo: if major changes or improvements have been introduced to one or more modules of the system, e.g. the NER or SRL modules, it is reasonable to recreate the index structures and positional information EXCERBT is based on for all processing steps downstream of the changed package. A de novo creation of the EXCERBT database may be considered for alterations of very fundamental processing steps, e.g. for exchanging the sentence splitting algorithm.

- Integration of new dictionary entries: this scenario occurs if new entity types have to be integrated into the system. For example, if a research group works on an entity type which is not yet part of the EXCERBT dictionary and requests an extension of the system, an appropriate ontology or other source for the entity names has to be parsed and the derived terms have to be added to the EXCERBT dictionary. The new terms then have to be searched in the integrated texts and the positional information gathered has to be integrated into the existing system. Major updates of already integrated ontologies may also be necessary from time to time in order to keep the dictionary up to date.

- Integration of new documents and sentences: the huge amount of literature published each day makes a regular update of the text resources necessary. At least once in a year the new publications in the integrated textual resources should be integrated to the system. Only the new sentences are then

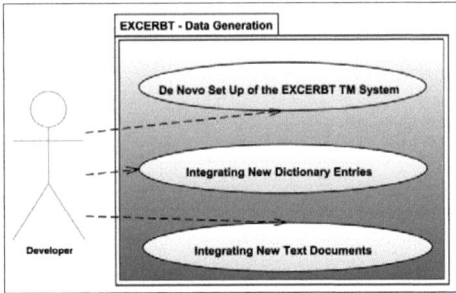

T

subjected to processing steps like SRL or NER.

4.1.2. LOGICAL VIEW

Figure 4-9 shows the working steps required to build up the data backbone of the EXCERBT TM system. At the beginning, a thorough analysis of the current and future research topics which shall be covered by EXCERBT has to be performed. The following questions have to be discussed in order to avoid frequent updates of the system:

- Dictionary: it is necessary to specify which kind of entity types are of interest for the researchers. Research groups solely working on miRNA may not only have an interest in this topic type but also on potential phenotypes influenced by miRNAs. The question, which ontological or database resource shall be used as the source for the name list for a certain entity type is also important and requires a sound biological as well as technical background. The chosen database has to cover the research area of interest and should not contain mixtures of entities of different types. It should not contain plural and singular forms as these forms are normalized by EXCERBT with the help of stemming. The terms contained in the parsed ontology should be as close as possible to the terms actually used in scientific publications. As the EXCERBT system has been implemented as one additional knowledge resource of the GeKnowME data integration system, it is also important to consider which other knowledge resources have already been integrated to GeKnowME when selecting resources for the dictionary: data derived from independent GeKnowME resources can be mapped by the names as well as by the identifiers to each other. If an external data resource has already been integrated to GeKnowME, this is an additional argument to use this resource as a source of biomedical terms for the EXCERBT dictionary.

- Relation types: relation types currently supported by EXCERBT are, in addition to cooccurrence: "activation", "regulation", "inhibition", "phosphorylation", "methylation", "is a" relation, "binding to", "functions as" relation and "transportation". It is possible to define relation types with a broad application scope such as "inhibition" (464 mapped verbs) but also with narrow scope such as "phosphorylation" (12 mapped verbs).

- Text resources: the most prominent resource of biomedical literature is the MEDLINE collection of abstracts. However, many molecular interactions are lost if only abstracts and not full text articles are integrated. Due to licensing issues, only a fraction of the PubMed Central full text article resource, the open access part, is available for third-party large scale analysis. There exist several additional possible literature resources such as patents (access to data-mining suited file formats liable to pay costs), the metabo cards of the Human Metabolome Database HMDB (*Wishart, 2007*), geneRIFs, Wikipedia or the "grey literature" of the World Wide Web. Depending on the research focus and the financial considerations, the text resources have to be chosen and licenses have to be applied for.

4. THE EXCERBT TM SYSTEM

After deciding on those basic questions, the EXCERBT database can be created and filled with data. The following section describes the workflow for the first use case of creating the database from scratch.

1. Creating the core EXCERBT database: In order to raise database performance, I developed a specially adapted database schema. The schema comprises the partitioning of large tables and the distribution of tablespaces containing data and PostgreSQL indices over several independent hard drives. At first, the directory structure on the database server, the PostgreSQL table spaces, the database tables, triggers and rules have to be created. This is done by various SQL commands and shell scripts encoded in the DBManagement module. In addition, verbs were collected from VerbNet (*Kipper-Schuler, 2005*) and manually enriched with additional biomedical verbs, e.g. "phosphorylates". Currently, more than 12.500 verbs are part of the EXCERBT database. A core set of relation types is added to the relationtypes table and mapped to the corresponding verb list. *Figure 4-4* depicts three tables linking verbs to relation types. This linking of relation types to a set of verbs defines the core semantic relation backbone of EXCERBT. The PASs structures are mapped via their verb to this backbone. One verb can be mapped to multiple relation types, e.g. the verb "inhibits" to the relation types "inhibition" and "regulation". A broadening or narrowing of a relation type can be accomplished simply by adding or removing a mapping entry between verbs and a relation type stored in the verbs_relationtypes table.

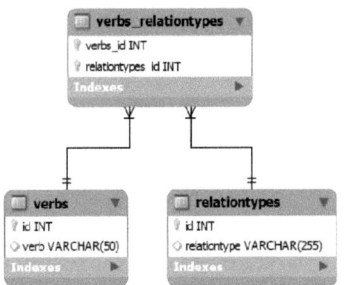

Figure 4-4: Modeling relation types in EXCERBT

2. Dictionary generation: The EXCERBT dictionary contains information on the entity names used in the NER step, original identifier and type of that entity as well as the name and URL of the source ontology. Ambiguous terms of different entity types may be contained more than once in the database. For example, the name "DMS" once stands for a metabolite (Dimethyl sulfoxide) mapped to the KEGG compound identifier "C11143". The second "DMS" dictionary element, however, stands for a disease (diffuse mesangial sclerosis) mapped to the OMIM record "#256370". The mapping of terms to original database identifier is anything but trivial as several independent ontologies have to be used to cover an entity type as comprehensively as possible. Usually, there

exist overlaps between those ontologies. Many OMIM disease terms, for example, are also contained in the list of the MESH disease ontology. In order to avoid duplications of names within one entity type, new original identifiers have to be mapped to terms from other dictionary resources which have already been integrated to the system. For some words, a case-sensitive search algorithm (see NER step) will be more appropriate than a case-insensitive search. Those words, mainly short gene names but also acronyms for phenotypes or other entity types, can usually be considered as candidates for this search type and are flagged with the sign "searchcasesensitive" = "true". The EXCERBT dictionary is part of the EXCERBT database and consists of a set of five tables depicted in *Figure 4-5*.

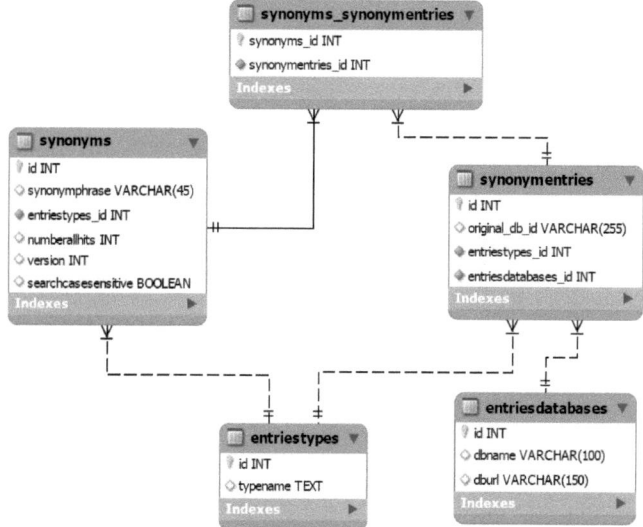

Figure 4-5: The EXCERBT dictionary. The synonyms table contains the names for the integrated entities in the synonymphrase table. As several overlapping ontological resources may be used to cover one entity type, only the original identifiers of an entity, not its associated synonym, is mapped to a database or ontological resource which is stored in the entriesdatabases table. The mapping between synonyms and synonymentries (n to m mapping) is contained in the synonyms_synonymentries table.

3. Sentence extraction: EXCERBT is a sentence based RE system. Sentence-based cooccurrence is less sensitive than document-based cooccurrence as this approach misses relations not expressed within one sentence. On the other hand, the results obtained by sentence-based cooccurrence are of higher reliability than those based on only document wide cooccurrence. In addition, most NLP programs such as syntactic parsers or SRL systems require a sentence as input. Due to the advantages of sentence-based cooccurrence and the requirements of advanced NLP methods, sentences were chosen as basic unit

4. THE EXCERBT TM SYSTEM

for all further processing steps. At first, the flat files containing the selected text resources such as PubMed abstracts or the open access part of PubMed Central have to be downloaded and parsed. Each single abstract or article has to be split into sentences which are stored to the EXCERBT database. EXCERBT uses the alias-i LingPipe[10] Java library collection in order to parse MEDLINE citations and for the task of sentence splitting.

4. <u>Sentence-based Indexing:</u> For a performant search of a large number of terms in large text resources, simple string-matching algorithms do not suffice, neither regarding processing speed nor regarding the accuracy of the matching procedure. Rather, an index has to be generated from the text resource (here: the extracted sentences) which allows a fast retrieval of all text sections mentioning a given term. For this purpose, the Java-based text search engine library Lucene[11] was used which is able to generate *inverted indices*. While the "conventional" sentence-centric view connects a single sentence to a list of terms, an *"inverted"* index focuses on a set of unique *terms* extracted from the total text resource. Each term in this index is linked to all sentences mentioning it. During the indexing process, all sentences are split into terms (tokens). Every new term is added to the inverted term-index of Lucene. For each term, this index contains all references to sentences and positions where the term was originally mentioned. By looking up the index for the term of interest, all sentences originally mentioning it can be retrieved very quickly, a feature which is crucial to the subsequent NER step. The disadvantage of the index-based search approach compared to, for example, alignment-based text matching approaches, is the fact that only exact matches regarding capitalization and term boundaries will be found. A dictionary containing only the term "lung" will not be applicable to find sentences mentioning the term "lungs" or "Lungs" based on a standard tokenization in combination with a case-sensitive indexing strategy. For many short gene names, elements or acronyms, however, a case sensitive search is mandatory, e.g. for the gene name 'merE' which could otherwise not be discriminated from the common term 'mere'. For this reason, the dictionary content as well as the search strategy in the NER step has to fit to the index generation strategy applied. To avoid losses caused by singular or plural forms, tokens can be reduced to their word stem ("stemming process") before they are added to the index. Not only plural or singular forms and capitalization matter but also the characters and rules that determine the token boundaries. If a hyphen is used as a tokenization signal, the two words "glucose phosphate" and "glucose-phosphate" both will be split into the words "glucose" and "phosphate" which are each considered as independent, unique index-entries. If a hyphen is not considered as a tokenization signal, "glucose-phosphate", other than "glucose phosphate", will be indexed as one single index entry. Hyphens are very common in metabolite- and substance names consisting of several chemical subunits. However, the usage of hyphens often varies from author to author but also from chemical ontology to ontology used for dictionary generation. Even within one and the same ontology like KEGG compound, hyphenisation is not always consistently applied. The possibility space of using a hyphen at a given position in a chemical name composed of 4-5

---

[10] LingPipe: http://alias-i.com/lingpipe/index.html
[11] Lucene provided by the Apache Software Foundation: http://lucene.apache.org/java/2_0_0/index.html

sub-parts is huge and the inclusion of all theoretically possible spelling variants regarding hyphen-usage would tremendously blow up the dictionary. While capitalization is usually irrelevant for phenotype names such as "high blood pressure", it is a very useful feature for the recognition of some gene names. The sentences mentioning the merE gene (RefSeq id: 2653933), for example, would be lost in thousands of sentences mentioning the common term "mere" if a case-insensitive index would be used for searching this gene name. While the reduction of tokens to their word stem is a valuable help to index polymorphous phenotype terms, this process can lead to artifacts when applied to acronyms or gene names: If the gene name "NETS" (RefSeq id: 11005) is stemmed, the word stem "NET" is generated which is the name for a completely different gene (RefSeq id: 7216908). In order to address those problems, the following indexing strategies were applied: I modified the default tokenization process in Lucene. In addition to the default Lucene tokenization signals, also hyphens were considered as defining a token boundary. This modification allows an accurate and consistent indexing and retrieval of compound names containing hyphens as it is often the case in metabolite names. As shown in *Figure 4-11*, two different index types are generated in this step: The first type uses a tokenization process in which the case of the tokens is not considered (case-insensitive tokenization and indexing). In addition, this index type applies stemming, so instead of indexing "lung" and "lungs" independently in different entries, only the word stem "lung" is indexed in both cases. This first index type is the default index type used to look up 98% of the ~3 million terms currently contained in the EXCERBT dictionary. For very short terms and acronyms flagged in the dictionary with "searchcasesensitive", a second index type is generated. The tokenization process for this index is case-sensitive leading to different entries for words differing from each other only regarding their capitalization. Stemming is not applied in this case. At the end of the presented working step, two types of indices have been created connecting terms to sentences and database sentence identifiers mentioning them: A "fuzzy" case-insensitive, stemmed index for searching the majority of dictionary terms and a second, case-sensitive, un-stemmed, "strict" index type for short names (e.g. some gene and element names) and acronyms.

5. Sentence-based Named Entity Recognition (NER): The goal of this step is to connect the terms contained in the EXCERBT dictionary to positions within sentences. For each dictionary term, the appropriate index and tokenization approach is selected automatically. Terms flagged with "searchcasesensitive" are searched in the "strict" index while all other terms are searched in the "fuzzy" Lucene index. In addition to selecting the appropriate index for each single term, the search algorithm also depends on the term's entity type. The description of phenotypes is highly polymorph. Singular as well as plural forms are used, the order of words often varies and word insertions my occur ("blood pressure increased", "increased blood pressure", "blood pressure significantly increased"). For gene or protein names, which are not distinguished here, the order of words usually is relevant ("brca 1" != "1 brca") and word insertions are not tolerated ("imidazoline receptor" != "imidazoline antagonist receptor"). The same applies also to metabolite names. Lucene's "span near query" functionality offers the possibility to smoothly define search strategies of different fuzziness for each entity type by varying the number of allowed word insertions and optionally tolerating a deviant term order in the text compared to the search

phrase. Although it is not possible to guarantee the optimum search strategy for each of the 3 million dictionary terms integrated in EXCERBT, the multitude of entity type specific search strategies in combination with the two available index types of different fuzziness makes a flexible and fine-grained adaptation of the chosen NER search strategy to a broad range of different dictionary entries possible. The positional information gathered in this step is finally stored to the EXCERBT database ("hits" table). The information gathered until this step is in principle sufficient to allow cooccurrence based association queries. It is also possible to retrieve all sentences or documents mentioning an entity of interest or to select all entities mentioned in a given sentence or document based on the positional data stored in the database. However, those queries cannot be processed efficiently at that time. The data has to be reorganized within the database beforehand. In addition, the system lacks any possibility to do a semantic search, the second supporting leg of the relation search functionality. It is also not possible to do a definition search. Those two functions depend on Semantic Role Labeling, which is explained in the next paragraph. As *Figure 4-9* shows, sentence-based indexing and sentence-based NER are no prerequisites of Semantic Role Labeling and its subsequent working steps. It is possible to begin with the SRL step right after storing the extracted sentences to the EXCERBT database. However, cooccurrence-based relation search as well as the correct assignments of biomedical terms to their positions in text depends on sentence-based indexing and NER. If the final TM system is intended to provide this functionalities, these steps have to be accomplished somewhere in the process of data generation after the storage of the sentences to the EXCERBT database.

6. <u>Semantic Role Labeling (SRL):</u> The annotation of the extracted sentences with semantic role tags is a prerequisite for the definition search and for semantic association queries. In the presented TM system, the neural network based SRL program SENNA was chosen for this task. All sentences are extracted from the EXCERBT database and labeled by SENNA with semantic tags according to the PropBank annotation schema. The output consists of tagged sentences, so called predicate-argument-structures (PASs). The number of PASs extracted for each sentence depends on the number of verbs and ranges from zero to a small dozen PASs. PASs containing at least one ARG0 and one ARG1 role are extracted and stored to the database. Each PAS entry refers to the sentence it was derived from. In addition, each PAS is linked by its verb_id column to the verbs table (see description of the first processing step) if the term recognized by SENNA as "verb" is contained in the verbs table.

4. THE EXCERBT TM SYSTEM

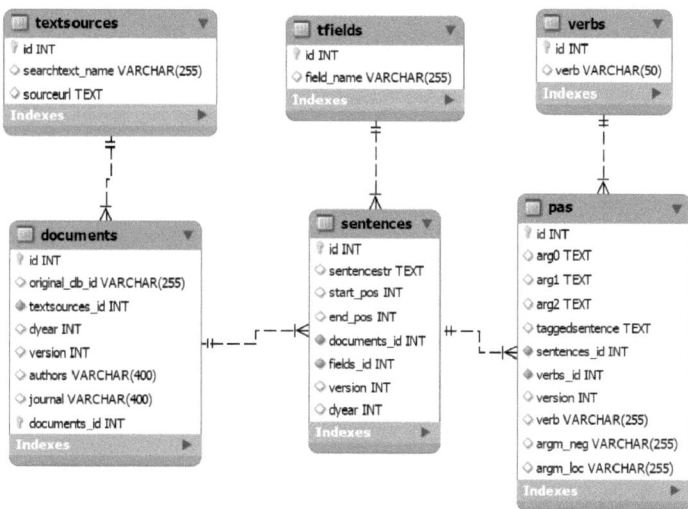

Figure 4-6: Storage of sentences and PASs in EXCERBT: each document is derived from a certain textsource like PubMed or HMDB. Each sentence is mapped to the document it was taken from by the documents_id column. In addition, a sentence has a foreign key column "fields_id" connecting it to the text section (tfields table) the sentence was derived from (e.g. title or text body). Each PAS is connected to its corresponding sentence by its sentence_id although not every sentence may have a PAS assigned. The core semantic PropBank arguments ARG0 to ARG2 as well as some modifier arguments are stored in the pas table in separate columns. The verbs_id column in the pas table connects each PAS to a verb in the verbs table, if its verb is the same as a verb string in the verbs table entry.

7. PAS-based index generation: This step is very similar to the sentence-based index generation despite the fact that not sentences are the text units used for indexing but the subject roles (ARG0) or argument roles (ARG1) contained in the PASs. The technical challenges and considerations regarding indexing strategy and search fuzziness affect this step in the same way as the sentence-based index generation procedure. Therefore, four index types are generated here: for the ARG0 roles as well as for the ARG1 roles, a case-insensitive, "fuzzy" index based on stemming and a case-sensitive, "strict" index without stemming is generated.

8. PAS-based Named Entity Recognition (NER): Functionally, this step corresponds to the sentence-based NER step. The purpose of this step is not to detect biomedical entities within whole sentences but within either the subject or the argument part of a sentence. The basic idea behind the semantic relation extraction of EXCERBT is the assumption that entities mentioned within the ARG0 (ARG1) role indeed act as (are affected as) subjects (arguments) in a way the verb implies. The positional data gathered in this step is stored to the

4. THE EXCERBT TM SYSTEM

EXCERBT database (synonyms_pasarg0 and synonyms_pasarg1 tables in *Figure 4-7*) and links entities from the dictionary to semantic roles of the PASs. The PASs, again, are semantically categorized depending on the mapping of their verb to the internal verb list of EXCERBT. At the end of this step, all data required for semantic association queries are contained in the EXCERBT database but still require reorganization for efficient data retrieval.

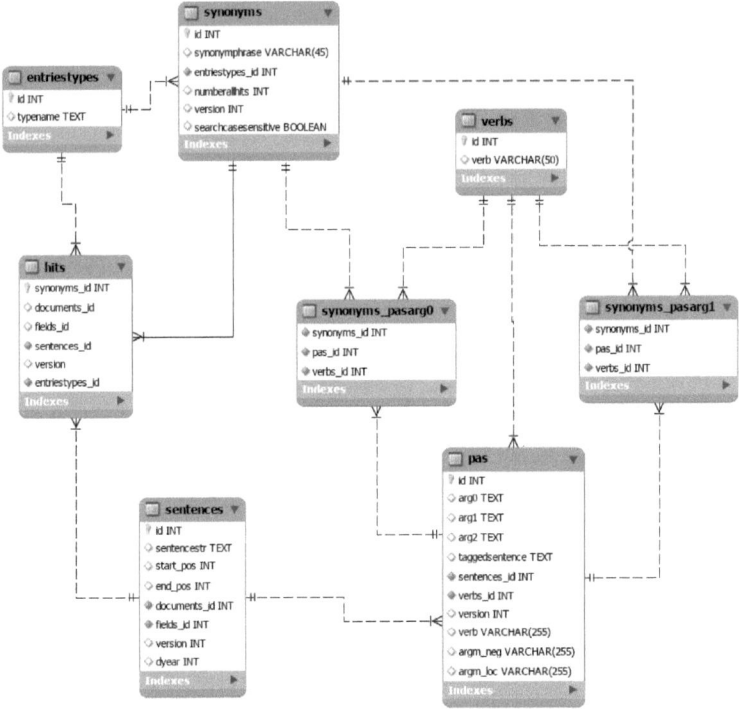

Figure 4-7: Storage of positional data in the EXCERBT database. All positional data linking sentences to synonyms are stored in the hits table. All positional data linking subject roles (ARG0) of a PAS to a synonym is stored in the synonyms_pasarg0 table which is mapped to a relation type via the corresponding pas, verbs and verbs_relationtypes table (see Figure 4-4). Accordingly, positional information of synonyms mentioned in the argument role (ARG1) is stored in the synonyms_pasarg1 table.

9. Definition index generation: This step is very similar to the PAS-based index generation for the ARG0 (subject) role. While the latter indexes all ARG0 roles generated in the SRL step, the definition index generation step indexes only subject roles of those PASs which are mapped by their verb to an "is a" or "functions as" relation type. Those relation types are considered as expressing a kind of "definition" for the ARG0 role and the entities mentioned therein. Due to this constraint, the definitions index is much smaller than the collection of all ARG0 indices. As the definition index is not used for any NER task, only the fuzzy index type is generated. The purpose of this index is not NER but providing the user with the possibility to submit an arbitrary term and efficiently retrieve definitions for this term which are linked to biomedical literature resources.

The task of data generation for EXCERBT de novo is accomplished after these nine steps. Due to the large amount of retrieved positional data (several hundred million positions for sentence based NER for 3 million biomedical terms), a reshuffling and partial duplication of the generated data stored in the EXCERBT database is required as depicted in *Figure 4-8*.

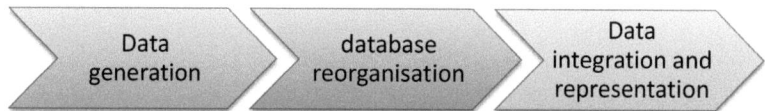

Figure 4-8: Overview on data generation workflow in EXCERBT

The aim of data reshuffling is to organize the sentence-centric positional data of the EXCERBT database in a way that allows a subject-centric representation and retrieval of relations within an acceptable frame of time.

The sequence of working steps is the same for the other two use cases where the dictionary or text resources have been updated and "new" terms have to be searched in "known" sentences or "known" terms have to be searched in "new" sentences. If new entries and terms are added to the EXCERBT dictionary, they are flagged with a version number. By considering only terms of this version number in the sentence- or PAS-based NER step it is possible to selectively extract positional information just for those freshly added terms. If new sentences are to be added to the system, the SRL step and the sentence- and PAS based indexing step have to be applied selectively on those new sentences (marked by the height of the internal database identifier). Then, all dictionary terms are searched in these new indices only. Finally, the freshly derived positional information is in both cases distributed in the database reshuffling step to the tables of their final destination in order to enable efficient data retrieval.

4. THE EXCERBT TM SYSTEM

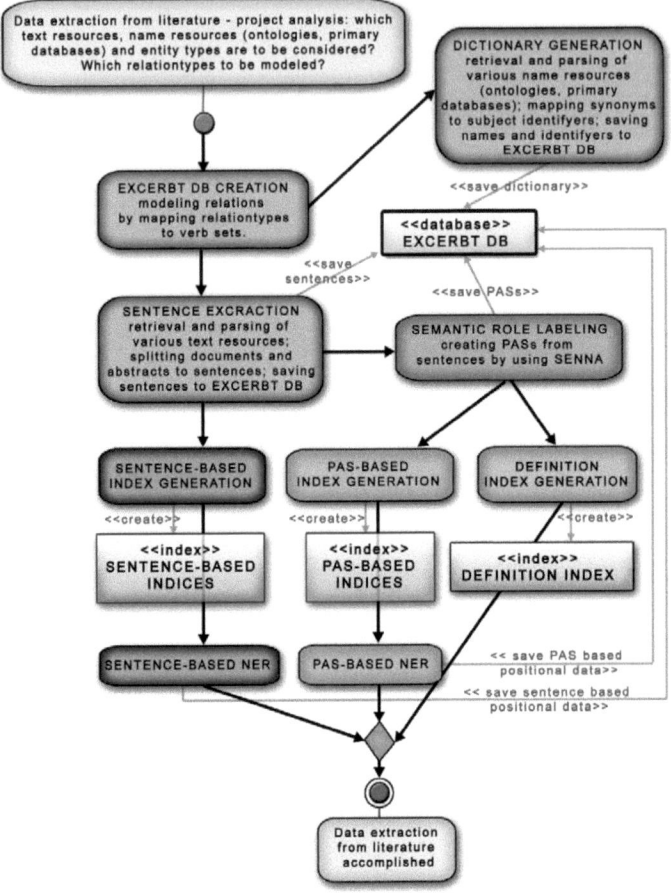

Figure 4-9: Activity diagram for literature based data extraction in EXCERBT. Dark blue: data generation steps required for cooccurrence based association queries. Pink: steps required for semantic queries (relation extraction and definition search). Green: Steps required for semantic relation extracting; Orange: data processing step required for definition search.

4.1.3. DEVELOPMENTAL VIEW

With only one exception (PASbasedIndexer), each fundamental data generation step presented in the process view corresponds to a particular Java software module. *Figure 4-10* shows the software packages required for data generation and their core classes and design patterns. With the exception of sharing some utility classes e.g. for reading or writing files contained in the TextSearchShared.jar Java library, these modules are completely decoupled. The shared "interface" is in fact the EXCERBT database schema and the index file structure. A change in the database schema may affect several modules and an altered indexing procedure regarding stemming or case sensitivity necessitates the adaptation of the search algorithms in the NER modules to the new indices.

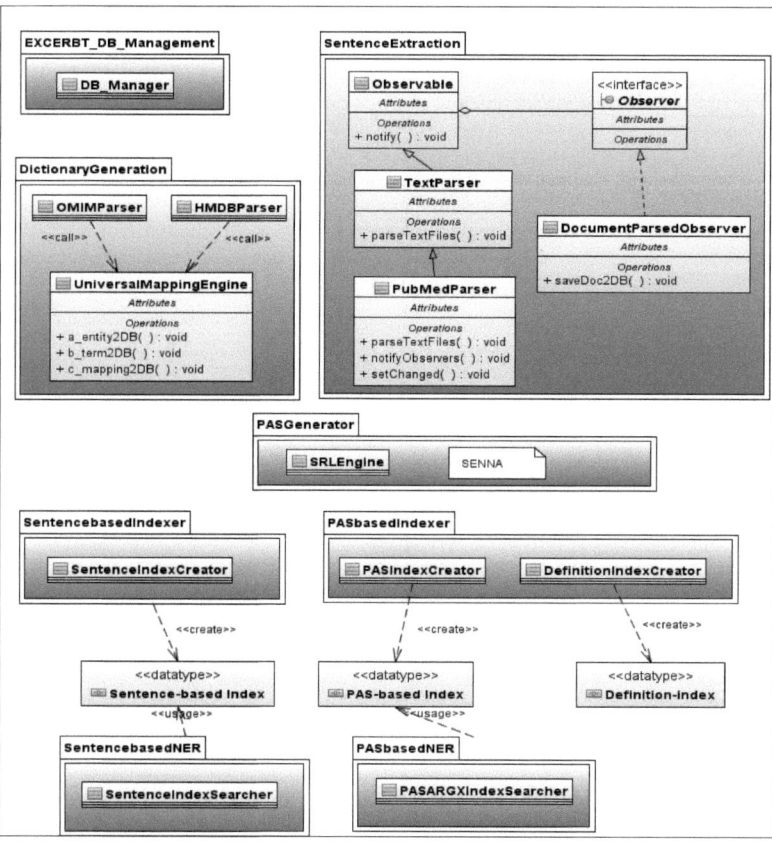

Figure 4-10: EXCERBT *Data Generation modules required for relation and definition search. Arrows indicate dependencies between different modules and data structures. As almost all modules read or write data from or to the* EXCERBT *database, the corresponding dependencies have therefore been omitted in this figure.*

4. THE EXCERBT TM SYSTEM

The following software modules (*Figure 4-10*) are assigned to the data generation steps depicted in *Figure 4-8*.

- EXCERBT_DB_Management: The core class of this module, DB_Manager, automatically generates scripts and SQL commands necessary for creating the table spaces and the database tables as well as for database reshuffling, maintenance and backup.

- DictionaryGeneration: This module consists of a set of classes parsing ontologies and database source files of various formats. The purpose of all these parser classes is to extract three types of files: one containing a list of non-redundant names, one file containing a list of non-redundant original identifiers and a third file mapping the names to the identifiers. The UniversalMapping-Engine class utilizes these files to add all names and identifiers not jet contained in the EXCERBT database to the corresponding tables. This class also updates the corresponding mapping of entity name and original identifier.

Table 4-1 lists the resources and ontologies used for generating the EXCERBT dictionary.

Table 4-1: databases and ontologies used to create the EXCERBT dictionary

ENTITY TYPE	DATABASE / ONTOLOGY
gene/protein names	• Entrez Gene (*Maglott et al., 2005*) • SwissProt (*Bairoch et al., 1999*) • Yeast SGD (*Cherry et al., 1998*) • Fusarium FGB (*Guldener et al., 2006*)
metabolite/ substance names	• KEGG Compound, KEGG drugs (*Ogata et al., 1999*) • MeSH (*Lindberg, 1990*) - chemicals • LIPID MAPS (*Schmelzer et al., 2007*) • Human Metabolome Database HMDB (*Wishart, 2007*)
phenotype/ disease names	• OMIM • Mammanian Phenotype Ontology (*Smith et al., 2005*) • MeSH (*Lindberg, 1990*) - disease
tissues	• Brenda Tissue Ontology (*Schomburg et al., 2004*) • MeSH (*Lindberg, 1990*) - anatomy
pathways	• KEGG pathway (*Ogata et al., 1999*)
domains	• InterPro (*Hunter et al., 2009*)

species	• NCBI taxonomy (*Wheeler et al., 2000*)
miRNA	• miRBase (*Griffiths-Jones et al., 2006*)
environmental factors	
methods	

In addition to the ontological resources used for dictionary creation, for every entity type also manually created term lists were added. Some categories currently contain only term lists manually compiled by me or other members of MIPS.

- SentenceExtraction: For each text resource, a parser class extracts one or several documents from the source file. The documents can be an abstract (PubMed), a large full text document (PMC), a database record (OMIM, HMDB) or even the complete text source (GeneRIF). All documents are split to sentences which are tagged depending on their localization as title- abstract or full text sentences. The DocumentParsedObserver class retrieves the extracted documents and sentences and stores them to the database.

  The following text sources are currently integrated to EXCERBT:

  o 19 million MEDLINE citations
  o 114.000 full text articles from the open access part of PubMed Central
  o 22.000 OMIM records
  o 7.500 METABOCARDS from HMDB (*Wishart, 2007*)
  o GeneRIF (Wheeler *et al.*, 2000) (440.000 sentences)
  o GenBank summaries for human proteins (24.000 sentences)

- SentencebasedIndexer: All sentences including their EXCERBT database identifiers are extracted. The SentenceIndexCreator class initiates the creation of the "fuzzy" as well as the "strict" index type. In order to enable high-speed NER in the next step, more than 100 non-overlapping indices were created each containing at max. 1 million sentences.

- SentencebasedNER: The Lucene search API employed for this module allows searching very large indices but the default Lucene search variant is too slow for processing large text corpora and dictionaries. An alternative search strategy based on loading the Lucene index into the working memory, however, is very fast. Not the searching of terms but the storing of positional information to the database is the time critical task. To ensure that each index can be held in memory, each index type does not consist of one large index but of about 100 sub-indices of 1 million sentences each of which is small enough to fit into the working memory. The positional information consists of the sentence id, dictionary-term id as well as the start and stop position of the term. Almost 600.000 terms of the 3.1 million terms containing EXCERBT dictionary were mentioned at least once in a sentence resulting in 450 million positional entries. The main class of this software module is the SentenceIndexSearcher.

4. THE EXCERBT TM SYSTEM

- PASsGenerator: This module is responsible for the Semantic Role Labeling step. Currently, it is based on the SENNA SRL system (*Barnickel T. et al., 2009*) but in principle, any SRL system or syntactic parser being able to label sentences with roles according to the PropBank schema can be used here. If faster or more accurate SRL engines are released in the future, they can be employed for this task instead of SENNA without any major changes to the system architecture.

- PASbasedIndexer: This module is functionally equivalent to the Sentencebased-Indexer module. Instead of full sentences, either the subject (ARG0) or the argument (ARG1) part of a PAS is indexed. The module creates four different types of indices (fuzzy and strict ARG0 and ARG1 indices). Each index type physically consists of more than 100 sub-indices each containing 1 million "ARG0" or "ARG1" arguments. The DefinitionIndexCreator class makes use of utility classes needed for creating the PAS-based indices and is therefore also a part of this software module. Other than the PASIndexCreator class, it does not include all ARG0 and ARG1 sentence parts in the indexing process. Rather, only the subject (ARG0) parts of sentences resembling an "is a" or "functions as" relation are considered. Other than the Sentence- and PAS-based indices, the definition index is not constructed for any NER task. Rather, it is used to extract defining sentences for arbitrary terms which do not have to be contained in the EXCERBT dictionary. Therefore, only one large, single definition index of the fuzzy type is created. Large indices which do not necessarily fit into memory are better suited for small-scale searches as required for a user-interactive system. This search variant has the advantage that the index does not have to be completely loaded to the working memory resulting in a faster initialization of the index. Other than the indices for the NER task, the definition index is used to dynamically retrieve data for user requests, and long initialization times would negatively affect the usability of the system. The other indices are never accessed by the user directly; they are solely used to extract positional information during NER. For those indices, the time required for searching three million terms is much more important than the initialization time. *Figure 4-11* depicts the physical structure of the generated index files.

- PASbasedNER: The positional information gathered in this module by the PASARGXIndexSearcher class connects terms of the dictionary to the subject or argument parts of a PAS. Terms mentioned in the subject and object part of the same PASs are thereby semantically connected to each other by the verb of the PAS. The positional information of a term being mentioned within the ARG0/ARG1 PAS part in combination with the mapping of PAS to verbs and the mapping of verbs to relationtypes defines the backbone of semantic relation representation in the EXCERBT database. After the data reshuffling step exercised by the EXCERBT_DB_Management module, this data is the basis for any semantic relation search.

4.1.4. PHYSICAL AND PROCESS VIEW

The modules for data generation are decoupled regarding their software architecture as well as their physical location. In the following paragraphs, the physical distribution of the EXCERBT data generation modules on different hardware resources and the requirements accounting for this distribution are explained.

Development machine: Tasks like dictionary generation, extracting sentences from source files or extracting PASs from the SENNA output files can be done on any standard development machine supplied with at least 3 GB memory and sufficient hard disc size to store the source files of the integrated ontologies and texts. The java modules on the development machine fulfilling these tasks are connected to the PostgreSQL database server hosting the EXCERBT database via JDBC connections. The generation of the definition index is also accomplished on the development machine. Scripts for database maintenance (EXCERBT_DB_manager), for starting several parallel indexing or NER processes on various clusters are also created on this machine by utility classes of the corresponding modules (sentence- and PAS- based indexing and NER). The PASsGenerator module creates scripts to run the SRL program SENNA on a cluster while the core functional classes of this module extract PAS structures from the SENNA output files on the development machine and store them in the database.

MIPS Quad core cluster (Sun Grid Engine): The creation of all indices (except definition index), Semantic Role Labeling and NER on the sentence as well as PAS argument indices have to be done on a cluster due to their high CPU power requirements. The quad core cluster consisting of four servers and 16 CPUs in total was chosen for the index generation and NER because these tasks require the availability of large amounts of disc space for creating and accessing the indices. The physical structure and size of these indices is depicted in *Figure 4-11* and *Table 4-2*. Depending on the workload of the cluster, the creation of all sentence- and PAS-based indices requires 5 – 10 days. This is also the time frame necessary to search the whole dictionary de novo and store the positional information via JDBC to the EXCERBT database. Searching a short list of only several thousand terms also requires at least 1-2 days time due to the time necessary to initiate several hundred indices. For redistributing the generated positional data, additional 2 days for pooling old and new positional data and redistributing it to the proper tables should be scheduled.

4. THE EXCERBT TM SYSTEM

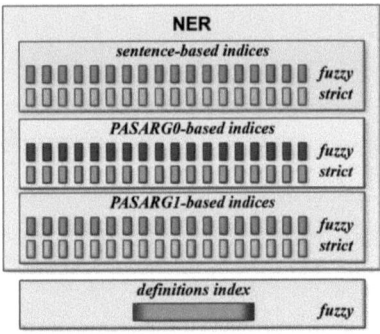

Figure 4-11: Physical structure of the definition index and the indices required for NER.

Table 4-2: Disc space required by the Lucene indices

INDEX	TOTAL SIZE [GB]
sentence-based – fuzzy	95 GB
sentence-based - strict	98 GB
PASARG0-based – fuzzy	14 GB
PASARG0-based - strict	15 GB
PASARG1-based – fuzzy	25 GB
PASARG1-based - strict	25 GB
definition index – fuzzy	1 GB

The BIM cluster (Sun Grid Engine): The BIM cluster consists of 104 CPUs and was chosen to perform the most resource demanding task, Semantic Role Labeling. JDBC connections from a machine outside the Helmholtz computational environment are prohibited due to security considerations. Therefore, the sentences have to be extracted as flat files from the EXCERBT database and copied to the BIM cluster. The output created by SENNA contains the PASs generated for each of those sentences. The output files have to be transferred back to the development machine where they are parsed by the PASsGenerator module.

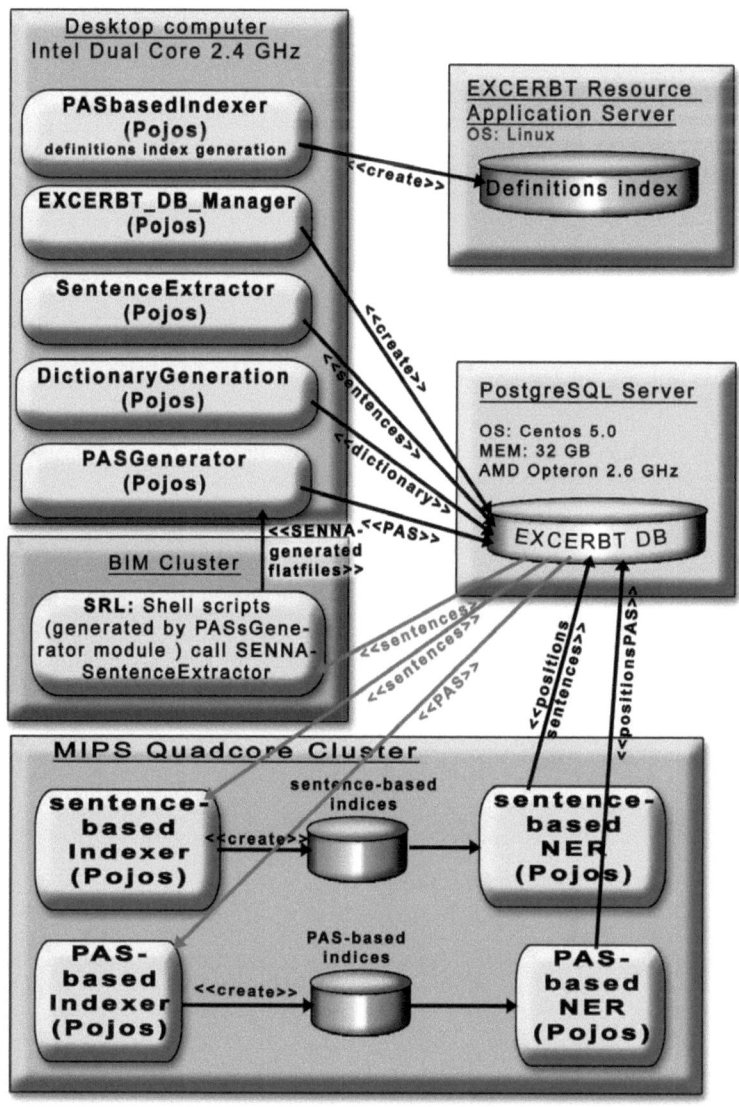

Figure 4-12: EXCERBT *data generation – physical view*

4. THE EXCERBT TM SYSTEM

4.2. Data Representation in EXCERBT

A key feature of the EXCERBT system is the transformation of the document- or sentence-centric positional data into a subject-centric representation. While the first representation connects concepts to pieces of literature, the latter connects semantic concepts or "subjects" to each other, e.g. by stating that a certain protein phosphorylates another. The linking of subject centric relations to their literature evidence is still present in the system and is of relevance if the user is interested in the literature evidence for an extracted relation. However, the relation type human researchers usually are interested first of all in order to build models or design experiments are subject-centric relations between genes, diseases, or metabolites. The second reason for the development of a subject centric TM system is the goal to connect the literature-based relations to relations derived from other knowledge resources. The GeKnowME system developed at MIPS by Dr. Karamfilka Nenova is a subject-centric, semantic information integration system. GeKnowME is based on the TopicMaps technology and allows the connection of heterogeneous and distributed knowledge resources by generating semantic domain models for each resource which are mapped to each other based on shared semantic categories, e.g. genes or phenotypes. In order to connect the results gathered from text mining with e.g. protein-protein interaction data contained in the Corum database (*Ruepp et al., 2008*), the data generated by EXCERBT has to be represented in a subject-centric way.

The database reshuffling step linking the data-generation to the data-representation part of EXCERBT plays a key role in this subject-centric representation. In this step, no data is generated. Instead, the positional data in the EXCERBT database is duplicated, distributed to several extensively partitioned tables and indexed in a way that subject-centric queries can be submitted and returned based on merely "document centric", positional information. Such queries ("List all proteins phosphorylated by Lrrk2 ordered depending on the number of supporting sentences") can require the consideration of several million pieces of positional information. In addition, the system has to "know" which terms belong to the category "protein" and are mentioned within the subject/argument parts of PAS structures representing a phosphorylation relation. Based on the data distribution achieved by the reshuffling step, the transformation from positional information to subject relations can be performed implicitly by appropriate SQL queries.

The EXCERBT data representation modules were developed as components of the GeKnowME system and implement the interfaces provided by this system. As the core design principles of GeKnowME have been described elsewhere (*Nenova, 2009*), the following chapters will focus on system aspects characteristic for the EXCERBT system but not on the information integration process realized by GeKnowME.

EXCERBT Relation Search

The Relation Search functionality of EXCERBT aims at extracting triples of subject, relation type and argument. Such a triple is the smallest, elementary piece of information in relation search. It can be extended by additional data on that triple, e.g. by the sentences supporting a relation triple of interest, or by definitions retrieved for the subject or argument phrase. Several dozens or thousands of such triples can be assembled to a literature based network.

Semantic relations expressed in the ARG0, verb and ARG1 sentence parts extracted by Semantic Role Labeling stand at the center of semantic relation extraction in EXCERBT. Cooccurrence based relation search does not require the semantic relations extracted by SRL but relies solely on the sentence-based NER step. For this reason, the process of data generation and storage is different for cooccurrence-based and semantic search. The two conceptual parts of relation extraction address different user requirements: The high recall and low accuracy values of cooccurrence based relation extraction makes this approach especially suited for rarely mentioned terms while SRL based semantic relation extraction is of high practical value for examining frequently mentioned terms like "diabetes" or "cancer". On the data presentation level, however, these computational differences are hidden behind uniform retrieval interfaces.

While cooccurrence scores are universally applicable but lack semantic information, this is not the case for the reliability of semantic relation extraction based on the proposed approach. A relation type in EXCERBT, defined by a set of verbs, can represent a semantically narrow concept such as phosphorylation with only several relevant verbs, but also a very broad concept like "activation" mapped to a large list of verbs such diverse as "accelerates", "triggers" or "causes". It can therefore not be assumed that the accuracy of the SRL based RE is the same for all integrated relation types. What can be expected to hold true for all forms of semantic as well as cooccurrence based relations is the assumption that a relation supported by a larger number of "evidence" sentences is in general more reliable than a relation based on only one single sentence. The results returned by the relation search queries are therefore ordered depending on the number of supporting sentences. The higher the number of evidence sentences, the higher the rank of the related entity pair delivered by EXCERBT.

EXCERBT Definition Search

A thesaurus is a controlled vocabulary of terms connected to each other by a relation, while a lexicon is a reference work connecting a term or phrase with factual information. A growing number of thesauri and ontologies like MESH terms, gene-ontology (*Ashburner et al., 2000*), GENIA ontology (*Ohta T. et al., 2002*) and others are available covering many different concepts and research areas in the biomedical domain. In contrast, the number of biomedical lexicons is comparatively small although some commercial vendors allow searching their lexicons online[12] and much information is scattered among various databases such as OMIM or HMDB (*Wishart, 2007*). One reason for this difference may be the fact that the manual compilation of a lexicon is very time consuming and factual information becomes much faster outdated than conceptual information reflected in thesauri and ontologies. The need for a lexical resource integrating a wide range of biomedical research domains and concepts updated on a regular basis makes an automated solution to the depicted problem highly desirable.

The EXCERBT definition search function is a SRL based method to automatically create such a lexicon from the subject (ARG0) parts of sentences labeled with SRL tags stating an "is a" or "functions as" relationship. Provided that the size of the processed

---

[12] e.g. www.medilexicon.com, www.medcyclopaedia.com

text corpus is large enough, this method is able to generate a comprehensive lexicon covering concrete technical as well as abstract terms. The lexicon can be search for any kind of term being explained within the processed biomedical literature. Clearly, a list of definition sentences may contain redundant information and is not a coherent piece of text following one line of thought as it is the case in manually created lexicons. However, due the automated creation process, it covers a broad amount of topics and literature resources and can be kept up-to-date comparatively easy. New drug, gene and disease names are integrated to the lexicon automatically provided that the authors give some definition of the new terms in the processed texts.

Two main use cases can be imagined:

- Classical lexicon function: medical practitioners, students, scientists and other employee groups working in the life science domain often are confronted with new scientific or technical terms belonging to an unknown field of research. If the term has just recently come into existence, the chance is low that it has found its way to a lexical resource relevant to that subdomain of research, e.g. OMIM for diseases. Searching PubMed or PubMed Central directly for the term of interest may imply reading several dozens of abstracts or full text articles until a text section is found giving sufficient information to define the submitted term. Here, EXCERBT can help to quickly retrieve only those pieces of literature containing information defining the concept of interest.

- Automated annotation: The emergence of several new 'omic' disciplines led to the production of large knowledge networks connecting genes with genes, phenotypes and a multitude of other types of entities. For those networks or other HT datasets, a method for annotating large lists of terms is urgently required. Often, these networks have to be analyzed and interpreted by human readers which usually are familiar only to a limited subset of terms and have to manually look up PubMed or several distinct lexical resources in order to understand the meaning of the nodes of the network. The definition search of EXERBT provides the option to link the node terms of any knowledge network or database with definitions derived from biomedical texts. For providers of primary databases containing empirically derived information on genes, microRNAs or other entities, the connection of their data to literature resources would raise the usefulness of their resources for third party users.

In summary, the definition search function of EXCERBT can be used for automated lexicon generation and maintenance, automated annotation of terms with information derived from the literature and for manually looking up unknown concepts and terms by students or researchers starting to work in a new area of research.

4.2.1. USECASE VIEW

Figure 4-13 lists the core query types which are available by using the graphical user interface (GUI) of EXCERBT. These queries can also be submitted to the JAVA API of the GeKnowME system.

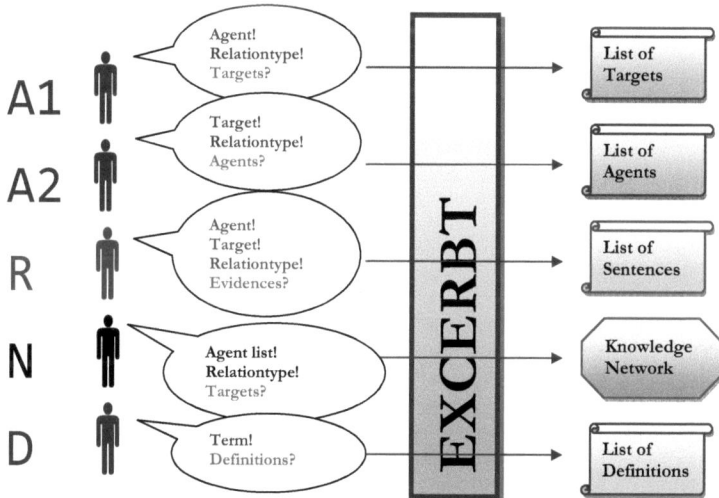

Figure 4-13: Five usecase scenarios for EXCERBT queries

Association queries (A1 and A2): These query types stand at the core of the relation search functionality of EXCERBT. The relation search connects a submitted entity (defined by entity name and type) with a list of entities by a semantic relation type or by cooccurrence. Although the representation of the semantic and cooccurrence based relations in the EXCERBT database is different, the query interfaces presented to the user is the same for both types. Association queries require the submission of a term, its type, the relation type of interest and the type of the requested agent or target, e.g. "borrelia", "species", "activates" and "phenotype".

Two sub-cases of the association search can be distinguished:

- The "active voice query" (A1) requires the submission of the name and type of the active player ("agent") and the relation type and returns a list of "target" entities. For example, a user interested in all proteins phosphorylated by the Lrrk2 protein would have to specify the agent entity as "Lrrk2" of type "gene", the relation type as "phosphorylates" and the target entity as "any" of type "gene" (gene names are often used in biomedical literature to refer to their gene products, therefore EXCERBT does not distinguish between genes and proteins). A list of proteins phosphorylated by Lrrk2 will be returned listed in descending order depending on the number of sentences supporting the proposed relation.

4. THE EXCERBT TM SYSTEM

- The "passive voice query" (A2) requires the submission of the name and type of the passive player ("target") and the relation type to return a list of "agent" entities. A user interested in all proteins phosphorylating BRCA1 would have to specify the target as "Brca1" of type "gene", the agent entity as "any" of type "gene" and the relation type as "phosphorylates" to retrieve the list of proteins phosphorylating BRCA1. The need for the active as well as passive voice is caused by the fact that the semantic relation types are directed. For the undirected relation type "cooccurrence", the voice of the query has no influence on the returned result list.

Reification Query (R): Reification in the TopicMap standard is a means of adding information to an association between two topics (entities). In EXCERBT, reification queries are used to retrieve sentences supporting the proposed relation between two entities. Usually, a user at first submits an association query and retrieves a list of entity pairs where the agent is connected to the target by the selected relation type. By selecting one entity pair from that list presented in the GUI, the user automatically submits a reification query for this association. The query returns all sentences supporting the connection of the selected agent, target and relation type. The main purpose of this query type is therefore to provide the user with additional information helping to decide if the proposed relation was correctly retrieved and to link the relation to the original literature resources, e.g. a PubMed abstract. In case the user already knows or speculates about the existence of a certain relation type between two entities, he can use this query type to directly retrieve all sentences supporting his hypothesis. For the reification search, name and type of the agent and target entity as well as the relation type have to be submitted.

Network Query (N): A network query is a special form of association query. Instead of submitting a singular agent entity, a list of agent terms is submitted. The output consists of a TopicMap containing the relations of all the agents and targets. This TopicMap is represented in the GUI in the form of a Pajek graph that is visualized with the help of layout algorithms provided with the Java Jung graph library. The purpose of this query type is the connection of a multitude of agents with a multitude of targets and the visualization of the extracted relations in the form of a graph. While A1 and A2 queries reveal only direct relations, the network query can reveal indirect relations between the submitted terms.

Definition Query (D): The A1, A2, R and N query types make use of the relation extraction functionality of the EXCERBT TM system (*Figure 4-2*). These queries are all centered in one form or other on the information triple of agent entity, relation type and target entity. The second functional core of EXCERBT is the definition search. Definition queries retrieve for a submitted term all sentences connected to a PAS where the term is mentioned in the PAS's ARG0 part and the PAS's verb expresses an "is a" or "functions as" relationship. The ability of the relation type queries to connect a submitted entity to other entities of a certain type is possible because the dictionary contains terms of a certain biomedical type and provides EXCERBT with a "background knowledge" on which terms belong to which type of entity (gene, species, phenotype or other). It is therefore not possible to submit or retrieve entities to any of the relation type queries which are not contained in the EXCERBT dictionary. The definition search, however, does not rely on this "background knowledge" provided by the dictionary or on any positional information generated by the NER step. Therefore, arbitrary terms can be submitted in the definition search. As result, a list of definitions (sentences) linked to their original PubMed or MEDLINE text sources is returned. The fuzziness parameter which can be adjusted by the user ("strict", "relaxed", "fuzzy" and "very fuzzy") is not identical to the fuzziness described in the index generation section. Rather, "strict" definition searches consider only those ARG0 (subject) phrases which are of (almost) identical length as the submitted term. Increasing the fuzziness of the definition search implies accepting also ARG0 phrases which are considerably longer than the submitted term or that contain all words of a submitted multi-word phrase but in a deviant word order or with word insertions. For example, a very fuzzy search for the term dopamine will result in a list of definitions where some definitions actually define "dopamine antagonists" or "dopamine receptors". If only definitions for "dopamine" and not the "dopamine receptor" shall be retrieved, the strict search should be chosen. However, definitions like "Dopamine (DA) is a free radical scavenger that attenuates apoptosis" will be lost by the strict variant because "dopamine (DA)" does not match exactly to the submitted term "dopamine". As a rule of thumb, a "strict" or "relaxed" search should be chosen at the beginning. Only in case the number of retrieved definition is not sufficient, the fuzziness of the definition query should be raised.

Table 4-3: EXCERBT Query Types

	QUERY TYPE	REQUIRED INPUT	EXAMPLES
RELATION SEARCH	A1 (Association Query Type 1)	agent name defined agent type defined target type defined target name NOT defined relation type defined	• Which diseases are caused by the wrn gene? • Which diseases are caused by species borrelia? • Which genes cooccur with miRNA-24? • Which metabolites inhibit the phenotype headache?
RELATION SEARCH	A2 (Association Query Type 2)	target name defined target type defined agent type defined agent name NOT defined relation type defined	• Which proteins phosphorylate the Brca1 protein? • Which metabolites activate ventricular arrhythmia phenotype? • Which tissues cooccur with the gene exportin 1? • Which tissues express the gene CD45?
RELATION SEARCH	R (Reification Query)	agent name defined agent type defined target name defined target type defined relation type defined	• Which sentences both mention the gene Brca1 and the phenotype breast cancer (cooccurrence)? • Which sentences support the view that metabolite caffeine inhibits phenotype headache? • Which sentences support the view that aurora A protein phosphorylates Brca1 protein?
RELATION SEARCH	N (Network Query)	Queue of A1 queries	• Network: All diseases activated by the submitted list of genes? • Network: All Metabolites cooccurring with a list of submitted diseases ?
DEFINITION SEARCH	D (Definition Query)	term to be defined	• Proper nouns, e.g. "Brc1", "phenylketonuria", "Lrrk2" • Abstract concepts: "bioinformatics", "patents"

In chapter 4.3, the graphical user interface for the presented five query types is described, while the developmental view deals with the Java interfaces lying behind the graphical front end. As EXCERBT has been implemented as one additional component of the GeKnowME system, in the following chapters only those aspects of the logical, developmental and physical view will be discussed which are specific for EXCERBT and which have therefore not been mentioned in *Nenova K., 2009*.

4. THE EXCERBT TM SYSTEM

4.2.2. LOGICAL VIEW

A key application scenario for TM systems is the generation or expansion of a model on a biochemical processes, diseases or a gene regulatory network. Models are proposed to help in understanding complex phenomena by representing only a reduced, relevant part of the available data. Therefore, the width (number of neighbors considered in each association query) and depth (number of association search steps applied) depends on the complexity of the biochemical phenomenon and on the biomedical question the user wants to model. Given one or a couple of entities and a relation type of interest, EXCERBT can retrieve related, direct neighbors, e.g. proteins phosphorylated by the submitted protein(s). The network can be expanded in the second step by taking one or all of those neighbors as input for a second relation search step, e.g. searching for metabolites regulating the retrieved kinases. *Figure 4-14* depicts the workflow of semi-automated literature based knowledge extraction with ECERBT. As will be discussed in chapter 5.2, a fully automated model generation by subsequently submitting relation searches taking the results of the preceding step as inputs is in principle possible but appears not to be recommendable. Instead, a semi-automated strategy has been successfully applied to generate literature based models of Parkinsonism. The strategy is described in detail in chapter 5.2. This semi-automated approach to model generation consisted of an alteration between knowledge expansion (A1, A2 queries) and manual inspection of the results for correctness and relevance (R and D queries). Only those terms and entities were considered in the next expansion step which appeared relevant for the phenomenon to be modeled. Especially the information provided by the definition search are helpful to decide if a retrieved entity is of relevance in the examined context, e.g. a disease, and should be taken as a starting point for expanding the knowledge network in the subsequent step.

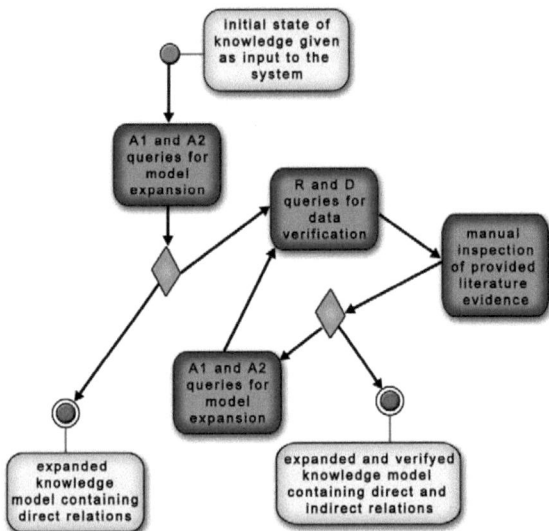

Figure 4-14: acitivty diagram of building literature-based biological models based on an alternation of A1, A2, R and D queries, the main data retrieval and representation procedures in EXCERBT

4. THE EXCERBT TM SYSTEM

4.2.3. DEVELOPMENTAL VIEW

The EXCERBT system can be accessed in two ways: by the graphical user interface (GUI), implemented as EXCERBT presentation module and the Java API provided by the GeKnowME system. The GUI is based on the Liferay Portal TM system and retrieves the requested data by calling the GeKnowME – SemanticManager class. The results are returned in the form of an XML document *Figure 4-15* shows that EXCERBT is only one resource among others which can be integrated and accessed by the Semantic Layer of GeKnowME.

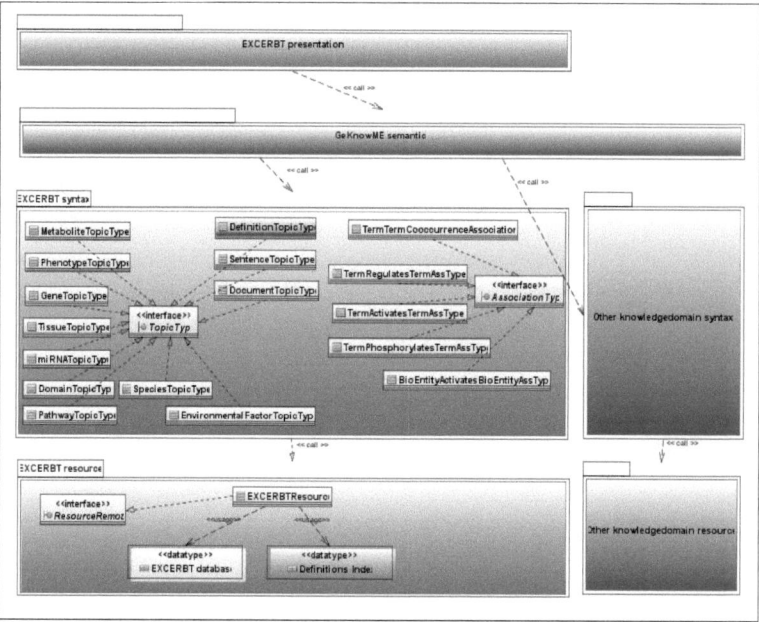

Figure 4-15: Layer model: EXCERBT data presentation. Grey squares: modules belonging to other GeKnowME resources; orange: modules or data structures relevant for definition search only.

The software layers required for data integration are listed below in a bottom-up order:

- EXCERBT_Resource: This module is called from the EXCERBT syntax layer and retrieves the requested data from two core data repositories, the EXCERBT PostgreSQL database and the definitions index. The data is returned in the form of an XML file.

4. THE EXCERBT TM SYSTEM

- EXCERBT_Syntax: For each entity- and relation type of EXCERBT, this module contains a TopicType and AssociationType class which implement the TopicType and AssociationType class provided by the GeKnowME system. This layer hands requests from the semantic layer down to the resource layer and processes the returned XML file. The syntax layer returns the extracted topics and association in the form of a TopicMap file.

- GeKnowME_Semantic: The GeKnowME SemanticManager, the core class of the semantic layer, links different knowledge resources to each other by mapping of shared concepts. This can be accomplished by merging the TopicMap files retrieved from the Syntactic module of several different resources.

- EXCERBT_representation: The representation layer actually consists of three modules. The core module is the EXCERBT_Portal module which makes use of two utility modules (GraphApplets module for the visual representation of the generated networks and the EXCERBTPortal_flashdocu module containing some flash videos for demonstration purposes). Each portlet of the GUI corresponds to one portlet class in the EXCERBT_Portal module. The EXCERBT_Portal module calls the SemanticManager class of the semantic layer and presents the results contained in the retrieved TopicMap file in the form of various portlets.

4.2.4. PHYSICAL AND PROCESS VIEW

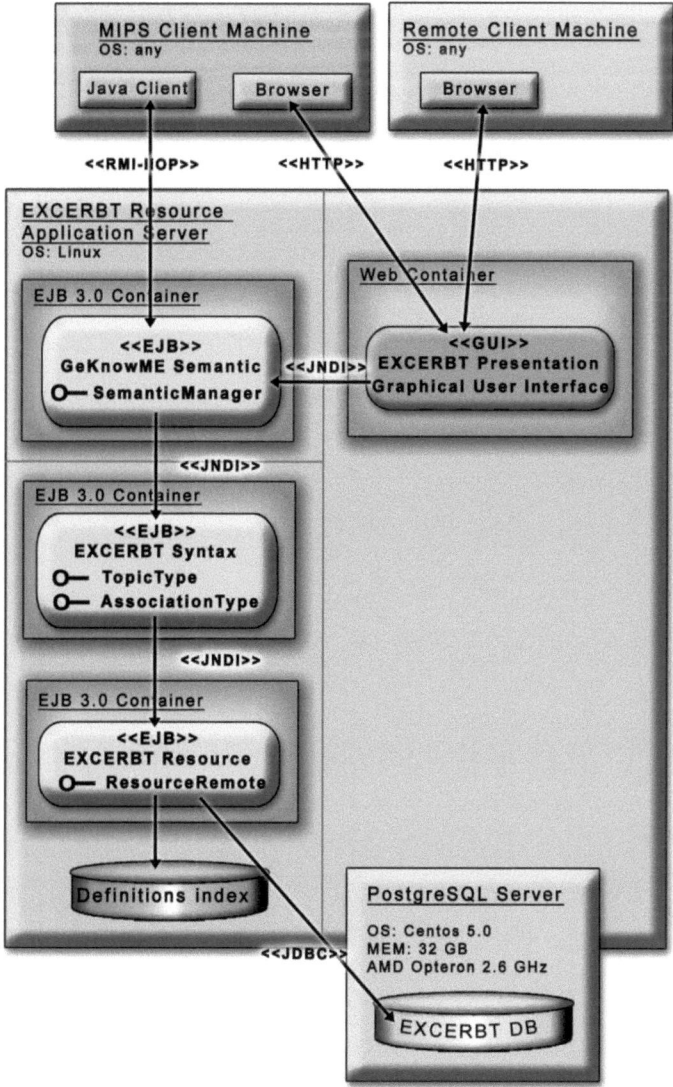

Figure 4-16: EXCERBT data presentation – physical view

4. THE EXCERBT TM SYSTEM

The GeKnowME system has been developed as a multi-tier software system. This architecture allows the integration of different resources hosted on physically separated machines. Currently, the resource-, syntax-, semantic- and presentation layers of EXCERBT/GeKnowME are deployed on a standard developmental machine (Intel Pentium Dual Core 2.4 GHz, 4 GB memory). The red lines in *Figure 4-16* indicate that each of these software components could also be hosted on physically distinct machines provided an application server with an EJB3.0 container for the EJB components and a web container for the portlets is installed. The definition index is directly accessed by the EXCERBT resource module; it must therefore be accessible in the file system of that machine to which the EXCERBT resource component is deployed. The EXCERBT database is accessed by the resource via JDBC.

4. THE EXCERBT TM SYSTEM

4.3. EXCERBT Graphical User Interface

The EXCERBT graphical user interface (GUI - *Figure 4-17*) is based on the Liferay Portal system which provides the possibility to encapsulate and represent functional units in the form of portlets. The web-interface of EXCERBT consists of three main pages for relation search, definition search and network (clustering) search. Each portal page consists of several portlets fulfilling a defined functional unit.

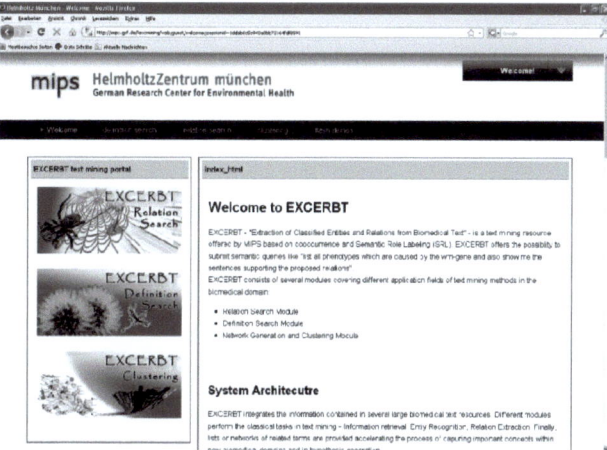

mips.helmholtz-

4. THE EXCERBT TM SYSTEM

4.3.1. RELATION SEARCH

Figure 4-18 shows the core portlets for the semantic A1 relation query "which phenotypes are caused by the wrn gene?". The user has the option to map the agent and target terms to their original database entry ("map terms to ids"). This option leads to a consideration of synonym terms in the query. However, due to the n-to-m mapping of names and identifiers and the increased risk to obtain false positive results due to common-English synonyms, this option is for most cases, especially gene names, not recommended.

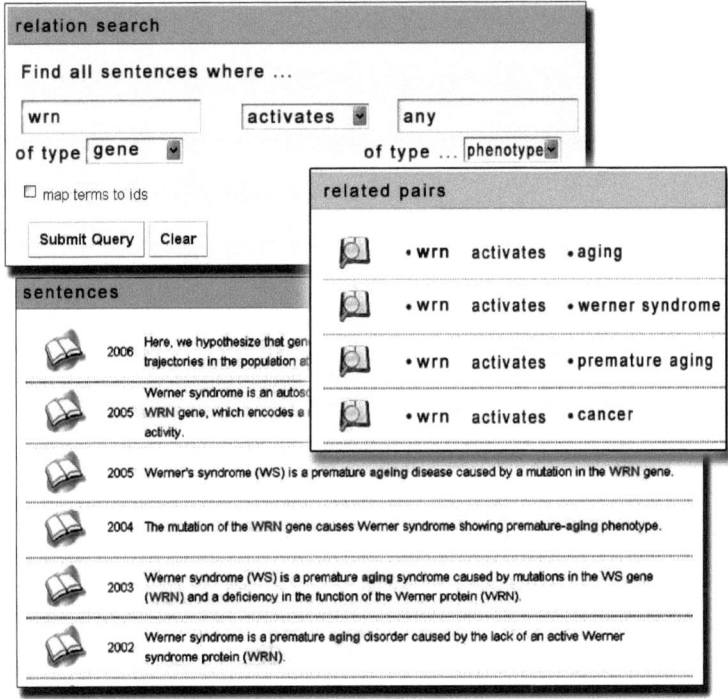

Figure 4-18: core relation search portlets: "relation search" portlet for A1, A2 and R- type queries (top); The "related pairs" portlet lists related entities ordered by the number of evidence-sentences (middle) for A1 and A2 queries; the "sentences" portlet (bottom) lists evidence sentences for R queries ("reification"). R queries are submitted by the user clicking on the book icon of a pair presented in the pairs portlet.

76

4. THE EXCERBT TM SYSTEM

4.3.2. NETWORK SEARCH

The submission of network queries via the GUI is currently constricted to 12 terms. Per term, at maximum 1000 related neighbor terms can be considered and added to the network. The size of the term list was limited to ensure that the extracted network can be held in memory. The network is returned in the Pajek graph format that can be transferred to the Java applet of the clustering portlet. The following example depicts the generation of a phosphorylation network by submitting a list of 11 proteins. The proteins of this list are linked to each other in the generated network by shared phosphorylation substrates.

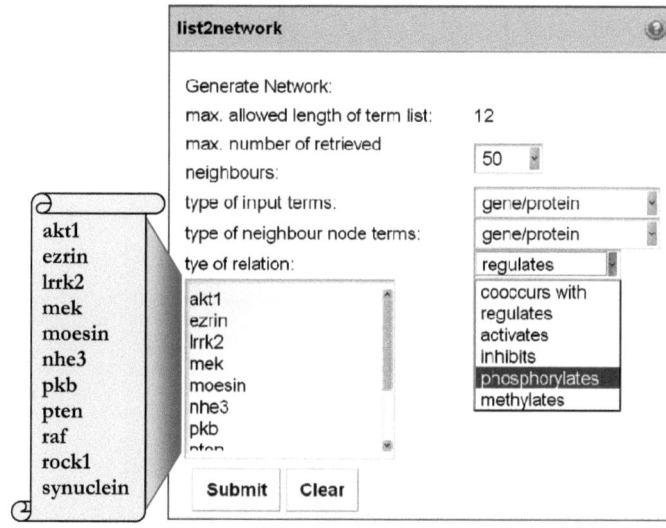

Figure 4-19: list2network portlet for submitting lists of agent terms for the N-query type; maximum number of retrieved neighbours(targets) per submitted term: 50; agent and target types: gene/protein; relationtype: phosphorylation

4. THE EXCERBT TM SYSTEM

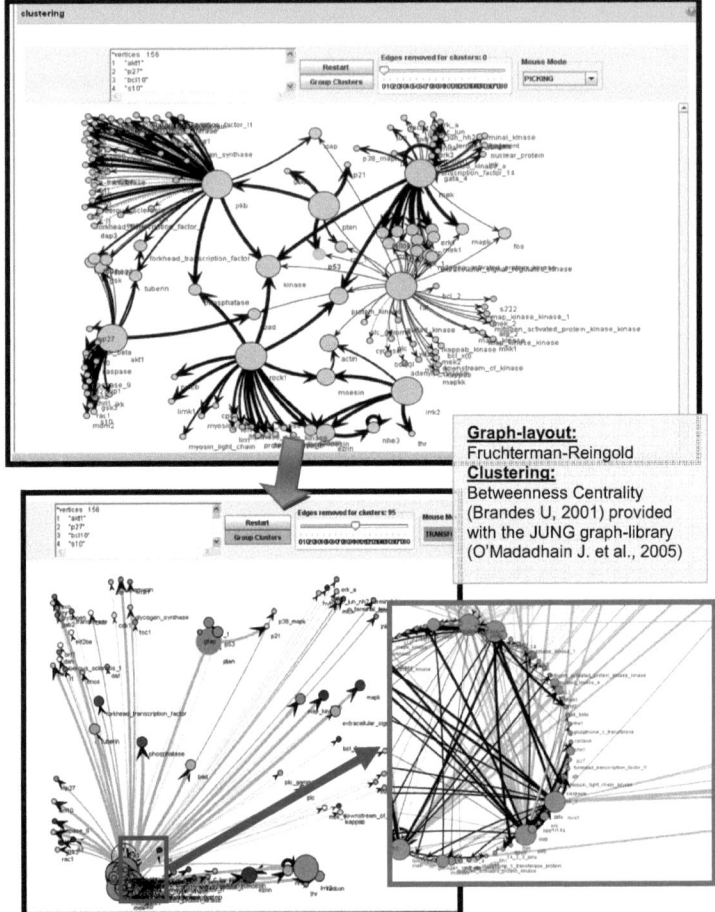

Figure 4-20: Network generation and clustering portlet. The applet contained in this portlet is based on the Jung graph library supporting the Fruchterman-Reingold layout algorithm and Betweennes Centrality Clustering.

The N-Query and clustering page of the EXCERBT portal allows submitting batch association queries to indirectly connect the terms in the submitted list with each other. The layout and clustering algorithms assist the user in getting a clear, visual impression of the detected direct and indirect relations.

4. THE EXCERBT TM SYSTEM

4.3.3. DEFINITION SEARCH

The definition search page hosts three portlets: One for entering one single term for which definitions shall be retrieved ("direct definition retrieval"), one portlet to show the defining sentences returned ("definitions portlet"), and one portlet for the context search which is also functionally connected to the definitions portlet.

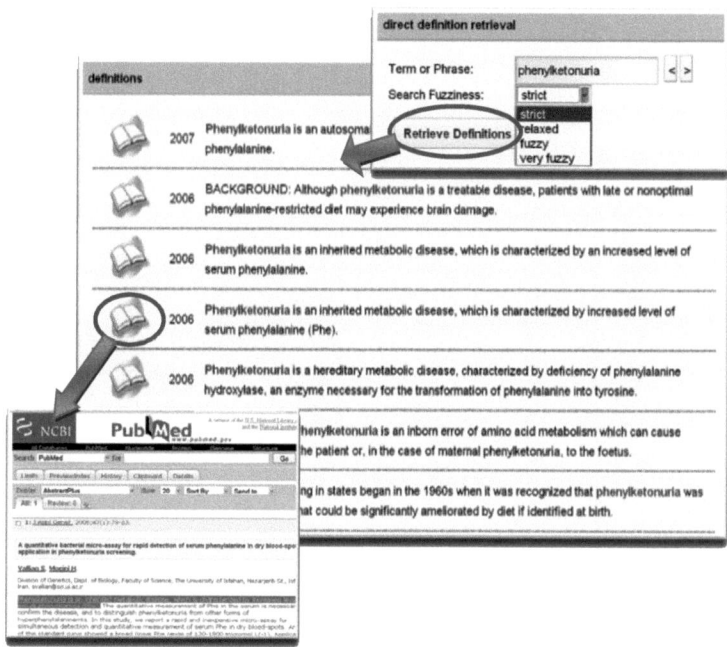

Figure 4-21: Definition search page - direct definition retrieval. The term "phenylketonuria" submitted in the first portlet via strict search returns a list of defining sentences. These "definitions" are listed in the "definitions portlet", e.g. "Phenylketonuria is an inherited metabolic disease, which is characterized by increased level of serum phenylalanine (Phe)". The definitions are ordered depending on the publication year of the corresponding text resource. The original publication can be quickly retrieved by clicking on the book symbol at the left side of each definintion which is linked to its corresponding abstract or fulltext article.

4. THE EXCERBT TM SYSTEM

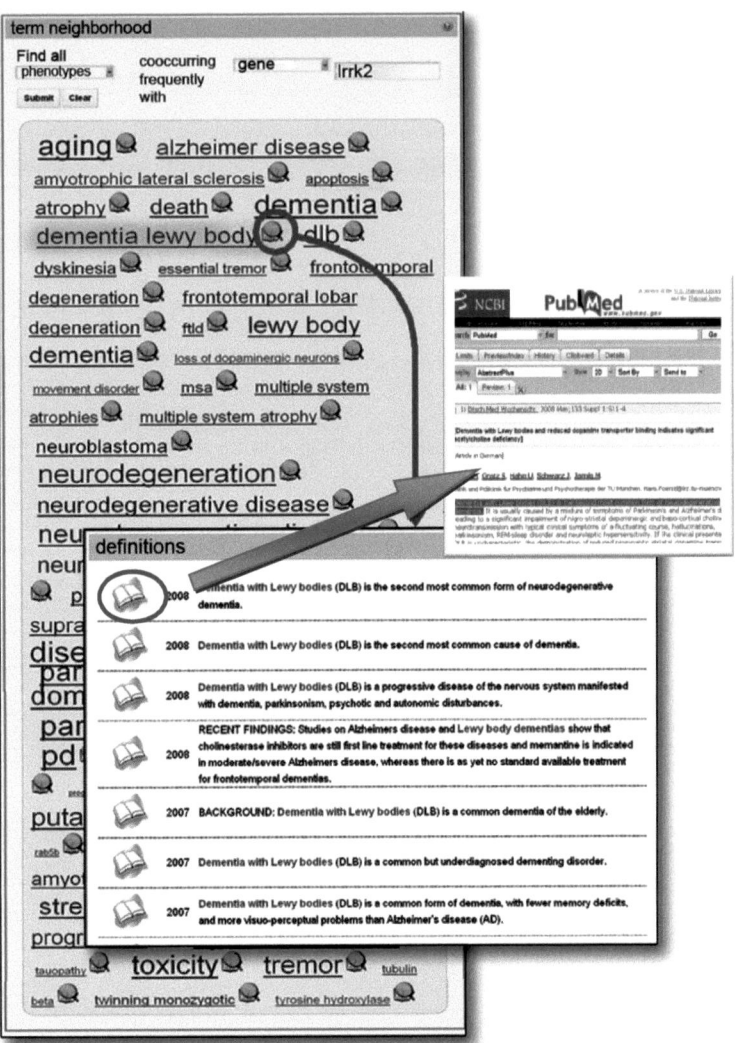

Figure 4-22: Definition search page - context search. The "term neighbourhood portlet", responsible for the context search, looks for terms of a certain entity type cooccurring frequently with the submitted term. The higher the numer of sentences mentioning both the submitted term and the "neighbour" term, the larger the font size of the neighbour term in the tag cloud. In this example, the phenotype-context for the lrrk2 gene are terms like "neurodegeneration", "tremor", "alzheimer disease" and "dementia lewy body". A click on the reading-glass icon to the right of each tag-cloud term starts a fuzzy definition search.The results of this search are displayed in the "definitions portlet", e.g. "Dementia with Lewy bodies (DLB) is the second most common form of neurodegenerative dementia". Each definition is linked to its original, external text resource.

5. APPLICATIONS

"In essence, science is a perpetual search for an intelligent and integrated comprehension of the world we live in."

Cornelius Bernardus Van Neil, U. S. microbiologist

EXCERBT can be used for speeding up the process of retrieving relevant information from literature, for semi-automated model generation and for annotating general terms and proper nouns of any type of biomedical category. In the following sections, some applications of the system will be discussed to explain how the TM system can help to solve these tasks in practice.

5.1. Speeding up Knowledge Retrieval

In order to evaluate if EXCERBT can accelerate literature based knowledge retrieval, two professional annotators were asked to measure the time they needed in order to answer and find literature evidence for the following two questions:

1. Which proteins phosphorylate Brca1?
2. Which proteins are phosphorylated by Aurora A?

The annotators were asked to use only PubMed, PubMed Central or OMIM as literature source. They were asked to stop after retrieving at least 9 different protein names or after 20 minutes working time at the latest even if they could not detect nine different names by then. The results are depicted in *Table 5-1*.

5. APPLICATIONS

Table 5-1: Comparison of time requirements and results of EXCERBT with that of two human annotators. The numbers in brackets indicate the time period in minutes at which the protein name was found.

QUERY TYPE	ANNOTATOR A	ANNOTATOR B	EXCERBT – UNCURATED	EXCERBT CURATED
Question I	Chk2 (3)	AKT (2)	(30 sec to retrieve the uncurated result list) 1. atr 2. kinase 3. atm 4. c abl 5. chek2 6. chk2 7. brca1 8. abl 9. protein kinase 10. checkpoint kinase 11. cell cycle checkpoint kinase 12. cdk4 13. ser 14. oncogene 15. gln 16. cyclin dependent kinase 2 17. cyclin dependent kinase 18. cyclin 19. cell cycle checkpoint kinase 2 20. aurora a	(additional 3 min, 30 sec to curate the list by manually inspecting the evidence sentences and removing redundancies) 1. atr 2. atm 3. c abl 4. chek2 5. chk2 6. cyclin dependent kinase 2 7. cdk4 8. cell cycle checkpoint kinase 2 9. aurora a
	ATM (9)	HRG (3)		
	ATR (9)	Casein-kinase 2 /CK2 (9)		
		Aurora-A (16)		
		ATM (20)		
		Chk2 (18)		
		ATR (22)		
		Cyclin-dependent kinase 2 /CDK2 (23)		
Question II	Eg 5 (3)	GSK-3 beta (1)	(35 sec to retrieve the uncurated result list) 1. tacc3 2. ndel1 3. cpeb 4. cenp a 5. ser 6. par 6 7. h3 8. cenpe 9. cdc25b	(additional 3 min for selecting and verifying the first nine entries of the list; five additional minutes to manually verify the remaining 11 protein names) 1. tacc3 2. ndel1 3. cpeb 4. cenp a
	Par-6 (4)	PLK 1 (3)		
	FAF-1 (4)	HURP (5)		
	HURP (6)	Histone H3 (8)		
	AIP (7)	Aurka (8)		
	ASAP (7)	AJP (9)		
	RASSF1A (8)	c-FOS (10)		
	TACC 3 (8)	ASAP (11)		

NDEL1 (9)	p53 (12)	10. brca1 11. par 12. hurp 13. transforming acidic coiled coil protein 14. tpx2 15. tacc 16. protein kinase c 17. protein kinase 18. plk1 19. parn a 20. parn 21. p53 22. numb 23. mbd3 24. kinase c 25. kinase 26. histone h3 27. histone 28. exonuclease 29. coiled coil protein 30. coil 31. centrosomal protein 32. cenps 33. cenpe a 34. atypical protein kinase c 35. atypical protein kinase c 36. asap 37. apkc	5. par 6 6. h3 7. cdc25b 8. brca1 9. par 10. hurp 11. tpx2 12. tacc 13. plk1 14. parn 15. p53 16. mbd3 17. histone h3 18. atypical protein kinase c 19. asap 20. apkc

The results clearly show that EXCERBT can help to speed up literature based knowledge retrieval significantly. While annotator A found only three proteins in the time span of 20 minutes, the second annotator found almost the same list of nine proteins which were returned by EXCERBT. Including manual inspection of the evidence sentences, the first question could be answered with the help of EXCERBT within four minutes instead of 23 minutes (annotator B). In order to retrieve the minimum of nine proteins for the second question from the literature, the annotators required 9 (annotator A) and 12 (annotator B) minutes. With the help of EXCERBT it would have been possible to retrieve a list of 20 rather than nine distinct and manually verified protein names. While the annotators had to consider only one "evidence sentence" per relation, the results returned by EXCERBT were often based on and connected to multiple sentences. If the annotators had been asked to search for multiple abstracts supporting each related kinase-substrate protein pair, the time gain by using EXCERBT would have been even larger.

5.2. A Literature Based Model for Parkinsonism

Parkinsonism is a neurodegenerative disorder characterized by the death of dopaminergic neurons, movement disabilities, tremor and postural instability. Environmental factors as well as genetic causes are known but the detailed biochemical pathways involved in the pathogenesis are still widely unknown. Oxidative stress responses,

5. APPLICATIONS

disturbance of the mitochondrial fusion and fission balance and impaired proteasomal degradation leading to the accumulation of Lewy bodies have been associated with the disease *(Henchcliffe and Beal, 2008)*. On the genetic level, some recessive as well as dominantly acting gene mutation have been characterized which lead to the development of Parkinsonism *(Gasser, 2009)*.

As the biomedical interaction cascades involved in the development of this disease have to a large extent not been experimentally characterized, it is not possible to extract this knowledge from literature. However, a linkage of macroscopic as well as genetic knowledge fragments with the help of literature mining appeared as a promising option to connect these two knowledge aspects as far as the current empirical knowledge allows and to elucidate biological relations scattered among several different publications.

Benedikt Wachinger and I used terms and relations stated in the Parkinsonism model of Henchcliffe et al. *(Henchcliffe et al., 2008)* as well as five Parkinson-related genes Lrrk2, synuclein, DJ-1, Pink1 and Htra2 as two independent starting points. In both cases, the aim was to connect the elements (e.g. pathway components and proteins) with each other with the help of the EXCERBT relation and definition search. At first, the comparatively restrictive "regulation" and "phosphorylation" searches were applied, in case of rarely mentioned terms the cooccurrence based search was used. Interesting "neighbors" were selected manually from the returned lists of related entities based on the inspection of the evidence sentences. Information on the retrieved genes and proteins provided by the definition search were also considered. In case the dictionary did not contain the required term, e.g. "mitochondrial fission", the search was done with the tissue term "mitochondrion" or by applying the definition search for the term "mitochondrial fission" which revealed a connection of this process with the Fis1 gene. With the help of EXCERBT, the network was built semi-automatically within about three days. Although neither Benedikt Wachinger nor I had deeper biological knowledge in the examined biomedical domain, a team of biologists with a strong background on Parkinsonism awarded the model to cover all relevant aspects currently discussed in the field. At least for this examined use-case, a biologically comprehensive network could be build although most of the information stated in the full text sections of the articles could not considered by EXCERBT due to license restrictions. In this use-case, EXCERBT proved to be a valuable help in accelerating knowledge retrieval from literature. It would not have been possible to build up this model containing also hidden relations interlinking two proteins via 4 or 5 intermediate relations by non-domain experts without this system in the same time. The network revealed some regulatory pathways connecting some of the five genes the model was started with to some phenotypic, Parkinson related traits. For example, it is known that mitochondrial fusion and fission play important roles for mitochondrial morphology and function *(Fritz et al., 2003)*. Mitochondrial fission is a response to stress that has an important role in neuronal cell death in neurodegenerative diseases *(Ju et al., 2007)*. *Figure 5-2* illustrates the molecular links between Pink1 and mitochondrial fusion/fission balance and shows that it shifts the balance towards fission via the OPA1 protein. *Figure 5-3* depicts a possible regulatory pathway connecting the MAO-B (mono-amine oxidase B), a well known target in anti-Parkinson therapies (MAO-B inhibitors) with DJ-1 via ROS, NO and possibly SUMO 1.

It should also be noted here that although the coverage of the semi-automatically extracted model was very good and only manually verified connections were integrated in the model, relations contained in those knowledge models should not be fully trusted

5. APPLICATIONS

without the analysis of a domain expert. The phosphorylation of moesin by lrrk2, for example, was correctly extracted from the literature by EXCERBT. The domain experts, however, rendered this relation as questionable as other groups had failed to reproduce this result. Clearly, this kind of knowledge is beyond the scope of an automated information extraction system as well as for biologists and curators lacking in-depth knowledge in the examined field.

The conventional way of retrieving answers to biomedical questions from literature has in the previous chapter been shown to be remarkably slower for each single semantic association than an EXCERBT supported knowledge retrieval. The time saving in the development of literature based biomedical models containing hundreds of such associations cannot be measured in minutes, but in working days.

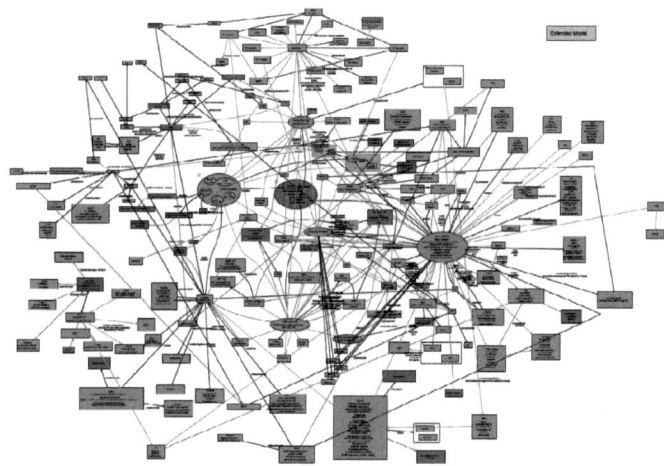

Figure 5-1: Literature based model for Parkinsonism starting from five Parkinson related genes depicted as ovals (Lrrk2, PINK1, DJ-1, alpha-synucleine, parkin)

5. APPLICATIONS

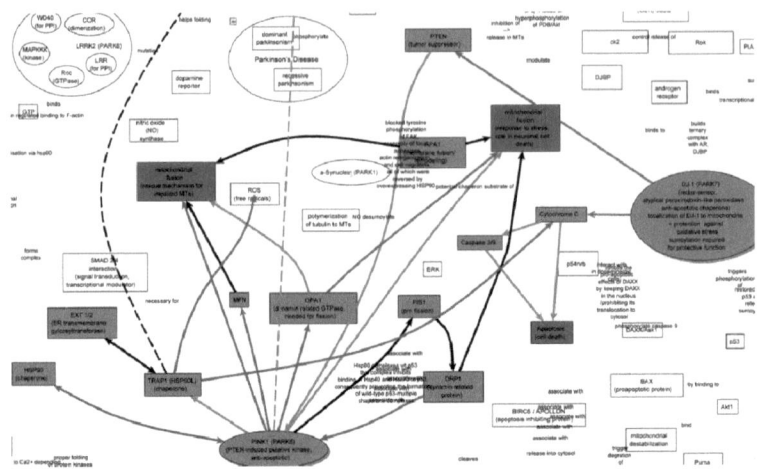

*a MFN, OPA1
tion; dotted blue:*

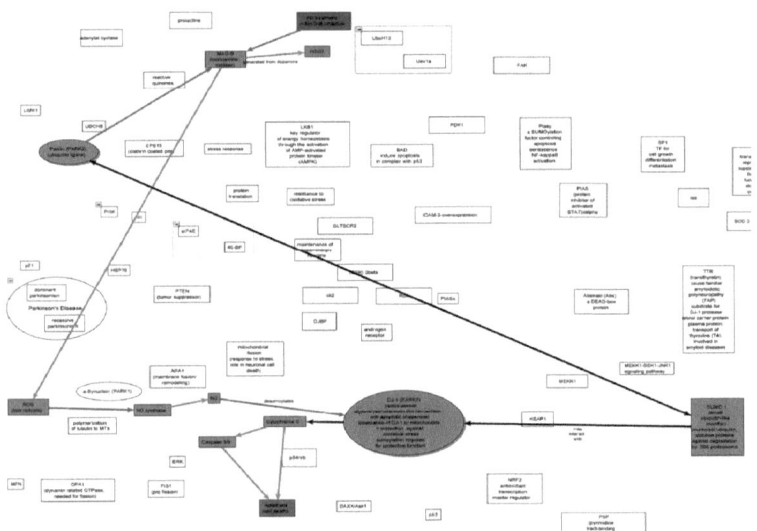

*nent anti-Parkinson
ylation of DJ-1 (by
stress. NO has been
ectly or indirectly via
egulatory connections*

86

5.3. Coverage Analysis I: Substances Affecting Parkinsonism

This use-case stands for a common problem in pharmaceutical industry and medical research: the search for substances with the potential to treat or even cure a disease. The purpose of this case study is to reveal the fraction of substance classes known to have an influence on the disease progression of Parkinsonism which could be detected by EXCERBT (evaluation of relation search coverage). In addition, definitions for all retrieved substance names were retrieved by applying the EXCERBT definition search (evaluation of definition search coverage).

Basically, there exist two ways of identifying drug candidates in EXCERBT, a direct and an indirect approach.

Direct Search

The system can be used to directly retrieve substances having an impact on a disease. Although this approach only reveals relations which have already been detected, this search is a good starting point for the following reasons:

- The returned list gives an overview on current treatments and approaches as well as on substances known to cause Parkinsonism.

- Several retrieved substances may have been tested on animal or cell culture models of a disease but have not (yet) been applied in clinical trials.

- The substances currently used for treatment belong to a chemical or physiological category, e.g. dopaminergic agonists. By looking for other substances belonging to that category, additional options for treatment may be revealed.

- The consideration of substances which have an exacerbating influence on a disease (by using a "regulation" instead of an "activation" search) can also be useful. Parkinson inducing or enhancing substances may reveal knowledge on biomedical interactions in the disease pathway that can be used to treat the disease due to inhibiting or reversing these interactions. For example, the herbicide *paraquat*, which is known to increase intracellular superoxide levels and oxidative stress, was reported to induce Parkinsonism. This finding renders anti-oxidative agents as possible drugs against oxidative-stress induced apoptosis of dopaminergic neurons leading to Parkinsonism.

Starting point and reference for the evaluation of this analysis is a statement made by (*LeWitt and Taylor, 2008*) on the current treatment options for Parkinsonism: "Although promising leads have arisen, no therapy has been proven to halt or slow disease progression. [...] This review summarizes findings from clinical trials with several classes of compounds, including monoamine oxidase-B inhibitors (selegiline, lazabemide, rasagiline), dopaminergic drugs (ropinirole, pramipexole, levodopa), antioxidant strategies (alpha-tocopherol), mitochondrial energy enhancers (coenzyme Q(10), creatine), antiapoptotic agents (TCH346, minocycline, CEP-1347), and antiglutamatergic compounds (riluzole). Beyond small-molecule pharmacology, gene therapy approaches, such as delivering neurotrophic substances (e.g., neurturin) by viral vector, are the next generation of treatment options."

5. APPLICATIONS

Appendix A lists all metabolites/substances retrieved by EXCERBT as having an impact on Parkinson disease (regulates-relation). The returned list consisted of 258 entities and was manually shortened to 185 entities by removing spelling variants and terms that were parts of other terms ("hexal" is part of "n-hexal"). The KEGG compound database that was used, among others, for the construction of the substance part of the EXCERBT dictionary, also contained some protein terms and environmental factors such as "smoking". Therefore, the substance list returned does also contain some entities of those categories. 1-3 sentences supporting the proposed relation between substance and disease were added to each entity pair to give an impression of the literature resources each proposed relation was based on. Errors introduced by the NER or RE step were marked with grey color, but even those sentences often revealed biomedical relevant information.

For all retrieved Parkinson-relevant agents, the definition search was applied in order to retrieve information on these entities. 1-5 defining sentences were added to each concept although in most cases more definitions could have been added. The substances preventing or ameliorating Parkinsonism retrieved by EXCERBT were compiled from the results in the appendix and categorized according to *LeWitt and Tayler in Table 5-2*.

Table 5-2: Substances with the potential to be used to treat Parkinsonism extracted with the help of EXCERBT.

SUBSTANCE CLASSES ACC. TO LEWITT AND TAYLER	EXCERBT RESULTS
Monoamine oxidase B inhibitors	• Selegiline • Pargyline
Dopaminergic drugs	• Pramipexole (according to definition search) • Levodopa • Apomorphine • Bromocriptine • Capergoline (according to definition search) • Pergolide • Terguride • Quinpirole [name not properly resolved – see "dopamine receptor]" • ML-23 and S-20928 [name not properly resolved – see "melatonine"]
Antioxidant strategies	• J-113397 NOP-receptor antagonist [name not properly resolved – see "benzimidazole"]
Mitochondrial energy enhancers	• -
Antiapoptotic agents	• Minocycline • In addition: several examples for pro-apoptotic agents causing Parkinson: MPTP, Beta-carbolines, ceramide, MPP, N-methyl(R)salsolinol)
Anti-glutaminergic compounds	• Riluzole • Baclofen (GABA-agonist)
other	• Amantadine - NMDA receptors antagonist • STN-DBS: Subthalamic nucleus deep brain stimulation • Implantation of fetal dopamine (DA) [-- see term "DA"] • Subtype-selective estrogen receptor-alpha (ERalpha) agonist SKF 82958 [name not properly resolved - see "dopamine receptor"] • Carbidopa = inhibitor of aromatic amino acid decarboxylase • Choline esterase inhibitor Rivastigmine [name not properly resolved - see " choline esterase"] • Isatin (atrial natriuretic peptide receptors antagonist) • Nerve growth factor NGF • smoking/nicotine • Oral administration of semisynthetic sphingolipids (mouse model!) • Possibly: neuronal nitric oxide synthase inhibitors, e.g. 7-NI, Dexamethasone or indomethacin • NADH may possibly ameliorate parkinsonism • Unilateral implantation of dopamine-loaded biodegradable hydrogel in the striatum

5. APPLICATIONS

The list of substances retrieved by EXCERBT shows a good overlap with the substances given by LeWitt and Tayler. All substance classes were covered by the EXCERBT result list except the mitochondrial energy enhancer class and the antioxidant strategy class which was only partially covered due to a name resolution error for J-113397 NOP-receptor antagonist. Notably, some additional substances and substance classes were contained in the EXCERBT result list like "NADH", "semisynthetic sphingolipids", "nicotine", the atrial natriuretic peptide receptor antagonist "Isatine" and others. The coverage of the relation search for the examined biomedical question appeared as very satisfying. This analysis reveals that the information contained in reviews and the information retrieved with the help of EXCERBT will usually contain significant overlaps (in this case five anti-Parkinson substances *Selegiline*, *Pramipexole*, *Levodopa*, *Minocycline* and *Riluzole*). But the review as well as the EXCERBT result list each contained several substances being not a member of the other data source. The reading of reviews and the usage of EXCERBT for information retrieval appear to complement rather than substitute each other. The substance list retrieved by EXCERBT as well as some evidence sentences for each relation can be examined in depth in Appendix A.

The second aim of this examination was to reveal the coverage and quality of the automatically generated lexicon (definition index). As can be seen in Appendix A, the lexicon covers a very broad spectrum of entities and concepts relevant for biomedical research. Only in five out of 185 cases, no appropriate definition could be retrieved. In the broad majority of cases, the listed definition sentences were highly accurate to describe the biomedical relevance of the substance of interest (see Appendix A).

There is much room for interpretation of the data in Appendix A by a human mind: Calcium antagonists like *flunarizine* have shown to induce Parkinsonism. Is the application of calcium agonists a way to ameliorate this disease? Hereditary Parkinsonism with dementia is caused by mutations in the *ATP13A2* gene encoding a lysosomal P-V type ATPase. Can this mutation be functionally examined in detail and reveal new options for treatment? It has been reported that intranigral iron injection induces biochemical Parkinsonism in rats. Do there exist substances being able to decrease iron levels in dopaminergic cells and can this impede the progression of this disease? An EXCERBT query for genes/proteins reducing the metabolite/substance "*iron*" suggested, among others, "*superoxide dismutase (SOD)*" (Nara et al., 1999; Cairo et al., 2002; Agrawal et al., 2001). According to a second query to EXCERBT, substances such as *Vitamin E* increase the *SOD* activity (*Mehta et al., 1999*). Interestingly, a protective effect of *Vitamin E* on Parkinson patients has been observed (*Agrawal et al., 2001*), that has been ascribed to the free radical scavenging capacities of *Vitamin E*. This connection reveals that the function of *SOD* as a radical scavenger may be not the only way in which this protein helps to protect against the break-out of Parkinsonism.

Indirect Search

While direct relations retrieved from literature resemble relations already known to the scientific community, indirect relations between two entities are not necessarily aware to even experts of a field of research. Indirect relations revealing new ideas on the treatment of a disease are of special interest to the pharmaceutical industry. Those relations connect, for example, a gene product known to have a causative or enhancing effect on a disease with a substance inhibiting this gene product. Some examples for such indirect relations will be given in the next paragraph. An inhibitory regulatory chain of three elements as depicted in *Figure 5-4* can consist of an inhibitory relation followed by a positive regulation. Alternatively, the chain can start with an activation and end with an inhibition. For (qualitative) regulatory chains of larger size, the overall output is always positive (enhancing) if no or an even number of negative regulatory steps is contained in the chain irrespective of the number of positive relations (edges). The overall effect of a regulatory chain is negative, if the number of inhibitory edges is odd. Although biochemical pathways can be of eminent complexity, for drug prediction task the length of the regulatory path connecting the drug target to the disease to be treated should be as short as possible to reduce the risk of interfering with non-disease associated biochemical pathways. In the following paragraphs, some examples for literature based drug candidate prediction based on the first of the two regulations schemas given in *Figure 5-4* will be discussed.

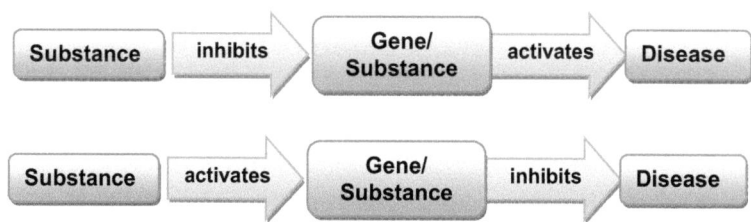

Figure 5-4: Regulatory schema for substances and potential drug candidates indirectly inhibiting a given phenotype

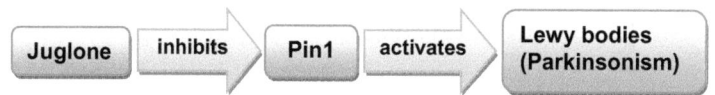

Figure 5-5: Regulatory schema for Juglone, Pin1 and Lewy bodies/Parkinsonism

Starting point of this examination is a publication by Ryo A. et al. (*Ryo et al., 2006*) stating that Pin1 overexpression facilitates the formation of alpha-synuclein inclusions. These inclusions play a key role in the development of several neurodegenerative diseases such as Parkinsonism or Alzheimer's disease (*Nowotny et al., 2007*). Based on Ryos observation, metabolites or substances with the potential to decrease the expression level or inhibit the function of Pin1 can be considered as potential drug candidates against Lewy body accumulation. Accordingly, an A2 query "list all metabolites/substances inhibiting the Pin1 gene!" was submitted to EXCERBT returning the following list of substances ordered by the number of "evidence sentences": juglone, rna, proteasome, glu, oxides, human chorionic gonadotropin, gonadotropin, gln, chorionic gonadotropin, amino acids, alanine. The amino acids returned were false positive results and the analysis was focused on Juglone.

5. APPLICATIONS

Subset of the evidence sentences for the proposed inhibitory relation between Juglone and PIN1:

- Shen et al. (2005) treated purified eosinophils with hyaluronic acid alone or with various concentrations of cyclosporin A (CsA), which inhibits PPIA (123840), FK506, which inhibits FKBP1A (186945), or juglone, which specifically and irreversibly inhibits PIN1, and assessed CSF2 (138960) secretion and eosinophil survival.
- Finally, the post-mitotic dephosphorylation of both CC-3 and MPM-2 antigens was prevented when cellular Pin1 activity was blocked by the selective inhibitor juglone.
- It has been shown that juglone inactivates Pin1 by forming a covalent bond through the sulfhydryl groups of cysteines in a slow and time-dependent fashion (12).
- The association of NHERF-1 with Pin1 facilitated dephosphorylation of NHERF-1, as shown in experiments in which cellular Pin1 activity was blocked by the selective inhibitor juglone.

The notion that juglone selectively inhibits Pin1 activity is important as this property helps to prevent undesirable side effects. A definition search to gather additional facts on juglone returned the following information:

- Juglone (5-hydroxy-1,4-napthoquinone) is a chemical released by walnut trees, which can be toxic at various levels to several plant species.
- The natural toxin juglone causes degradation of p53 and induces rapid H2AX phosphorylation and cell death in human fibroblasts.
- Juglone is the active ingredient of the green flesh of walnuts and is known to be a strong irritant.
- Juglone is a napthoquinone found in the bark of the black walnut (Juglans nigra), which has been used as an herbal medicine for its antihaemorrhagic and antifungal properties [33].
- The data indicate that juglone is an effective inhibitor of RNA polymerase II transcription and suggest that Pin1 may be involved.

Based on this examination, Juglone appears as a potential drug candidate as it has been reported to selectively inhibit a Parkinson-promoting protein, Pin1. As Juglone has already been used as antihaemorrhagic agent, some information on its usability for medical treatment should be available. There exists also information speaking against its usability as drug, e.g. the blocking of RNA polymerase II transcription. An in-depth analysis of the pharmaceutical applicability of juglone appears reasonable based on the extracted data.

In this example, the link between Pin1 and Parkinson was already known and only a comparatively small set of candidate drugs had to be extracted by EXCERBT and manually verified afterwards. The number of abstracts mentioning Pin1 and its biochemical relations is comparatively small.

A much greater challenge is the detection of drug candidates given only a disease name that have not yet been discussed in the scientific literature in the context of this disease. This task is especially challenging for buzzwords like "Parkinsonism". In order to reveal potential and not hitherto examined drug candidates, a Java Program was written searching for all metabolites or genes increasing "oxidative stress", a cell state known for its neurotoxic effects on dopaminergic cells potentially resulting in Parkinsonism. This step was accomplished by submitting appropriate association queries to the Java interfaces of the EXCERBT TM system. In the second step, for each gene or substance of that list, an association query was submitted to EXCERBT retrieving all substances having an inhibitory influence on that oxidative stress – causing substance or gene. The substance list returned after this second step consisted of several thousand entries. Many of them were known to have an impact on Parkinsonism. In order to exclude those "known" substances, an association query for substances cooccurring with the term "parkinsonism" or "Parkinson disease" was submitted to EXCERBT. The returned terms were considered as "not new" in the context of Parkinson and used to cleanse and down-size the result list returned in the step before. Finally, a file still containing several thousand entries connecting a potential drug with "oxidative stress" according to *Figure 5-6* was generated. A fraction of the relations contained in this file was used for manual verification of the results.

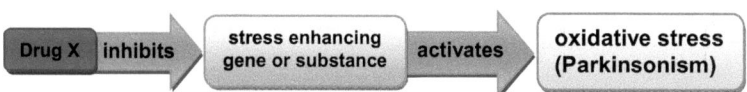

Figure 5-6: Potential drug, oxidative stress enhancer, ocidative stress/Parkinsonism

Most of the returned results could be excluded as potential drugs by looking on the evidence sentences for the two relations or by submitting some additional definition searches or PubMed queries. The main reason for false positive drug candidates were errors in the NER or RE step in one of the two edges and the finding that a substance was already known in the context of Parkinsonism. The filtering step sorting out all metabolites co-mentioned on the sentence level (EXCERBT) did not rule out all those substances known to have an impact on Parkinsonism and mentioned together with this disease on the abstract or document level. In several cases, the definition search revealed that a substance was highly toxic or could not be administered properly. Still, after about seven hours manual inspection of the results, a list of more than ten potential drugs for the treatment of Parkinson could be compiled which can be considered as "new" drug candidates. If queries submitted to PubMed as well as PubMed Central for the substance name in combination with the term "Parkinson" did not return an appropriate result, the detected relation was considered as "new". Although no in-depth analysis on all information available to the proposed substances was made which could render some of the list item as toxic or otherwise problematic, the examples show that with the help of EXCERBT the task of literature based hypothesis generation and drug candidate detection can be significantly accelerated.

Table 5-3, the color of the cells corresponds to the node- and arrow- colors given in *Figure 5-6*.

5. APPLICATIONS

Substance	Evidence	Stress Enhancer	Disease
Oxidative stresses induced by reactive oxygen species (ROS) have been shown to be involved in several physiological and pathophysiological processes, such as cell proliferation and differentiation. (PMID: 18716444)			
Peanut and Olive oil **Remark**: Although searching for one of those oils in combination to "Parkinson" will return no results in the two most prominent biomedical text resources (except for some papers where peanut oil is used as solution for the application of other substances), a study has been published revealing that a diet high on unsaturated fatty acids prevents against Parkinsonism: PMID:15985568. Interestingly, peanut as well as olive oil contains a high fraction of omega-9 fatty acids.	Peanut oil and olive oil feeding also lowered the extent of ROS generation in macrophages compared to those from coconut oil fed animals. (PMID: 7981240)	ROS	Oxidative Stress
Phenyllactate / Hydroxyphenyllactate definition search: Phenyllactic acid is a product of phenylalanine catabolism.	Phenyllactate, small er, Cyrillic-hydroxyphenyllactate, and p-hydroxyphenylacetate inhibited the production of ROS and pore opening, acting as antioxidants. (PMID: 18634861)	ROS	Oxidative Stress
Anticarcinogenic agents: Chlorophyllin definition search: Chlorophyllin (CHL) is a chlorophyll derivative with anticarcinogen and antioxidant activities. **Remark**: according to PMID 14644357, porphyrin compounds, e.g. chlorophyllin (CHL) and tetrakis(4-benzoic acid)porphyrin (TBAP), belong to those anticarcinogenic substances that reduce ROS production. No connection to Parkinson was found in PubMed and PMC for Chlorophyllin. Two 2 abstracts/5 PMC articles mentioning Parkinson and MnTBAP were found, one of them stating that provision of mnTBAP can indeed rescue a genetically introduced form of Parkinsonism in mice (PMID: 9462746).	A number of structurally different anticarcinogenic agents inhibit inflammation and tumor promotion as they reduce ROS. (PMID: 14644357 – the paper discusses Chlorophyllin)	ROS	Oxidative Stress

5. APPLICATIONS

Zopolrestat definition search: Zopolrestat (Alond) is a new (1998) drug that is being evaluated as an aldose reductase inhibitor for the treatment of diabetic complications. **Remark**: Although neither in PubMed nor PubMed Central a connection between the two terms "Zopolrestat" and "Parkinson" could be found, a patent exists (Patent WO/2002/043763) for the combined administration of GABA agonists and aldose reductase inhibitors, among the latter: Zopolrestat	Both the aldose reductase specific inhibitor (zopolrestat) or transfection with aldose reductase antisense oligonucleotide blocked the phosphorylation of JAK2, the production of ROS, and proliferation of VSMC induced by HG, but it had no effect on the Ang II-induced activation of these parameters in both NG and HG. (PMID: 12777386)	ROS	Oxidative Stress
Zafirlukast definition search: Zafirlukast is a potent and selective cysteinyl leukotriene receptor antagonist which is used mainly in the prophylaxis of bronchial asthma.	In agreement with our results, LTD4 has been proposed to increase production of superoxide anion [54], while, more recently, zafirlukast has been shown to interfere with the release of ROS during respiratory bursts of human polymorphonuclear neutrophils or eosinophils [55,56]. (PMCID: PMC1488842)	ROS	Oxidative Stress
Midostaurin definition search: Because OSM sensitizes rat osteosarcoma to apoptosis/necrosis, the use of kinase inhibitors such as Midostaurin in association with OSM could represent new adjuvant treatments for this aggressive malignancy.	Oral treatment with the PKC inhibitor midostaurin reduced aortic Nox1 expression, diminished ROS production, and reversed eNOS uncoupling in SHR. (PMID: 16781385)	ROS	Oxidative Stress
Allantoin / Allantoate definition search: Allantoic acid is the END product of Allantoicase [EC:3.5.3.4], an enzyme involved in uric acid degradation (Purine metabolism). Allantoin is a botanical extract of the comfrey plant and is used for its healing, soothing, and anti-irritating properties. Allantoin is a nonenzymatic oxidative product of uric acid in human.	Interestingly, the level of ROS and mortality could be attenuated by the addition of allantoin and allantoate, suggesting that these metabolites can act as scavengers of ROS. (PMID: 18266920)	ROS	Oxidative Stress

Exposure to TNF-alpha induced oxidative stress and inflammatory mediators, such as p38 mitogen-activated protein kinase (MAPK), nuclear factor kappaB, COX-2, and PGE(2), which were all amplified by preenrichment with linoleic acid but blocked or reduced by alpha-linolenic acid..(PMID: 18803934)

5. APPLICATIONS

Gentianine definition search: Gentianine and gentianal were the important bioactive metabolites of gentiopicroside in rats.	For the first time, we found that oral administration of gentianine (10-100 mg/kg) suppressed the increases in tumor necrosis factor-alpha (TNF-alpha) (ED(50), 37.7 mg/kg) and interleukin (IL)-6 (ED(50), 38.5 mg/kg) in the sera from the rats challenged with bacterial LPS (100 microg/kg; i.p.).). (PMID: 15802824)	TNF alpha	Oxidative Stress
Polyacetylene constituents (Falcarinol and Falcarindiol) definition search: In conclusion, pre-incubation with low concentrations of both polyacetylenes prior to H(2)O(2) exposure induced a cytoprotective effect whereas higher concentrations had adverse effects. Thus, the effects of falcarinol on CaCo-2 cells appear to be biphasic, inducing pro-proliferative and apoptotic characteristics at low and high concentrations of falcarinol, respectively. These results suggest that excessive NO production plays an important role in the neurotoxic effect, and falcarindiol is a potential inhibitor in NO-mediated neuronal death. **Remark**: no abstracts or papers mentioning both "Parkinson" and "Falcarindiol" were found, but one publication supports the relation to Falcarindiol: "Falcarindiol inhibits nitric oxide-mediated neuronal death" (PMID: 14561925)	In in vitro experiments, coumarin constituents (hyuganins A-D, anomalin, pteryxin, isopteryxin, and suksdorfin) and polyacetylene constituents [(-)-falcarinol and falcarindiol] substantially inhibited LPS-induced NO and/or TNF-alpha production in mouse peritoneal macrophages, and isoepoxypteryxin inhibited D-GalN-induced cytotoxicity in primary cultured rat hepatocytes. (PMID: 16226032: Falcarinol and Falcarindiol are discussed)	TNF alpha	Oxidative Stress
Anthocyanidin (e.g. cyanidin chloride) definition search: Anthocyanidin is a type of the plant pigments distributed very extensively, in traditional Chinese herbal products as well. Like other flavonoids, anthocyanidins are also expected to have antioxidative and anti-mutagenic properties in vivo, although only few data are available. Anthocyanidins are the aglycon nucleuses of anthocyanins, which are reddish pigments widely spread in colored fruits and vegetables	Lipopolysaccharide (LPS)-induced TNF-alpha production from macrophages was inhibited by treatment with flavone (luteolin, apigenin, and chrysin), flavonol (quercetin and myricetin), flavanonol (taxifolin), and anthocyanidin (cyanidin chloride) in vitro. (PMID: 14745173)	TNF alpha	Oxidative Stress

5. APPLICATIONS

Myricetin definition search: Myricetin is a novel natural inhibitor of neoplastic cell transformation and MEK1. Myricetin is a naturally occurring flavonoid that is commonly found in tea, berries, fruits, vegetables, and medicinal herbs. This showed that myricetin was a good inhibitor of lipid peroxidation in this model and that the intermediate generation of phenoxyl radicals might contribute to the antioxidant mechanism of myricetin. **Remark**: It has been observed that Myricetin reduces 6-hydroxydopamine-induced dopamine neuron degeneration in rats. (PMID: 17589323)	Lipopolysaccharide (LPS)-induced TNF-alpha production from macrophages was inhibited by treatment with flavone (luteolin, apigenin, and chrysin), flavonol (quercetin and myricetin), flavanonol (taxifolin), and anthocyanidin (cyanidin chloride) in vitro. (PMID: 14745173) Release of IL-6, IL-8 and TNF-alpha was inhibited by 82-93% at 100 microM quercetin and kaempferol, and 31-70% by myricetin and morin (PMID: 15912140).	TNF alpha / Oxidative Stress
Yangonin, Desmethoxyyangonin (Wikipedia: Yangonin belongs to a substance group of Kavapyrones (Styryl-alpha-Pyrones) derived from the Kava-plant. Kavalactones derived from the roots and bark oft he Kava-plant have anxiolytic, moderately analgetic and antioxidative properties.) **Remark**: Yangonin administration resulted in a decrease of dopamine levels to below the detection limit while desmethoxyyangonin, an other Kavapyrone, increased dopamine levels. (PLMID: 9829291)	5,6-Dehydrokawain (desmethoxyyangonin)(1) and yangonin (4) significantly inhibited TNF-alpha release with IC50 values of 17 microM and 40 microM; a potency as great as (-)-epigallocatechin gallate (EGCG) isolated from green tea extract. (PMID: 12809361).	TNF alpha / Oxidative Stress

Table 5-3: Potential drug candidates for the treatment of Parkinsonism based on a manual inspection of a fraction of the predictions generated by EXCERBT

Although a clinical trial is the ultimate test to evaluate the applicability of a predicted drug, this case study looks promising even in the absence of such an empirical test: A connection between Zopolrestat and Parkinsonism could not be retrieved by searching PubMed or PubMed Central. The connection between these entities in this case study was derived only indirectly via "ROS" and "oxidative stress". However, a patent exists claiming Zopolrestat to be, in combination with other substances, applicable against Parkinsonism. Patent literature has not yet been integrated into EXCERBT, but this example shows that based on the indirect relations contained in MEDLINE, a relation could be predicted that was contained in a different text resource directly. For other substances (peanut oil, Chlorophyllin) there exist examples where a chemically or functionally related substance have been observed to have the predicted inhibitory influence on Parkinsonism/neuronal cell death (unsaturated fatty acids, MnTBAP).

5. APPLICATIONS

5.4. Coverage Analysis II: Diseases Caused by Borrelia

According to the Online-Encyclopedia Wikipedia on Borreliosis, "[…] early manifestations of infection may include fever, headache, fatigue, depression, and a characteristic skin rash called erythema migrans. Left untreated, late manifestations involving the joints, heart, and nervous system can occur […]".

Querying EXCERBT for all disease traits caused by the pathogen species Borrelia resulted in a list of 174 disease or phenotype terms. This list was manually reduced to 150 terms by removing duplications due to spelling variants ("non Hodgkin lymphoma", "non Hodgkin's lymphoma") or terms standing for a gene, not for a disease. The list of induced phenotypes given in Appendix B very well elucidates the spectrum of phenotypes that is associated with a tick bite induced borrelia infection. Each phenotype is connected to at least one scientific article or text resource supporting or citing the proposed relation. Among the list of induced phenotypes are, backed by the highest number of "evidence sentences": "Lyme disease", "borreliosis", "tick borne fever", "erythema", "facial palsies" and "meningitis".

6. DISCUSSION

"It is a capital mistake to theorise before one has data. Insensibly one begins to twist facts to suit theories instead of theories to suit facts"

Sherlock Holmes, a fictional creation of Arthur Conan Doyle

The aim of my doctorate was the development of a text mining system being capable to facilitate and accelerate literature based knowledge retrieval for biomedical questions. The construction of qualitative models of various sizes and the prediction of drugs for complex, multifactorial diseases such as Parkinsonism have been successfully applied with the help of the EXCERBT system much faster than it would have been possible based on conventional information retrieval strategies. A technical challenge was the generation of a database schema for semantic knowledge extraction and representation covering a multitude of relation types in a uniform, maintainable and extendable way. In addition, the very large amount of extracted information had to be represented in a subject-centric way. Relation retrieval was supposed to scale to a very broad range of term frequencies and should be able to connect a broad range of diverse semantic concepts and their interrelations with the underlying literature evidence as well as to other knowledge resources integrated in the GeKnowME system.

6.1. Accuracy Evaluation

Two basic evaluation approaches for TM systems exist, a "bottom-up" and a "top down" approach. The "bottom up" approach evaluates error rates for each single step applied during knowledge extraction. A final score for all involved text processing, NER and RE steps is calculated by considering and integrating the accuracy values of all single steps. In this evaluation approach, the accuracy of each processing step has to be determined separately in an appropriate test. This evaluation approach was not addressed for the following reasons: for many of the mentioned tasks, no annotated test corpora exist, e.g. for relations regarding miRNAs. The time required for annotating such corpora covering all integrated entity types, text resources (abstracts and full texts) and relation types and being of sufficient size to extrapolate the results on a text resource of more than 100 million sentences and 3 million dictionary terms would require several man-years of work. Therefore, the top-down evaluation approach was applied and the results presented in the application section of this thesis: The relations and definitions retrieved by the final EXCERBT system were manually evaluated regarding the ability to retrieve comprehensive and sufficiently accurate biomedical knowledge on a certain topic. The amount of time required with or without the help of EXCERBT to extract the knowledge required to model a biochemical phenomenon or answer a biological question was assessed. Clearly, these examples are of anecdotal character given the amount of data and relations contained in MEDLINE and in the whole EXCERBT database. Never the less, the obtained results appear very promising regarding the speed of knowledge retrieval as well as its accuracy.

This observation is at the first place surprising as the specificity and recall values obtained for the RE step (P/R) were only 71% and 43% and additional errors introduced by sentence splitting and the NER step were not covered by this values. The reasons for this observation are as follows:

6. DISCUSSION

- The low recall values retrieved for the SRL based RE step were measured on a per sentence basis. For the generation of literature based biomedical models, the consideration of just one single sentence describing a certain relation is sufficient. In practice, most relations between two entities are stated several times, so the recall value on the "relation level" will be notably higher.

- The SENNA/SRL based extraction of subject-predicate-argument relationships performs much worse for nominalizations than for verbal forms. The majority of the relations missed in the RE evaluation consisted of relations being expressed as nominalization, e.g. "gene X transcriptional inhibitor Z". It appears questionable if an author would use this syntactical structure in order to express a newly detected relationship. If a relation between two entities is considered by the author as being new and relevant, a verbal form will probably be preferred. This syntactical form directs the attention of the reader much more to the proposed relation than a nominalization, which is a condensed form of relational expression. In addition, for some relation types, the nominalization form is highly unusual. While "A, the activator of B" is a common syntactical form for well known activating relations, the expression "A, the phosphorylator/methylator of B" is not. Of 110 million biomedical sentences contained in EXCERBT (*Barnickel T. et al., 2009*), only three contained the term "phosphorylator" but 88.440 contained the term "activator". The fraction of nominalizations for relational expression varies depending on the verb and relation type. As the sensitivity of the introduced SRL based RE approach strongly depends on the ratio of nominal- to verbal forms of relational expression, and this ratio depends on the relation type, an overall accuracy value for SRL based relation extraction cannot be given. The evaluation done for the RE step presented in chapter 3.7 was based on text corpora mainly containing regulatory protein protein relationships. The sensitivity and accuracy of the phosphorylation relation can be expected to be significantly higher than the values observed for the regulatory relations as nominalizations occur much less frequent for this relation type.

Due to the large number of integrated entity types, relation types, text sources and dictionary terms, a comprehensive, quantitative analysis of the coverage and accuracy of EXCERBT for all possible combinations of entity types and relation types is not feasible. The accuracy values retrieved in the evaluation based on protein-protein relationships can for reasons given beforehand be considered as the lower bound of relation extraction accuracies reached by EXCERBT. The application scenarios presented in the preceding chapter as well as the data listed in the appendices are highly promising examples for the potential of the system to tackle biomedical questions and problems in practice.

6. DISCUSSION

6.2. Literature Based Model Generation with EXCERBT

Accuracy values for NER and RE are not the only aspects of relevance for literature based model generation in biology. An important finding during the development of the model for Parkinson genesis was that even a text mining system with 100% accuracy is probably unable to fully automatically build biochemical models deeper than one to two expansion steps. This is caused by the way experimentally derived, scientific knowledge is gained and presented to the public. *Figure 6-1* depicts the problem: the "real" biochemical regulatory pathway is shown at the top. "A" has a promotional effect on "B", "B" has a promotional effect on "C" while "C" inhibits "D". The effects in the "real" regulatory chain are based on direct molecular interactions. Before these "real" relations are understood on the molecular basis, researchers of different laboratories may have observed that an increase of "A" as well as "B" has an inhibitory effect on "D". This observation is reported in scientific publications and does not imply that the effect of "A" on "D" is introduced via physical interaction. As a consequence, a regulatory network consisting of four nodes and three edges can lead to a literature derived model with up to six edges even if the TM system applied would reach 100% accuracy and would not extract one single false positive relation.

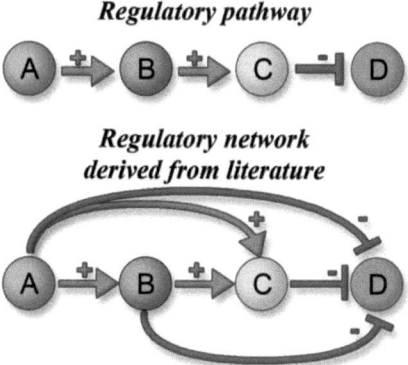

Figure 6-1: Literature based regulatory networks contain more edges than regulatory networks based on physical interaction even if no false positive relations have been introduced.

For this reason, a fully automated expansion of a regulatory network for more than one or two steps will lead to the generation of a network too big and too complex to be understood by a human, though this is the actual goal of any model. Even for relation types where the extracted relations can always be expected to be physical interactions, e.g. for phosphorylation, a human mind is necessary for model interpretation: a phosphorylation event correctly extracted from literature may have been detected solely in vitro, not in vivo. The animal models used in different publications which contribute

6. DISCUSSION

to the model may be based on different, hardly comparable animal models, and this information may not be available by considering only the abstracts of a paper. These are principle obstacles for automated literature based model generations which are accompanied and aggravated by term ambiguity and technical problems.

Given this constraints, the aim of EXCERBT is not and cannot be to render human interpretation of literature derived knowledge unnecessary. Rather, EXCERBT has proven in several real world scenarios that it can assist and accelerate relation extraction and information retrieval from literature and can reveal interesting biomolecular relations hidden in the vast amount of publications. In the case of the model for Parkinson genesis, the ideal work flow turned out to be an alteration between automated model expansion and semi-automated model verification (*Figure 4-14*). At first, a "knowledge germ" derived from a paper or review in the form of five Parkinson related genes was expanded using EXCERBT's open semantic querying interface in active and passive voice (A1 and A2 queries). These queries returned lists of, for example, proteins regulated by the Pink1 protein or a list of proteins regulating DJ-1. As proteins may be responsible for different physiological functions depending on their cellular context, each element of the result list of proteins was checked with the help of the EXCERBT definition search if at least one functional annotation existed linking a protein to a Parkinsonism related phenotypic or molecular trait. If the definition search revealed that a certain protein was involved in apoptosis, the defense of oxidative stress, in the maintenance of the cytoskeleton or mitochondrial fission or fusion dynamics, those proteins were rendered as especially interesting and relevant. They were the primary candidates used to expand the network by additional A1 and A2 queries in subsequent network expansion steps. Therefore, the relation search functionality of EXCERBT used for model generation and expansion is ideally complemented by the definition search functionality in order to select the starting points for the next model expansion step. If both search approaches are combined during the process of model generation, it is possible even for non-domain experts to quickly generate and expand biological models not by simply aggregating any entity somehow related to the topic of interest but to make informed decisions on which relations and entities to be included in the model and which not. The model for the genesis of Parkinsonism was evaluated by several domain experts of the field who attested the model to cover all relevant aspects currently discussed in this field of research and even to contain relations they had not been aware of so far.

In addition to the examples explained in the application section of this thesis, EXCERBT has been successfully applied in the modeling of regulatory connections between genes and miRNAs involved in acute myeloid leukaemia (AML). It is currently used to elucidate virus- and host interactions involved in the Hepatitis B virus (HBV) life cycle.

6.3. Knowledge integration

The text mining approach presented here is based on a subject centric representation of the extracted positional information. This is a prerequisite for a seamless integration of the literature derived relations to the GeKnowME system allowing the connection and superposition of knowledge derived from different resources. Automatically derived literature networks are not free of errors due to well known conceptional and technical problems. As explained previously, a superposition of data from different resources can help to detect those relations supported by several independent knowledge resources. With the help of the GeKnowME infrastructure,

EXCERBT can be used to link those resources to relations and concept definitions contained in the ever growing amount of scientific literature.

6.4. Summary

To the best knowledge of the author, EXCERBT is the only publicly available text mining system for the biomedical domain enabling the user to submit open, semantic queries for a very broad range of entity and relation types. Other than in most existing publicly available system, the NLP procedures for NER and RE are fast enough to cover not only the whole MEDLINE text corpus, but also some additional literature sources like OMIM or HMDB. Many existing TM solutions are, due to processing speed constraints, confined to fractions of the available literature (Texpresso, Chilibot) or abstain from semantic analysis in favor of faster cooccurrence based approaches (iHop).

The possibility to submit open, semantic queries is, however, a key functionality for any relation extraction system. Especially for hub terms, merely cooccurrence based approaches will not be restrictive enough and the user will still lose much time for evaluating the long list of unspecifically retrieved results. User queries have to be submittable as "open queries", because this way of proposing a question ensures that the user provides only information on what he is interested in while the task of hypothesis generation and knowledge extraction is completely at the hand of the text mining system. A conventional MEDLINE search via the PubMed interface, on the contrary, often implies the submission of additional search terms to reduce the list of returned documents, but this method also implies submitting relational data the user already knows about instead of letting the system find the relevant relations.

Semantically open queries can only be answered by a computer-based system if the system possesses some internal ontological knowledge on some aspects of the world. The EXCERBT dictionary used to answer such open queries comprises a higher number of biomedical entity types and names than any other online resource for biomedical literature mining currently available. The dictionary was derived from a multitude of different databases and ontologies and manually stocked up with additional terms in order to ensure a good coverage of names for any integrated entity type.

The strict modularity of the system architecture ensures that additional entity and relation types can be seamlessly integrated to EXCERBT. Molecular biology is a highly dynamic field, and the detection of regulatory pathways governed by the action of miRNAs has shown that a highly flexible software architecture is a prerequisite to ensure that all relation- and entity types relevant for model generation in Systems Biology can be covered by a text mining system also in future times.

6. DISCUSSION

7. CONCLUSION

"Data is not information, information is not knowledge, knowledge is not understanding, understanding is not wisdom"

Clifford Stoll

The EXCERBT text mining system presented in this thesis is a broad scale system for extracting a multitude of semantic relations from biomedical scientific literature. Several conceptional as well as technical problems were addressed to generate a tool capable of accelerating literature based knowledge retrieval by researchers, students and annotators in the life science domain.

In recent years, several specialized approaches for extracting protein protein interactions or phosphorylation events have been presented. The goal behind the development of EXCERBT was not the generation of one additional, highly adapted system for one singular relation type not jet covered by these systems. Rather, EXCERBT was developed as a broad-range text mining system covering a higher number of semantic relation types and entity types than any competing system. EXCERBT's accuracy has been shown in several use cases as being well capable of speeding up the process of knowledge retrieval from literature. In order to understand complex biomedical pathways, a broad coverage of concepts and relation types is necessary to interlink all relevant interactions and interdependencies. This can currently not be achieved in a satisfying way by using a large set of different publicly available TM systems, e.g. RLIMS-P for phosphorylation interactions, iHop for gene/protein relations or MEDIE for gene-phenotype interactions. The heterogeneity regarding functionality and user interfaces of all these different tools implies that the user has to get used to multiple interfaces and multiple technically different approaches (cooccurrence, semantically enriched or real semantic queries) and text sources. An automated interconnection of the results obtained from these different tools is in most cases not possible although the coverage and connection of different relation and entity types is necessary, e.g. for drug candidate prediction (see application section). For some relation and entity types, no online-available TM tool exists, e.g. for miRNAs. An additional obstacle for data connection and integration is the fact that many of the existing systems generate document-centric rather than subject centric networks and can therefore not be connected to subject-based approaches or directly be used for network generation.

In order to tackle those obstacles for literature mining in Systems Biology, EXCERBT covers a multitude of relation and entity types making them accessible for the user via one single system and one graphical user interface. EXCERBT provides the user with the convenience of a subject centric representation of the results. These results are gathered from several text resources and link related concepts to each other, to evidence sentences as well as to the ontological resources the concepts were derived from.

Thanks to the implementation of EXCERBT as one additional component of the GeKnowME information integration system, the semantic interlinking of concepts is possible not only for heterogeneous data derived from literature but also for literature-based results and information derived from in house or external databases and resources. The predicate-verb-argument based approach of EXCERBT ideally fits to the TopicMap

7. CONCLUSION

based semantic information representation schema applied in the GeKnowME system. Therefore, the system fulfills a dual function: it is a stand-alone, publicly available, semantic TM system but it can also be semantically linked to non-literature based knowledge domains with the help of GeKnowME. The Java interfaces implemented by the information representation modules of EXCERBT ensure that automated access to the system is possible. In future times, these interfaces may also be used for the implementation of Web Services in order to allow, in addition to the graphical user interface, automated access to the system from outside of MIPS.

The definition search functionality provided by EXCERBT is, to my knowledge, the first publicly-available example of an automatically generated lexicon for the biomedical domain. It is capable of automatically linking arbitrary terms to factual knowledge on those terms described in scientific publications. Although this lexicon has been realized with focus on the life science domain, this approach is applicable to any domain provided a text corpus in English of sufficient size is available. The retrieved definitions may contain redundant information and the retrieved list of definition sentences does not follow a single line of logical argumentation like it is the case for classic lexica or Wikipedia. However, the time necessary to build the definition search lexicon covering diverse fields of research is marginal compared to the time required for building up and maintaining such a lexicon manually. In addition, each definition sentence is linked to its text source which is an important aspect for citation purposes. The group of possible beneficiaries ranges from students searching for unknown biomedical terms for their studies to researchers and medical practitioners interested on background information on a gene or disease. It can also be used for automated functional annotation of biomedical databases and ontologies. The definition search significantly improves the information value and relevance of the EXCERBT relation search designed to reveal unknown relations as this functionality immediately reveals the biological function of an unknown gene or phenotype returned by the relation search. It has been exhaustively applied during the generation of the biomedical models presented in this thesis and has also been used for citation purposes in several pieces of writings (diploma and doctoral thesis) at MIPS. A possible technical further development of this functionality could be the implementation of a plug-in for MS Word or other text processing applications that retrieves definitions and their corresponding literature reference via a web service from EXCERBT.

There has been a lot of press coverage lately regarding the need for semantic search strategies in various areas of working and everyday life. Wolfram Alpha[13], released in Mai 2009, has gained much attention as a possible successor to Google but the system turned out to be more a math- and number centric question answering system rather than a fully automated semantic search engine based on text processing. At least for the near future, the system will therefore be more a supplement rather than competitor to Google which does not contradict the possibility that Wolfram Alpha is very helpful for several scientific and math-centric application scenarios. The considerable worldwide attention attracted by Wolfram Alpha shows the widespread need for systems that do not only return lists of potentially relevant documents but rather provide some kind of semantic answer to a submitted question. Ideally, a text mining system should be able to do this task automatically without the need for manually selecting and interpreting parts of the available literature by a group of human annotators or data curators as it is currently the case for Wolfram Alpha. The constantly increasing amount of literature requires

---

[13] http://www.wolframalpha.com/

7. CONCLUSION

automated solutions to semantically structure and interpret the flood of data hidden in natural language text. For manual text interpretation, the amount of available literature is far out of reach already today. On the other hand, without a minimum, core ontological framework built up manually by humans that has to be integrated into the text processing system, a TM system will not be able to interpret any text input semantically. A core ontological framework is required in order to map singular pieces of data extracted from text to ontological knowledge shared also by humans. EXCERBT resembles a new approach based on Semantic Role Labeling to semantically structure and interpret large amounts of text. It has a simple ontological framework or "semantic backbone" in the form of a set of possible relation types each defined by a list of verbs and a set of entity types defined by a list of entity names belonging to that that category, e.g. genes or metabolites. Based on this ontological semantic backbone, the system allows the submission of a broad range of open semantic questions which are very close to the syntax of human every-day speech. Other than Wolfram Alpha, the answers returned by the system are gathered completely automatically and no manual curation or structurisation of the knowledge gained from literature is necessary. Although the system is currently based on biomedical scientific publications, biomedically relevant ontologies and verb sets, EXCERBT could equally well be used in other application scenarios, e.g. to extract knowledge from engineering or business related literature. Apart from introducing another semantic backbone by using other ontological sources for the EXCERBT dictionary and the definition of appropriate relation types based on sets of representative verbs, no change in the system architecture would be required.

EXCERBT has been designed as a tool bringing text mining approaches from theory to practice by not only focusing on improving the accuracy of a single TM step but rather trying to consider and optimize data representation, usability, access times, coverage of concepts as well as extensibility. The system meets the conceptual as well as technological requirements of a text mining system assisting in the task of literature based knowledge retrieval and model generation for Systems Biology. The broad range of integrated text sources, entity- and relation-types in combination with the definition search renders the EXCERBT TM system as a useful tool in practice to extract biomedical knowledge from literature. The presented applications show that the system has already been successfully applied to facilitate and accelerate literature based knowledge retrieval for question answering and drug candidate prediction. With the help of EXCERBT, the answering of typical biomedical questions could be completed within three minutes compared to 10-20 minutes required by professional human annotators with comparable or even better accuracy. The system has successfully been applied for the generation of several biological models. Its flexibility ensures that the system will be able to cover also new relation and entity types that may define the focus of interest of Systems Biology in future years.

7. CONCLUSION

LIST OF ABBREVIATIONS

DR	Document Retrieval
EXCERBT	Extraction of Classified Entities and Relations from Biomedical Text
GeKnowME	Generic Knowledge Modeling Environment
GeneRIF	Gene Reference Into Function
HT	High Throughput
HMDB	Human Metabolome Database
IE	Information Extraction
IR	Information Retrieval
IIS	Information Integration System
ME	Maximum Entropy
MIPS	Munich Information Center for Protein Sequences
NER	Named Entity Recognition
NLP	Natural Language Processing
OMIM	Online Mendelian Inheritance in Man
PAS	Predicate Argument Structure
RE	Relation Extraction
SGD	Saccharomyces Genome Database
SRL	Semantic Role Labeling
TM	Text Mining

List of Abbreviations

LIST OF FIGURES

Figure 1-1: A: Equation expressing the relationship between knowledge and data; B: Definition of "Interpretation" (derived from (Jack Par et al., 2002) 2

Figure 1-2: GeKnowME five tier system architecture (Figure taken from Nenova K., 2009). 5

Figure 2-1: Growth of MEDLINE: Number of new MEDLINE citations published per year (1960 - 2008) 11

Figure 2-2: Word usage per abstract for 13 countries. Dark blue bars: countries in which English is not the main language. Light blue bars: 6 countries in which English is the main language. The image lists two words not generally used in English-speaking countries (left side) and their equivalent words commonly used by native English speakers (right side) - (Netzel et al., 2003) 15

Figure 2-3: The three main levels of natural language text 17

Figure 2-4: Key steps in literature mining 21

Figure 2-5: Applying NER on a piece of biomedical text. Words resembling genes (blue) and phenotypes (red) have been detected, labeled and linked to the identifiers of Entrez Gene and OMIM. 23

Figure 2-6: Constituent tree generated by the lexicalized version of the Stanford Parser. Figure derived from (Clegg and Shepherd, 2007) 27

Figure 3-1: PropBank sentence with annotated semantic roles 31

Figure 3-2: Performance comparison of SENNA with common SRL programs and syntactic parsers. Performance time (ptime) of SENNA* (a slightly slower variant of SENNA), ASSERT, two variants of the Enju HPSG parser and Stanford PCFG and lexicalized parser were measured relative to SENNA 1.0 web version on four test sets of 500 sentences each. The length interval of the sentences ranged from 65-75 characters for the first test set to 235-245 characters in the fourth test set. 36

Figure 3-3: Length distribution for 89 million biomedical sentences from PubMed abstracts (including the titles), the open access part of PMC full text articles and OMIM records with lengths between 10 and 400 characters. Extremely short or long sentences often result from errors in the sentence splitting step 38

Figure 3-4: True positive relation extraction based on SRL 40

Figure 3-5: False positive relation extraction caused by errors in the NER step 40

Figure 3-6: False positives caused by additional words reversing the meaning of the verb (here: "loss of") 40

Figure 4-1: Two central data processing tasks in EXCERBT 44

Figure 4-2: Two functional cores of EXCERBT 44

Figure 4-3: Use case view for data generation in EXCERBT 46

Figure 4-4: Modeling relation types in EXCERBT 48

Figure 4-5: The EXCERBT dictionary. The synonyms table contains the names for the integrated entities in the synonymphrase table. As several overlapping ontological resources may be used to cover one entity type, only the original identifiers of an entity, not its associated synonym, is mapped to a database or ontological resource which is stored in the entriesdatabases table. The mapping between synonyms and synonymentries (n to m mapping) is contained in the synonyms_synonymentries table. 49

Figure 4-6: Storage of sentences and PASs in EXCERBT: each document is derived from a certain textsource like PubMed or HMDB. Each sentence is mapped to the document it was taken from by the documents_id column. In addition, a sentence has a foreign key column "fields_id" connecting it to the text section (tfields table) the sentence was derived from (e.g. title or text body). Each PAS is connected to its corresponding sentence by its sentence_id although not every sentence may have a PAS assigned. The core semantic PropBank arguments ARG0 to ARG2 as well as some modifier arguments are stored in the pas table in separate columns. The verbs_id column in the pas table connects each PAS to a verb in the verbs table, if its verb is the same as a verb string in the verbs table entry. 53

Figure 4-7: Storage of positional data in the EXCERBT database. All positional data linking sentences to synonyms are stored in the hits table. All positional data linking subject roles (ARG0) of a PAS to a synonym is stored in the synonyms_pasarg0 table which is mapped to a relation type via the corresponding pas, verbs and verbs_relationtypes table (see Figure 4-4). Accordingly, positional information of synonyms mentioned in the argument role (ARG1) is stored in the synonyms_pasarg1 table. 54

Figure 4-8: Overview on data generation workflow in EXCERBT 55

Figure 4-9: Activity diagram for literature based data extraction in EXCERBT. Dark blue: data generation steps required for cooccurrence based association queries. Pink: steps required for semantic queries (relation extraction and definition search). Green: Steps required for semantic relation extracting; Orange: data processing step required for definition search. 56

Figure 4-10: EXCERBT Data Generation modules required for relation and definition search. Arrows indicate dependencies between different modules and data structures. As almost all modules read or write data from or to the EXCERBT database, the corresponding dependencies have therefore been omitted in this figure. 57

Figure 4-11: Physical structure of the definition index and the indices required for NER. 62

Figure 4-12: EXCERBT data generation – physical view 63

Figure 4-13: Five usecase scenarios for EXCERBT queries 67

Figure 4-14: acitivty diagram of building literature-based biological models based on an alternation of A1, A2, R and D queries, the main data retrieval and representation procedures in EXCERBT. 70

Figure 4-15: Layer model: EXCERBT data presentation. Grey squares: modules belonging to other GeKnowME resources; orange: modules or data structures relevant for definition search only. 71

Figure 4-16: EXCERBT data presentation – physical view 73

Figure 4-17: Welcome screen of the EXCERBT system (www.mips.helmholtz-muenchen.de/geknowme/web/excerbt) 75

Figure 4-18: core relation search portlets: "relation search" portlet for A1, A2 and R-type queries (top); The "related pairs" portlet lists related entities ordered by the number of evidence-sentences (middle) for A1 and A2 queries; the "sentences" portlet (bottom) lists evidence sentences for R queries ("reification"). R queries are submitted by the user clicking on the book icon of a pair presented in the pairs portlet. 76

Figure 4-19: list2network portlet for submitting lists of agent terms for the N-query type; maximum number of retrieved neighbours(targets) per submitted term: 50; agent and target types: gene/protein; relationtype: phosphorylation 77

Figure 4-20: Network generation and clustering portlet. The applet contained in this portlet is based on the Jung graph library supporting the Fruchterman-Reingold layout algorithm and Betweennes Centrality Clustering. 78

Figure 4-21: Definition search page - direct definition retrieval. The term "phenylketonuria" submitted in the first portlet via strict search returns a list of defining sentences. These "definitions" are listed in the "definitions portlet", e.g. "Phenylketonuria is an inherited metabolic disease, which is characterized by increased

List of Figures

level of serum phenylalanine (Phe)". The definitions are ordered depending on the publication year of the corresponding text resource. The original publication can be quickly retrieved by clicking on the book symbol at the left side of each definintion which is linked to its corresponding abstract or fulltext article. 79

Figure 4-22: Definition search page - context search. The "term neighbourhood portlet", responsible for the context search, looks for terms of a certain entity type cooccurring frequently with the submitted term. The higher the numer of sentences mentioning both the submitted term and the "neighbour" term, the larger the font size of the neighbour term in the tag cloud. In this example, the phenotype-context for the lrrk2 gene are terms like "neurodegeneration", "tremor", "alzheimer disease" and "dementia lewy body". A click on the reading-glass icon to the right of each tag-cloud term starts a fuzzy definition search.The results of this search are displayed in the "definitions portlet", e.g. "Dementia with Lewy bodies (DLB) is the second most common form of neurodegenerative dementia". Each definition is linked to its original, external text resource. 80

Figure 5-1: Literature based model for Parkinsonism starting from five Parkinson related genes depicted as ovals (Lrrk2, PINK1, DJ-1, alpha-synucleine, parkin) 85

Figure 5-2: The impact of PINK1 on mitochondrial fission and fusion balance via MFN, OPA1 and DRP1; black: regulation; red: inhibition; green: activation; blue: phosphorylation; dotted blue: hypothetical relation between a known kinase and the phosphoprotein Lrrk2. 86

Figure 5-3: Literature based model for Parkinsonism: Linking MAO-B, a prominent anti-Parkinson drug target, with a Parkinson related gene, DJ-1, via ROS and NO. The sumoylation of DJ-1 (by SUMO 1?) is required for the proper function of DJ-1, a protector against oxidative stress. NO has been shown to desumoylate DJ-1 in neural cells, and it has been reported that ROS directly or indirectly via the NO synthase inhibits NO levels. The depicted pahthway reveals potential regulatory connections between known Parkinson related entities. 86

Figure 5-4: Regulatory schema for substances and potential drug candidates indirectly inhibiting a given phenotype...91

Figure 5-5: Regulatory schema for Juglone, Pin1 and Lewy bodies/Parkinsonism 91

Figure 5-6: Potential drug, oxidative stress enhancer, ocidative stress/Parkinsonism.....93

Figure 6-1: Literature based regulatory networks contain more edges than regulatory networks based on physical interaction even if no false positive relations have been introduced...101

List of Figures

LIST OF TABLES

Table 3-1: Core set of PropBank Semantic Role Labels 32
Table 3-2: Three exemplary frames and associated semantic roles of the core arguments (Palmer et al., 2005) 32
Table 3-3: Multiple frame sets for the polysemous verb "decline" (Palmer et al., 2005) 33
Table 3-4: Evaluation of average sentence length in characters for the two test sets as well as for three sources of biomedical literature. *) including titles, **) excluding titles 38
Table 3-5: Evaluation of SENNA based RE on LLL'05 training- and BC-PPI corpus .. 39
Table 4-1: databases and ontologies used to create the EXCERBT dictionary 58
Table 4-2: Disc space required by the Lucene indices 62
Table 4-3: EXCERBT Query Types 69
Table 5-1: Comparison of time requirements and results of EXCERBT with that of two human annotators. The numbers in brackets indicate the time period in minutes at which the protein name was found. 82
Table 5-2: Substances with the potential to be used to treat Parkinsonism extracted with the help of EXCERBT. 89
Table 5-3: Potential drug candidates for the treatment of Parkinsonism based on a manual inspection of a fraction of the predictions generated by EXCERBT 97

List of Tables

REFERENCES

1. Ackermann H (2008) Cerebellar contributions to speech production and speech perception: psycholinguistic and neurobiological perspectives. *Trends Neurosci,* 31, 265-272.

2. Agrawal R, Sharma PK, and Rao GS (2001) Release of iron from ferritin by metabolites of benzene and superoxide radical generating agents. *Toxicology,* 168, 223-230.

3. Altman RB, Bergman CM, Blake J, Blaschke C, Cohen A, Gannon F, Grivell L, Hahn U, Hersh W, Hirschman L, Jensen LJ, Krallinger M, Mons B, O'Donoghue SI, Peitsch MC, Rebholz-Schuhmann D, Shatkay H, and Valencia A (2008) Text mining for biology--the way forward: opinions from leading scientists. *Genome Biol,* 9 Suppl 2, S7.

4. Ambros V (2008) The evolution of our thinking about microRNAs. *Nat Med,* 14, 1036-1040.

5. Ananiadou S and McNaught J (2006). *Text Mining for Biology and Biomedicine.* Norwood, MA 02062.

6. Angle J and Wissmann DA (1978) Age, reading, and myopia. *Am J Optom Physiol Opt,* 55, 302-308.

7. Aruga J, Odaka YS, Kamiya A, and Furuya H (2007) Dicyema Pax6 and Zic: tool-kit genes in a highly simplified bilaterian. *BMC Evol Biol,* 7, 201.

8. Ashburner M, Ball CA, Blake JA, Botstein D, Butler H, Cherry JM, Davis AP, Dolinski K, Dwight SS, Eppig JT, Harris MA, Hill DP, Issel-Tarver L, Kasarskis A, Lewis S, Matese JC, Richardson JE, Ringwald M, Rubin GM, and Sherlock G (2000) Gene ontology: tool for the unification of biology. The Gene Ontology Consortium. *Nat Genet,* 25, 25-29.

9. Babu PA, Udyama J, Kumar RK, Boddepalli R, Mangala DS, and Rao GN (2007) DoD2007: 1082 molecular biology databases. *Bioinformation,* 2, 64-67.

10. Bairoch A and Apweiler R (1999) The SWISS-PROT protein sequence data bank and its supplement TrEMBL in 1999. *Nucleic Acids Res,* 27, 49-54.

11. Baldock R and Burger A (2005) Anatomical ontologies: names and places in biology. *Genome Biol,* 6, 108.

12. Berger R (2008). *Warum der Mensch spricht.* Eichborg AG, Frankfurt am Main.

13. Bovino JA and Marcus DF (1982) The mechanism of transient myopia induced by sulfonamide therapy. *Am J Ophthalmol,* 94, 99-102.

References

14. Box GEP (1979). *Robustness in Statistics - "Robustness in the strategy of scientific model building".* Academic Press, New York.

15. Buxton B, Hayward V, Pearson I, Karkkainen L, Greiner H, Dyson E, Ito J, Chung A, Kelly K, and Schillace S (2008) Big data: the next Google. Interview by Duncan Graham-Rowe. *Nature,* 455, 8-9.

16. Cairo G, Ronchi R, Recalcati S, Campanella A, and Minotti G (2002) Nitric oxide and peroxynitrite activate the iron regulatory protein-1 of J774A.1 macrophages by direct disassembly of the Fe-S cluster of cytoplasmic aconitase. *Biochemistry,* 41, 7435-7442.

17. Charniak E (2000) A maximum-Entropy-Inspired Parser. *Proceedings of the NAACL-2000,* 132-139.

18. Chen H and Sharp BM (2004) Content-rich biological network constructed by mining PubMed abstracts. *BMC Bioinformatics,* 5, 147.

19. Cheng D, Knox C, Young N, Stothard P, Damaraju S, and Wishart DS (2008) PolySearch: a web-based text mining system for extracting relationships between human diseases, genes, mutations, drugs and metabolites 1. *Nucleic Acids Res,* 36, W399-W405.

20. Cherry JM, Adler C, Ball C, Chervitz SA, Dwight SS, Hester ET, Jia Y, Juvik G, Roe T, Schroeder M, Weng S, and Botstein D (1998) SGD: Saccharomyces Genome Database. *Nucleic Acids Res,* 26, 73-79.

21. Chiou GC (2001) Review: effects of nitric oxide on eye diseases and their treatment. *J Ocul Pharmacol Ther,* 17, 189-198.

22. Chun HW, Tsuruoka Y, Kim JD, Shiba R, Nagata N, Hishiki T, and Tsujii J (2006) Extraction of gene-disease relations from Medline using domain dictionaries and machine learning. *Pac Symp Biocomput,* 4-15.

23. Clegg AB and Shepherd AJ (2007) Benchmarking natural-language parsers for biological applications using dependency graphs. *BMC Bioinformatics,* 8, 24.

24. Cohen KB and Hunter L (2008) Getting started in text mining. *PLoS Comput Biol,* 4, e20.

25. Cohen WW and Minkov E (2006) A graph-search framework for associating gene identifiers with documents. *BMC Bioinformatics,* 7, 440.

26. Coiras M, Camafeita E, Lopez-Huertas MR, Calvo E, Lopez JA, and Alcami J (2008) Application of proteomics technology for analyzing the interactions between host cells and intracellular infectious agents. *Proteomics,* 8, 852-873.

27. Collobert R and Weston J. Fast Semantic Extraction Using a Novel Neural Network Architecture. 45th Annual Meeting of the Association for Computational Linguistics, Proceedings of the Conference . 2007.

28. Collobert R and Weston J. Fast Semantic Extraction Using a Novel Neural Network Architecture. 45th Annual Meeting of the Association for

Computational Linguistics, Proceedings of the Conference . 2007.

29. Collobert R and Weston J (2008) A Unified Architecture for Natural Language Processing: Deep Neural Networks with Multitask Learning. *Proceedings of the 25th international conference on Machine learning.*

30. Coop G, Bullaughey K, Luca F, and Przeworski M (2008) The timing of selection at the human FOXP2 gene. *Mol Biol Evol,* 25, 1257-1259.

31. Craven M and Kumlien J (1999) Constructing biological knowledge bases by extracting information from text sources. *Proc Int Conf Intell Syst Mol Biol,* 77-86.

32. Divita G, Browne AC, and Loane R (2006) dTagger: a POS tagger. *AMIA Annu Symp Proc,* 200-203.

33. Doms A and Schroeder M (2005) GoPubMed: exploring PubMed with the Gene Ontology. *Nucleic Acids Res,* 33, W783-W786.

34. Donaldson I, Martin J, de Bruijn B, Wolting C, Lay V, Tuekam B, Zhang S, Baskin B, Bader GD, Michalickova K, Pawson T, and Hogue C (2003) PreBIND and Textomy--mining the biomedical literature for protein-protein interactions using a support vector machine. *BMC Bioinformatics,* 4, 11.

35. Enard W, Przeworski M, Fisher SE, Lai CS, Wiebe V, Kitano T, Monaco AP, and Paabo S (2002) Molecular evolution of FOXP2, a gene involved in speech and language. *Nature,* 418, 869-872.

36. Ferland RJ, Cherry TJ, Preware PO, Morrisey EE, and Walsh CA (2003) Characterization of Foxp2 and Foxp1 mRNA and protein in the developing and mature brain. *J Comp Neurol,* 460, 266-279.

37. Fritz S, Weinbach N, and Westermann B (2003) Mdm30 is an F-box protein required for maintenance of fusion-competent mitochondria in yeast. *Mol Biol Cell,* 14, 2303-2313.

38. Fundel K, Kuffner R, and Zimmer R (2007) RelEx--relation extraction using dependency parse trees. *Bioinformatics,* 23, 365-371.

39. Gasser T (2009) Mendelian forms of Parkinson's disease. *Biochim Biophys Acta.*

40. Gerhard Vollmer (2002). *Evolutionäre Erkenntnistheorie. Angeborene Erkenntnisstrukturen im Kontext von Biologie, Psychologie, Linguistik, Philosophie und Wissenschaftstheorie.* Hirzel, Stuttgart.

41. Gerhard Vollmer (2003). *Wieso können wir die Welt erkennen?: Neue Beiträge zur Wissenschaftstheorie.* Hirzel, Stuttgart.

42. Gerstein M, Serinhaus M, and Fields S (2007) Correspondence: Structured digital abstract makes text mining easy. *Nature,* 142.

43. Gopnik M (1999) Familial language impairment: more English evidence. *Folia Phoniatr Logop,* 51, 5-19.

References

44. Goss DA and Jackson TW (1996) Clinical findings before the onset of myopia in youth: 4. Parental history of myopia. *Optom Vis Sci*, 73, 279-282.

45. Griffiths-Jones S, Grocock RJ, van DS, Bateman A, and Enright AJ (2006) miRBase: microRNA sequences, targets and gene nomenclature. *Nucleic Acids Res*, 34, D140-D144.

46. Grishman R (2001) Adaptive information extraction and sublanguage analysis. *Proceedings of the Workshop on Adaptive Text Extraction and Mining, at the 17th International Joint Conference on Artificial Intelligence.*

47. Guldener U, Mannhaupt G, Munsterkotter M, Haase D, Oesterheld M, Stumpflen V, Mewes HW, and Adam G (2006) FGDB: a comprehensive fungal genome resource on the plant pathogen Fusarium graminearum. *Nucleic Acids Res*, 34, D456-D458.

48. Haesler S (2007) Studien zur Evolution und Funktion des FoxP2-Gens in Singvögeln. *Dissertation, FU Berlin.*

49. Haesler S, Rochefort C, Georgi B, Licznerski P, Osten P, and Scharff C (2007) Incomplete and inaccurate vocal imitation after knockdown of FoxP2 in songbird basal ganglia nucleus Area X. *PLoS Biol*, 5, e321.

50. Hahn U, Wermter J, Blaczyk R, and Horn AP (2007) Correspondence: Text mining: powering the database revolution. *Nature*, 130.

51. Henchcliffe C and Beal MF (2008) Mitochondrial biology and oxidative stress in Parkinson disease pathogenesis. *Nat Clin Pract Neurol*, 4, 600-609.

52. Hirschman L, Yeh A, Blaschke C, and Valencia A (2005) Overview of BioCreAtIvE: critical assessment of information extraction for biology. *BMC Bioinformatics*, 6 Suppl 1, S1.

53. Hoffmann R and Valencia A (2004) A gene network for navigating the literature. *Nat Genet*, 36, 664.

54. Hunter L and Cohen KB (2006) Biomedical language processing: what's beyond PubMed? *Mol Cell*, 21, 589-594.

55. Hunter S, Apweiler R, Attwood TK, Bairoch A, Bateman A, Binns D, Bork P, Das U, Daugherty L, Duquenne L, Finn RD, Gough J, Haft D, Hulo N, Kahn D, Kelly E, Laugraud A, Letunic I, Lonsdale D, Lopez R, Madera M, Maslen J, McAnulla C, McDowall J, Mistry J, Mitchell A, Mulder N, Natale D, Orengo C, Quinn AF, Selengut JD, Sigrist CJ, Thimma M, Thomas PD, Valentin F, Wilson D, Wu CH, and Yeats C (2009) InterPro: the integrative protein signature database. *Nucleic Acids Res*, 37, D211-D215.

56. Ip JM, Saw SM, Rose KA, Morgan IG, Kifley A, Wang JJ, and Mitchell P (2008) Role of near work in myopia: findings in a sample of Australian school children. *Invest Ophthalmol Vis Sci*, 49, 2903-2910.

57. Jack Par, Sam Hunting, and Douglas C.Engelbart (2002). *XML Topic Maps: Creating and Using Topic Maps for the Web.*

58. Jensen LJ, Saric J, and Bork P (2006) Literature mining for the biologist: from information retrieval to biological discovery. *Nat Rev Genet,* 7, 119-129.

59. Ju WK, Liu Q, Kim KY, Crowston JG, Lindsey JD, Agarwal N, Ellisman MH, Perkins GA, and Weinreb RN (2007) Elevated hydrostatic pressure triggers mitochondrial fission and decreases cellular ATP in differentiated RGC-5 cells. *Invest Ophthalmol Vis Sci,* 48, 2145-2151.

60. Kim JD, Ohta T, Tateisi Y, and Tsujii J (2003) GENIA corpus--semantically annotated corpus for bio-textmining. *Bioinformatics,* 19 Suppl 1, i180-i182.

61. Kipper-Schuler K. VerbNet: A broad-coverage, comprehensive verb lexicon. 2005. University of Pennsylvania, Dissertation

62. Klein D and Manning C (2003) Accurate Unlexicalized Parsing. *Proceedings of the 41st Meeting of the Association for Computational Linguistics,* 423-430.

63. Kogan Y, Collier N, Pakhomov S, and Krauthammer M (2005) Towards semantic role labeling & IE in the medical literature. *AMIA Annu Symp Proc,* 410-414.

64. Krallinger M, Valencia A, and Hirschman L (2008) Linking genes to literature: text mining, information extraction, and retrieval applications for biology. *Genome Biol,* 9 Suppl 2, S8.

65. Krause J, Lalueza-Fox C, Orlando L, Enard W, Green RE, Burbano HA, Hublin JJ, Hanni C, Fortea J, de la RM, Bertranpetit J, Rosas A, and Paabo S (2007) The derived FOXP2 variant of modern humans was shared with Neandertals. *Curr Biol,* 17, 1908-1912.

66. Lease M and Charniak E (2005) Parsing Biomedical Literature. *Proceedings of the Second International Joint Conference on Natural Language Processing (IJCNLP'05),* 58-69.

67. LeWitt PA and Taylor DC (2008) Protection against Parkinson's disease progression: clinical experience. *Neurotherapeutics,* 5, 210-225.

68. Lindberg C (1990) The Unified Medical Language System (UMLS) of the National Library of Medicine. *J Am Med Rec Assoc,* 61, 40-42.

69. Maglott D, Ostell J, Pruitt KD, and Tatusova T (2005) Entrez Gene: gene-centered information at NCBI. *Nucleic Acids Res,* 33, D54-D58.

70. Marcus MP, Santorini B, and Marcinkiewicz MA (1994) Building a Large Annotated Corpus of English: The Penn Treebank. *Computational Linguistics,* 19, 313-330.

71. Markgraf E and Langer G (1975) Results of the surgical management of spontaneously ruptured long biceps tendons. *Beitr Orthop Traumatol,* 22, 68-70.

72. Mehta J, Li D, and Mehta JL (1999) Vitamins C and E prolong time to arterial thrombosis in rats. *J Nutr,* 129, 109-112.

References

73. Meystre SM, Savova GK, Kipper-Schuler KC, and Hurdle JF (2008) Extracting information from textual documents in the electronic health record: a review of recent research. *Yearb Med Inform*, 128-144.

74. Miyao Y and Tsujii J (2008) Feature forest models for probabilistic hpsg parsing. *Computational Linguistics*, 34.

75. Miyao Y and Tsujii J (2005) Probabilistic Disambiguation Models for Wide-Coverage HPSG Parsing. *ACL '05: Proceedings of the 43rd Annual Meeting on Association for Computational Linguistics*, 83-90.

76. Muller HM, Kenny EE, and Sternberg PW (2004) Textpresso: an ontology-based information retrieval and extraction system for biological literature. *PLoS Biol*, 2, e309.

77. Nadkarni PM (2002) An introduction to information retrieval: applications in genomics. *Pharmacogenomics J*, 2, 96-102.

78. Nara K, Konno D, Uchida J, Kiuchi Y, and Oguchi K (1999) Protective effect of nitric oxide against iron-induced neuronal damage. *J Neural Transm*, 106, 835-848.

79. Nedellec C (2005) Learning language in logic - genic interaction extraction challenge. *In Proceedings of the ICML-2005 Workshop on Learning Language in Logic (LLL05)*, 31-37.

80. Nenova K. Towards Effective Biomedical Knowledge Discovery through Subject-Centric Semantic Integration of the Life-Science Information Space. 2009. TU Munich, Dissertation

81. Netzel R, Perez-Iratxeta C, Bork P, and Andrade MA (2003) The way we write. *EMBO Rep*, 4, 446-451.

82. Newell A, Zlot A, Silvey K, and Arail K (2007) Addressing the obesity epidemic: a genomics perspective. *Prev Chronic Dis*, 4, A31.

83. Noble D (2008) Claude Bernard, the first systems biologist, and the future of physiology. *Exp Physiol*, 93, 16-26.

84. Nowotny P, Bertelsen S, Hinrichs AL, Kauwe JS, Mayo K, Jacquart S, Morris JC, and Goate A (2007) Association studies between common variants in prolyl isomerase Pin1 and the risk for late-onset Alzheimer's disease. *Neurosci Lett*, 419, 15-17.

85. Ogata H, Goto S, Sato K, Fujibuchi W, Bono H, and Kanehisa M (1999) KEGG: Kyoto Encyclopedia of Genes and Genomes. *Nucleic Acids Res*, 27, 29-34.

86. Ohta T, Tsuruoka Y, Takeuchi J, Kim JD, Miyao Y, Yakushiji A, Yoshida K, Tateisi Y, Ninomiya T, Masuda K, Hara T, and Tsujii J (2006) An intelligent search engine and GUI-based efficient MEDLINE search tool based on deep syntactic parsing. *Proceedings of the COLING/ACL on Interactive presentation sessions*, 17-20.

87. Osumi N, Shinohara H, Numayama-Tsuruta K, and Maekawa M (2008) Concise review: Pax6 transcription factor contributes to both embryonic and adult neurogenesis as a multifunctional regulator. *Stem Cells,* 26, 1663-1672.

88. Palakal M, Bright J, Sebastian T, and Hartanto S (2007) A comparative study of cells in inflammation, EAE and MS using biomedical literature data mining. *J Biomed Sci,* 14, 67-85.

89. Palmer M, Gildea D, and Kingsbury P (2005) The Proposition Bank: An Annotated Corpus of Semantic Roles. *Computational Linguistics Journal,* 31, 71-106.

90. Peckham CS, Gardiner PA, and Goldstein H (1977) Acquired myopia in 11-year-old children. *Br Med J,* 1, 542-545.

91. Pradhan S, Ward W, Hacioglu K, Martin J, and Jurafsky D (2004) Shallow Semantic Parsing using Support Vector Machines. *Proceedings of the Human Language Technology Conference/North American chapter of the Association for Computational Linguistic annual meeting (HL/NAACL).*

92. Richler A and Bear JC (1980) The distribution of refraction in three isolated communities in Western Newfoundland. *Am J Optom Physiol Opt,* 57, 861-871.

93. Ruepp A, Brauner B, Dunger-Kaltenbach I, Frishman G, Montrone C, Stransky M, Waegele B, Schmidt T, Doudieu ON, Stümpflen V, and Mewes HW (2008) CORUM: the comprehensive resource of mammalian protein complexes. *Nucleic Acids Res,* 36, D646-D650.

94. Ryo A, Togo T, Nakai T, Hirai A, Nishi M, Yamaguchi A, Suzuki K, Hirayasu Y, Kobayashi H, Perrem K, Liou YC, and Aoki I (2006) Prolyl-isomerase Pin1 accumulates in lewy bodies of parkinson disease and facilitates formation of alpha-synuclein inclusions. *J Biol Chem,* 281, 4117-4125.

95. Scharff C and Haesler S (2005) An evolutionary perspective on FoxP2: strictly for the birds? *Curr Opin Neurobiol,* 15, 694-703.

96. Schmelzer K, Fahy E, Subramaniam S, and Dennis EA (2007) The lipid maps initiative in lipidomics. *Methods Enzymol,* 432, 171-183.

97. Schomburg I, Chang A, Ebeling C, Gremse M, Heldt C, Huhn G, and Schomburg D (2004) BRENDA, the enzyme database: updates and major new developments. *Nucleic Acids Res,* 32, D431-D433.

98. Shang S and Tan DS (2005) Advancing chemistry and biology through diversity-oriented synthesis of natural product-like libraries. *Curr Opin Chem Biol,* 9, 248-258.

99. Shu W, Cho JY, Jiang Y, Zhang M, Weisz D, Elder GA, Schmeidler J, De GR, Sosa MA, Rabidou D, Santucci AC, Perl D, Morrisey E, and Buxbaum JD (2005) Altered ultrasonic vocalization in mice with a disruption in the Foxp2 gene. *Proc Natl Acad Sci U S A,* 102, 9643-9648.

100. Smith CL, Goldsmith CA, and Eppig JT (2005) The Mammalian Phenotype Ontology as a tool for annotating, analyzing and comparing phenotypic information. *Genome Biol,* 6, R7.

101. Smith L, Rindflesch T, and Wilbur WJ (2004) MedPost: a part-of-speech tagger for bioMedical text. *Bioinformatics,* 20, 2320-2321.

102. Sokal A, Bricmont J, Zimmer D, and Schwab J (1999). *Eleganter Unsinn. Wie die Denker der Postmoderne die Wissenschaften mißbrauchen.* C.H.Beck.

103. Takahashi H (2006) Language gene. *Rinsho Shinkeigaku,* 46, 848-850.

104. Teixeira AP, Carinhas N, Dias JM, Cruz P, Alves PM, Carrondo MJ, and Oliveira R (2007) Hybrid semi-parametric mathematical systems: bridging the gap between systems biology and process engineering. *J Biotechnol,* 132, 418-425.

105. Tokoro T, Suzuki K, Hayashi K, and Otsuka J (1976) Development of myopia induced by organic phosphoruous pesticide (Sumithion) in beagle dogs (author's transl). *Nippon Ganka Gakkai Zasshi,* 80, 51-53.

106. Tsai RT-H, Chou WC, Su YS, Lin YC, Sung CL, Dai HJ, Yeh IT-H, Ku W, Sung T-Y, and Hsu W-L (2007) BIOSMILE: a semantic role labeling system for biomedical verbs using a maximum-entropy model with automatically generated template features. *BMC Bioinformatics,* 8, 325.

107. Tsai TH, Wu CW, Lin Y-C, and Hsu W-L (2005) Exploiting full parsing information to label semantic roles using an ensemble of ME and SVM via integer linear programming. *CoNLL-05 Conference paper.*

108. Tsujii J (2006) Linking Text with Knowledge - Challenges in Text Mining for Biology. *ICSB 2006 presentation.*

109. Wattarujeekrit T, Shah PK, and Collier N (2004) PASBio: predicate-argument structures for event extraction in molecular biology. *BMC Bioinformatics,* 5, 155.

110. Wheeler DL, Chappey C, Lash AE, Leipe DD, Madden TL, Schuler GD, Tatusova TA, and Rapp BA (2000) Database resources of the National Center for Biotechnology Information. *Nucleic Acids Res,* 28, 10-14.

111. Wishart DS (2007) Human Metabolome Database: completing the 'human parts list'. *Pharmacogenomics,* 8, 683-686.

112. Yuan X, Hu ZZ, Wu HT, Torii M, Narayanaswamy M, Ravikumar KE, Vijay-Shanker K, and Wu CH (2006) An online literature mining tool for protein phosphorylation. *Bioinformatics,* 22, 1668-1669.

113. Zhang Q, Xiao X, Li S, Jia X, Yang Z, Huang S, Caruso RC, Guan T, Sergeev Y, Guo X, and Hejtmancik JF (2007) Mutations in NYX of individuals with high myopia, but without night blindness. *Mol Vis,* 13, 330-336.

114. Zhao K, Wang L, Wang L, Wang L, Zhang Q, and Wang Q (2001) Novel deletion of the RPGR gene in a Chinese family with X-linked retinitis pigmentosa. *Ophthalmic Genet,* 22, 187-194.

115. Zweigenbaum P, mner-Fushman D, Yu H, and Cohen KB (2007) Frontiers of biomedical text mining: current progress. *Brief Bioinform,* 8, 358-375.

References

APPENDIX A

Metabolites or substances affecting the development or severity of Parkinsonism. Errors caused during the NER step are indicated in the results list are by a grey background colour of the substance cells. Sentences supporting the extracted relation between a substance and Parkonsonism are listed in the "Evidence Sentences" column. Definitions revealing the biological function or impact of the retrieved substance is given in the "Definitions" column.

Metabolite or substance regulating Parkinsonism	Evidence Sentences (not exhaustive)	Definitions (not exhaustive)
1 benzyl 1,2,3,4 tetrahydroisoquinoline	Chronic administration of 1-benzyl-1,2,3,4-tetrahydroisoquinoline, an endogenous amine in the brain, induces parkinsonism in a primate.	1-Benzyl-1,2,3,4-tetrahydroisoquinoline is specifically increased in the cerebrospinal fluid of patients with Parkinson's disease and induces parkinsonian features in the monkey and mouse. 1,2,3,4-Tetrahydroisoquinoline (TIQ) and 1-benzyl-1,2,3,4-tetrahydroisoquinoline (1BnTIQ), which exist in the brain of several mammalian species, are parkinsonism-inducing substances, and 1-methyl-1,2,3,4-tetrahydroisoquinoline (1MeTIQ), which is enzymatically synthesized in rat brain, is a parkinsonism-preventing substance.
1 methyl 4 phenyl 1,2,3,6 tetrahydropyridine	The neurotoxin 1-methyl-4-phenyl-1,2,3,6-tetrahydropyridine (MPTP) has been shown to induce parkinsonism in man and non-human primates. The observations that rural residence and pesticide exposure increase the risk of developing PD, and that a synthetic drug, 1-methyl-4-phenyl-1,2,3,6-tetrahydropyridine, can cause parkinsonism, suggest that at least a subset of PD may be caused by a toxin.	We report that the prototypical parkinsonian neurotoxin, MPTP (1-methyl 4-phenyl 1,2,3,6-tetrahydropyridine), is a selective dopamine neuron toxin in the enteric nervous system (ENS). In 1983, 1-methyl-4-phenyl-1,2,3,6-tetrahydropyridine (MPTP), a contaminant of "synthetic heroin", has been reported to induce parkinsonian symptoms in humans, who were responsive to L-DOPA therapy, as a result of the degeneration of nigrostriatal neurons.
6 hydroxy dopamine	Eleven Sprague-Dawley rats with 6-hydroxy-dopamine (6-OHDA) induced hemi-parkinsonism were treated in the Leksell Gamma Knife using a single 4 mm collimator shot targeted to the ipsilateral (parkinsonian) caudate-putamen complex.	Application of the dopamine specific toxin 6-hydroxy dopamine (6-OHDA) induces a significant decline in tyrosine hydroxylase positive cell bodies and fibers.
6 hydroxydopamine	In view of the fact that 6-hydroxydopamine (6-OHDA) or MPTP causes parkinsonism by generating free radicals, and inducers of metallothionein (MT) isoforms avert the said neurotoxicity, we intended to learn whether MT isoforms were capable of scavenging free radicals.	DA and its metabolite, 6-hydroxydopamine (6-OHDA), induce apoptosis in different cell types. 6-Hydroxydopamine (6-OHDA) is a neurotoxin to produce an animal model of Parkinsons disease. Despite the availability of innovative models, 6-hydroxydopamine (6-OHDA) remains the most widely used tool to induce a nigrostriatal lesion in the animal (rat). 6-Hydroxydopamine (6-OHDA) induces oxidative stress and cell death in catecholaminergic cells.
acetogenins	These data are compatible with the theory that annonaceous acetogenins, such as annonacin, might be implicated in the aetiology of Guadeloupean parkinsonism and support the hypothesis that some forms of parkinsonism might be induced by environmental toxins.	Annonaceous acetogenins are a large family of natural polyketides. Acetogenins are a new chemical series with interesting in vitro antileishmanial activity and further studies will be focused on the understanding of this selectivity in regard to the membrane and mitochondrial action using specific probes. Annonaceous acetogenins represent a new class of bioactive compounds whose primary mode of action is the inhibition of NADH-ubiquinone oxidoreductase.

Appendix A

		Some natural acetogenins are the most potent inhibitors of bovine heart mitochondrial complex I. Annonaceous acetogenin (or polyketide) is a kind of potential antineoplastic agents from Annonaceae plants.
acetylcholine	Indeed, LID in parkinsonism can be modulated by drugs acting on different neurotransmitters including glutamate, gamma-aminobutyric acid, noradrenaline, acetylcholine, serotonin, adenosine, and cholecystokinin.	Acetylcholine is an important excitatory neurotransmitter, which plays a crucial role in synaptic transmission. Although acetylcholine is one of the most widely studied neurotransmitters in the retina, many questions remain about its downstream signaling mechanisms. As already mentioned, acetylcholine is a paracrine factor stimulating GH and PRL release but it becomes inhibitory in the presence of glucocorticoids, an effect possibly mediated through a paracrine inhibitory action of NO released from FS cells by acetylcholine. Acetylcholine is an important modulator of synaptic efficacy and is required for learning and memory tasks involving the visual cortex. Acetylcholine induces neurite outgrowth and modulates matrix metalloproteinase 2 and 9.
adenosin	Indeed, LID in parkinsonism can be modulated by drugs acting on different neurotransmitters including glutamate, gamma-aminobutyric acid, noradrenaline, acetylcholine, serotonin, adenosine, and cholecystokinin.	Adenosine is an endogenous neuroprotectant regulated by adenosine kinase (ADK). Adenosine is a primordial signaling molecule present in every cell of the human body that mediates its physiological functions by interacting with 4 subtypes of G-protein-coupled receptors, termed A1, A2A, A2B and A3. Adenosine acts as an extracellular signaling molecule in various tissues and in liver this nucleoside exerts protective effects. Adenosine is an endogenous byproduct of metabolism that regulates cerebral blood flow and modulates neurotransmission. Adenosine is a prototypical neuromodulator, which mainly controls excitatory transmission through the activation of widespread inhibitory A1 receptors and synaptically located A2A receptors. Definition search for LID: [LID is a severe motor complication in advanced PD patients.]
adrenal	There are two major hypotheses proposed to explain why adrenal medullary grafts may promote functional recovery in human parkinsonism: (1) replacement of lost striatal neurotransmitter (dopamine) by the viable grafted tissue, or (2) induction of recovery of remaining host dopaminergic systems by the implantation procedure.	The adrenal medulla is an important part of the sympathoadrenal system. The adrenal medulla (as opposed to the direct sympathetic innervation) has been thought to play only a minor role in the catecholaminergic regulation of white adipose tissue. Such a biochemical deficit is likely to originate from the adrenal medulla, which is the primary site of EPI synthesis. Adrenaline isolated from extracts of adrenal medulla was the first intercellular messenger to be chemically identified and synthesized. The adrenal medulla is a typical paraganglion, having the same origin as the sympathetic ganglia, and contains at least two types of parenchymal cells: chromaffin cells and supporting cells. The adrenal medulla was the richest source of both bFGF and IGF-I mRNA in both control and experimental rat adrenals. It is concluded that adrenal medulla autotransplantation is an experimental approach and not a treatment for Parkinson's disease. Adrenaline acted as an inoconstrictor, dobutamine an inodilator and milrinone predominantly a vasodilator Adrenaline is a critical mediator of acute exercise-induced AMP-activated protein kinase activation in adipocytes. Adrenaline is a potent respiratory regulator. Adrenaline is a highly effective stimulator of cyclic AMP (cAMP) production in microvascular endothelial cells (ECs) - HMEC-1
alanine	Repeated dietary consumption of the neurotoxic amino acid beta-N-methylamino-L-alanine (BMAA), found in the seeds of Cycas circinalis, has been postulated as causing both amyotrophic lateral sclerosis (ALS) and the parkinsonism-dementia syndrome (PD) that were formerly very prevalent among the indigenous people of the Marianas Islands.	Alanine is the main second amino acid in vertebrate proteins and its coding entails increased use of the rare codon GCG. Alanine intrinsically may not play a role in hypoxic stress tolerance, but rather alanine production may be a mechanism by which the plant stores nitrogen, in preparation for the return to normal oxygen condition as proposed by Miyashita et al. (2007). Alanine is the most effective precursor for gluconeogenesis among amino acids, and the initial reaction is catalyzed by alanine aminotransferase (AlaAT). Alanine is the amino acid with the highest concentration (mean = 1200 microg/g) followed by asparagine (mean = 680 microg/g) in robusta and 800 microg/g and 360 microg/g in arabica respectively. Alanine is a nonessential amino acid made in the body from the conversion of the carbohydrate pyruvate or the breakdown of DNA and the dipeptides carnosine and anserine. Alanine is an important participant as well as regulator in glucose metabolism.
alcohol	Chronic alcohol use can produce a	Alcohol is a well-known risk factor for liver damage and is one of the

Appendix A

	wide spectrum of movement disorders including tremor, withdrawal parkinsonism and dyskinesias, cerebellar ataxia, and asterixis. Seven chronic alcoholics, aged 53 to 70, demonstrated transient signs of parkinsonism provoked by alcohol withdrawal or chronic severe intoxication. Alcohol is a risk factor for several types of cancer.	major causes of liver disease worldwide. Alcohol is the most commonly abused drug among young adults Alcohol induces Ca(2+)-dependent intracellular trypsinogen activation in the apical granular area via non-oxidative metabolites, such as fatty acid ethyl esters and fatty acids. Alcohol can induce adipogenesis by bone marrow stromal cells and may cause osteonecrosis of the femoral head. Despite the generally held view that alcohol is an unspecific pharmacological agent, recent molecular pharmacology studies demonstrated that alcohol has only a few known primary targets.
amantadine	Especially in akinetic crisis and in combination with L-Dops amantadine improves the major symptoms of parkinsonism if L-Dopa alone is no more sufficient.	Amantadine is the only medication available with demonstrated ability to reduce the expression of established LID without reducing antiparkinsonian benefit. Amantadine is a well-known medication involved in drug-induced livedo reticularis (LR), yet remains under-reported in the English literature. Amantadine is a reasonable option for improving cognition and reducing agitation following a TBI but confirmatory evidence of the efficacy the drug is necessary. Amantadine is a well tolerated medication when it is used in pediatric patients with traumatic brain injury. Amantadine is an antiviral agent that may have activity against hepatitis C virus. Amantadine is the first antiviral drug for human which was developed by duPont chemical company in 1964. Amantadine, is a non competitive NMDA receptors antagonist that has been proved beneficial in Parkinson's disease. Amantadine is an antiviral agent active against the influenza A virus that has been used in cases of chronic hepatitis C. Amantadine is an antiviral agent that was unexpectedly found to cause symptomatic improvement in patients with Parkinsonism, although its mechanism of action remains to be elucidated. Amantadine is a better tolerated agent for elderly patients, with similar efficacy to the anticholinergic agents. Amantadine appears to show a remarkable antidepressive efficacy in BDV-infected depressive patients.
amine	On the other hand, 1-methyl TIQ (1MeTIQ), an endogenous amine in the brain, prevented 1BnTIQ-induced parkinsonism in mice. Chronic administration of 1-benzyl-1,2,3,4-tetrahydroisoquinoline, an endogenous amine in the brain, induces parkinsonism in a primate.	Amines can induce toxicological responses that are relevant in biochemical treatment processes, as well as in natural waters. amines acted as weak inhibitors, whereas catechols had a more pronounced inhibitory effect on the aldehyde oxidase activity. Amines are a powerful group of small molecular weight asthmatogens that are commonly used in various types of industries locally and should be recognised in the clinical evaluation of workers with asthma. Amines are a group of highly important compounds of biological importance; they are known promoters of cell growth, can complex with nucleic acids and can stimulate DNA-primed RNA polymerase activity. So 1MeTIQ is a candidate for anti-parkinsonian drugs. We speculate that 1MeTIQ-synthesizing enzyme may play an important role in idiopathic Parkinson's disease. The compounds 1,2,3,4-tetrahydroisoquinoline (TIQ) and 1-methyl-1,2,3,4-tetrahydroisoquinoline (1-MeTIQ) are endogenous in humans and rats. 1,2,3,4-Tetrahydroisoquinoline (TIQ) and 1-benzyl-1,2,3,4-tetrahydroisoquinoline (1BnTIQ), which exist in the brain of several mammalian species, are parkinsonism-inducing substances, and 1-methyl-1,2,3,4-tetrahydroisoquinoline (1MeTIQ), which is enzymatically synthesized in rat brain, is a parkinsonism-preventing substance. Chronic administration of 1-benzyl-1,2,3,4-tetrahydroisoquinoline, an endogenous amine in the brain, induces parkinsonism in a primate. 1-Benzyl-1,2,3,4-tetrahydroisoquinoline is specifically increased in the cerebrospinal fluid of patients with Parkinson's disease and induces parkinsonian features in the monkey and mouse.
aminobutyric acid	Indeed, LID in parkinsonism can be modulated by drugs acting on different neurotransmitters including glutamate, gamma-aminobutyric acid, noradrenaline, acetylcholine, serotonin, adenosine, and cholecystokinin.	Gamma-aminobutyric acid is an inhibitory neurotransmitter, synthesized by two isoforms of glutamate decarboxylase (GAD), GAD65 and -67. gamma-aminobutyric acid is a strong modulator of dorsal raphe nucleus serotonergic neurons, and that this modulation is important in the regulation of slow wave sleep, rapid eye movement sleep and waking. Gabergic model: gamma aminobutyric acid is an inhibitory aminoacid with a specific, but limited, distribution in the CNS. gamma-Aminobutyric acid is an inhibitory neurotransmitter restricting

Appendix A

annonaceous acetogenins (↑ acetogenins)			the release of luteinizing hormone-releasing hormone before the onset of puberty.
		These data are compatible with the theory that annonaceous acetogenins, such as annonacin, might be implicated in the aetiology of Guadeloupean parkinsonism and support the hypothesis that some forms of parkinsonism might be induced by environmental toxins.	Annonaceous acetogenins represent a new class of bioactive compounds whose primary mode of action is the inhibition of NADH-ubiquinone oxidoreductase. The annonaceous acetogenins are the most potent of the known inhibitors of bovine heart mitochondrial complex I.
anti cholinergics		In a study on 144 chronic psychotic patients treated with neuroleptics, the authors tried to define a therapeutic schedule for anti-cholinergic drugs use to control parkinsonism induced by anti-psychotic drugs.	Anti-cholinergic drugs are the cornerstone of medical management of OAB. Anti-cholinergic drugs induce amnesia, which can be reversed by withdrawal of the medication. Anti-cholinergic drugs and anti-dopaminergic drugs easily induce adverse central nervous system reactions in patients with vascular depression demonstrating prominent neurological factors.
antioxidant		The view that melatonin may be unfavorable in the case of parkinsonism, was further supported by respective experiments using the (putative) melatonin receptor antagonists ML-23 and S-20928, which, again, improved motor functions and, in the case of ML-23, prevented 6-OHDA-induced mortality [309,310].These findings show that antioxidative protection and even potentially beneficial mitochondrial effects do not suffice for judging the value of a drug under systemic aspects.	In conclusion, these results provide evidence that the dietary antioxidants can play a fundamental role in inflammatory processes. Glial cell line-derived neurotrophic factor and antioxidants preserve the electrical responsiveness of the spiral ganglion neurons after experimentally induced deafness.
antipsycho-tic agent		Unfortunately, typical antipsychotic agents such as haloperidol, which selectively antagonizes dopamine D-2 receptors, can induce extrapyramidal syndromes such as tardive parkinsonism.	BACKGROUND: Antipsychotic agents are the drugs of choice in the treatment of schizophrenia. Antipsychotic agents play a dominant role in treatment, but, except for clozapine, no one drug has been proved more effective than any other.
antipsychotic drug		Although antipsychotic drugs produce this parkinsonism-like effect only after prolonged use, it is probable that diatrizoate produces the effect immediately by virtue of the high concentrations that may accumulate at the base of the brain after myelography. The difference among antipsychotic drugs in the potency to interact with the plasma membrane as revealed in the present study may be partly responsible for the difference among the drugs in the probability of inducing extrapyramidal side-effects such as parkinsonism and tardive dyskinesia. Compared with older agents, newer antipsychotic drugs are less likely to cause parkinsonism, akathisia, and dystonia and may cause TD less often. The treatment of Lewy body dementia (LBD) is particularly difficult for the co-occurrence of psychiatric and parkinsonian symptoms: antipsychotic drugs can worsen parkinsonism, and antiparkinsonian drugs can precipitate delusions and hallucinations. Antipsychotic drugs produce several neurologic complications	Antipsychotic drugs were the most frequently prescribed drugs (44%), regardless of diagnosis. Antipsychotic drugs are the most effective treatment for the psychotic symptoms of schizophrenia, yet their mechanism of action remains largely unknown. If sedative neuroleptics were excluded, antipsychotic drugs were the first prescribed neuroleptic drugs in a large proportion (80%) of patients. Antipsychotic drugs are the primary treatment for symptoms of delirium, but their side effects can be problematic. Antipsychotic drugs induce weight gain and metabolic abnormalities. Aripiprazole, an atypical antipsychotic drug, is a D(2) dopamine-receptor partial agonist, but also has affinity to several serotonin receptors (5-HT(1A,2A,2C,7)). Some cytokines such as granulocyte colony-stimulating factor, interferons and antipsychotic drugs have been shown to induce PG OBJECTIVE: Antipsychotic (AP) drugs frequently induce weight gain.

Appendix A

	including acute dyskinesia, parkinsonism, neuroleptic malignant syndrome, akathisia, and tardive dyskinesia.	
apomorphine	CONCLUSIONS: Subthreshold concentrations of apomorphine did not worsen parkinsonism, suggesting that presynaptic dopamine autoreceptors are not important to the motor response in moderate to advanced Parkinson disease. For instance, apomorphine prevents experimental parkinsonism induced by the neurotoxin 1-methyl-4-phenyl-1,2,3,6-tetrahydropyridine. The non-selective dopamine agonist apomorphine ameliorated the parkinsonism, but induced marked hyperactivity dose-dependently. Apomorphine alone also ameliorated the parkinsonism but induced marked hyperactivity.	Apomorphine is a potent short-acting dopamine agonist that rapidly ameliorates symptoms of PD. Apomorphine is a dopaminergic agent that has been known to the medical community for more than a century, but has only recently been developed to treat such motor fluctuations. Apomorphine induced a biphasic dose-response relationship, low doses producing hyperalgesia and high doses inducing antinociception. Apomorphine is a non-selective dopaminergic receptor agonist. Apomorphine is a dopamine D(1) and D(2) receptor agonist that has been approved for marketing in Europe. Apomorphine is a potent molecule for the treatment of Parkinson's disease (PD). RESULTS: Apomorphine is a dopaminergic agonist that acts directly on D2 receptors. Apomorphine is a dopamine agonist administered subcutaneously for the management of motor symptoms of Parkinson's disease (PD). Apomorphine is a non-narcotic morphine derivative that acts as a potent dopaminergic agonist.
atpase	Hereditary parkinsonism with dementia is caused by mutations in ATP13A2, encoding a lysosomal type 5 P-type ATPase. A number sign (#) is used with this entry because rapid-onset dystonia-parkinsonism (DYT12) is caused by mutation in the gene encoding the alpha-3 subunit of the N,K-ATPase (ATP1A3; 182350).	The Transport TheoryThe Na,K-ATPase is an ubiquitous membrane-bound enzyme complex that plays fundamental role in cellular function. The recent discovery that V-ATPase interacts with components of the endocytic transport machinery indicates that V-ATPase is also a pH sensor that regulates early to late endosomal transport [33]. The v-ATPase is a rotary molecular motor that uses hydrolysis of ATP to pump protons across membranes [44]. These results showed that the V-ATPase is a key regulator of mammalian acrosome pH, and that acrosome alkalinization is not the only prerequisite to activate proacrosin under in vivo conditions. The V-ATPases are a family of ATP-dependent proton pumps, involved in a variety of cellular processes, including bone breakdown. The V-ATPase is the dominant H(+)-pump at endomembranes of most plant cells, both in terms of protein amount and, frequently, also in activity. The Na+/K+ ATPase appears to play the major role and is largely responsible for the transient nature of the response to elevated [K+]o, whereas KIR channels primarily affect the duration and kinetics of the response. The Na+K+-ATPase is a known target of cardiac glycosides such as digitoxin and ouabain. The Na+/K+-ATPase is a ubiquitous plasma membrane ion pump that utilizes ATP hydrolysis to regulate the intracellular concentration of Na+ and K+. The Na-K-ATPase is a target for an EDHF displaying characteristics similar to potassium ions in the porcine renal interlobar artery. The Na+/K+-ATPase is a target protein for protein kinase C (PKC).
baclofen	Baclofen (20-120 mg daily) reduced the hyperkinesias (median score from 5 to 3, P less than 0.05) and increased the parkinsonism (median score from 5 to 7, P less than 0.01).	Baclofen is mainly an antispastic drug and the main indication of ITB is generalized lower limb spasticity in spinal cord injury and multiple sclerosis. Baclofen is a GABA-B agonist that may be useful in the treatment of substance use disorders, and also reduces binge-like eating in rodents. Baclofen was well tolerated by the participants. Baclofen is an effective drug for treatment of oromandibular dystonia. Baclofen is a centrally acting gamma-ammino butyric acid agonist that is used like muscular relaxant in disorders with spasticity and intractable hiccups. These results suggest that baclofen may represent a potentially effective medication in the treatment of alcohol-dependent patients. Baclofen is a GABA(B) agonist that is administered spinally via an implanted drug delivery device to treat spasticity. Baclofen is a stereoselective gamma-aminobutyric acid (GABAB) receptor agonist. However, baclofen induces sedation, hypothermia and muscle relaxation, which may interfere with its use in behavioral paradigms.
benzimidazole	We now present evidence that coadministration of the NOP receptor antagonist 1-[(3R,4R)-1-cyclooctylmethyl-3-hydroxymethyl-4-piperidyl]-3-ethyl-1,3-dihydro-2H	Benzimidazoles represent the dominating group of anthelmintics in sheep (78.3%), horses (42.1%), and pigs (42.0%) Benzimidazoles represent the only class of truly broad-spectrum anthelmintics, however, they also show activity against fungi and mammalian cells.

Appendix A

	benzimidazol-2-one (J-113397) and l-DOPA to 6-hydroxydopamine hemilesioned rats produced an additive attenuation of parkinsonism.	In summary, J-113397 is the first potent, selective ORL1 receptor antagonist that may be useful in elucidating the physiological roles of nociceptin/orphanin FQ. The present study also indicates that J-113397 is a potent ORL1 receptor antagonist. Taken together, these data indicate that J-113397 is a high-affinity, selective and competitive antagonist of the OP4 receptor; Definition search for op4 receptor: Nociceptin/orphanin FQ (NC) and its receptor (OP4) represent a novel peptide/receptor system which has been implicated in the regulation of various central functions, including pain. The results of these studies indicate that agents that selectively activate or block the OP4 receptor may represent new potential drugs for the treatment of human diseases.
beta carbolines	Endogenously occurring beta-carboline induces parkinsonism in nonprimate animals: a possible causative protoxin in idiopathic Parkinson's disease.	Beta-carbolines induce apoptosis in cultured cerebellar granule neurons via the mitochondrial pathway. beta-Carbolines show structural resemblance to the neurotoxic N-methyl-4-phenyl-1,2,3,6-tetrahydropyridine and are metabolized to mitochondrial toxicants. Thus, beta-carbolines represent a new class of insulin secretagogues, although it remains unclear whether their action is mediated solely by I(3) sites in the beta cell. Beta-carbolines induce apoptotic death of cerebellar granule neurones in culture.
biperiden	Perphenazine (20.5 mg/day), haloperidol (5.5 mg/day), and haloperidol (11 mg/day) + biperiden (7 mg/day) induced a moderate suppression of TD and at the same time produced a corresponding aggravation in parkinsonism.	Biperiden is an anticholinergic compound that has demonstrated effectiveness for treating organophosphate-induced seizure/convulsions. Biperiden is a cholinergic, muscarinic receptor antagonist that may preferentially block the M1 receptor subtype. Biperiden was less potent than atropine. Definition searches for perphenazine and haloperidol: Perphenazine is an old phenothiazine antipsychotic with a potency similar to haloperidol. Haloperidol is a classical neuroleptic drug that is still in use and can lead to abnormal motor activity such as tardive dyskinesia (TD) following repeated administration.
bromocriptine	However, because of variations in individual response, bromocriptine sometimes ameliorates the problems of prolonged levodopa therapy, i.e., declining efficacy, fluctuations in therapeutic response, and the development of disabling abnormal involuntary movements, Thus bromocriptine is a valuable adjunct in the treatment of parkinsonism. The results suggest that bromocriptine not only may improve the motor disorder of parkinsonism but also may reduce some side effects of levodopa therapy, such as depression, which could be due to serotonin depletion.	Bromocriptine is an oldest dopamine agonist. Bromocriptine induced a rapid but transient decrease in insulinemia in males only and biphasic increases in glucagon levels and a sustained stimulatory effect on circulating corticosterone in both sexes. Bromocriptine has the longest history of use and is a well-established, inexpensive, safe and effective therapy option. Bromocriptine is the preferred agent for treatment of hyperprolactin-induced anovulatory infertility. Bromocriptine induces regression of left ventricular hypertrophy in peritoneal dialysis patients. Bromocriptine is the only agonist approved for use in pediatric patients by the FDA. Bromocriptine is a selective agonist for dopamine D2-receptors and is used in the treatment of Parkinson's disease. We argue that bromocriptine may show both task-specific modulation and task-general inhibition of neural activity due to dopaminergic neurotransmission. Bromocriptine might induce 5-HT release by stimulating D1, D2 and 5-HT3 receptors and depolarizing neurons in the ileum. (1) Levodopa is the cornerstone of therapy for Parkinson's disease, and bromocriptine is the reference drug for patients who develop motor complications on levodopa. Bromocriptine is an ergot derivative, and other compounds that are structurally related to ergot have been developed.
buspirone	At daily dosages of 20 mg, buspirone might prove effective in reducing levodopa-induced dyskinesias without worsening of parkinsonism.	Buspirone is a potent anxiolytic that decreases serotonin transmission. Buspirone is a serotonin 5-HT(1A) receptor agonist licensed for the treatment of anxiety. The major metabolite of buspirone, 1-(2-pyrimidinyl)piperazine (1-PP) also increased and this further inhibited immobilization-induced hyperglycemia, since 1-PP increased serum insulin levels in both non-stressed and stressed mice, similar to the increases induced by buspirone. Buspirone induces a hypothermic response, which most likely is due to 5-HT(1A) autoreceptor stimulation, and growth hormone (GH) release, which probably is related to postsynaptic 5-HT(1A) receptor stimulation. Buspirone is a well-known and safe azapiron, which produces a fall in blood pressure. In addition, buspirone induces plasma adrenocorticotropic hormone (ACTH) and cortisol release [40]. All the premenopausal women were tested within the first two weeks of the menstrual cycle, i.e. in the

Appendix A

		follicular phase. Buspirone is an anxiolytic drug which exerts several central effects. Our 4 cases support the concept of buspirone acting as a full agonist at the presynaptic 5-HT1A somatodendritic receptors located on the cell bodies of raphe serotonergic neurons that project to the ventral tegmental area (VTA) of the midbrain. Buspirone is a member of the azapirone group of anxiolytic drugs and has one major metabolite, 1-(2-pyrimidinyl)piperazine (1-PP). Buspirone, but not sumatriptan, induces miosis in humans: relevance for a serotoninergic pupil control. Buspirone is a selective agonist at a subtype of serotonin receptor termed 5-HT1A, whereas fluoxetine is a selective inhibitor of the reuptake of 5-HT. Buspirone is an effective augmenting agent of serotonin selective re-uptake inhibitors in severe treatment-refractory depression. Buspirone is a nonsedating, nonbenzodiazepine anxiolytic with antidepressant properties. Buspirone induced prolactin release in mania. Buspirone is a novel agent which is clinically effective as an anxiolytic but which lacks the muscle relaxant, anticonvulsant and sedative effects of classical anxiolytics. Buspirone is a new drug with ansiolitic properties which chemical structure and mechanism of action is different from the classical drugs traditionally used for this symptom. Buspirone is a newer anxiolytic which differs chemically and pharmacologically from the benzodiazepines.
ca2+	Abnormal Ca2+-calmodulin-dependent protein kinase II function mediates synaptic and motor deficits in experimental parkinsonism.	Ca2+ is the most ubiquitous second messenger found in all cells. Ca2+ is essential for numerous physiological functions in our bodies. Ca2+ is a ubiquitous second messenger and triggers physiological changes in response to environmental stimuli [53]. Ca2+/calmodulin-dependent protein kinase II is a modulator of CARMA1-mediated NF-kappaB activation. Ca2+/calmodulin activated protein kinase II (CaMKII) is an oligomeric protein kinase with a unique holoenyzme architecture. Ca2+/calmodulin-dependent protein kinase II is an essential mediator in the coordinated regulation of electrocyte Ca2+-ATPase by calmodulin and protein kinase A.
cabergoline	Cabergoline and pramipexole fail to modify already established dyskinesias in an animal model of parkinsonism. With low doses (50%-amelioration doses), cabergoline or L-dopa alone improved the parkinsonism without induction of hyperactivity and dyskinesia, but the duration of action was brief.	Cabergoline is a potent D(2) agonist that is efficacious for the treatment of PD and is marketed throughout Europe. Cabergoline is a new, long acting, dopamine agonist that is more effective and better tolerated than bromocriptine in patients with hyperprolactinemia. The results of this study suggest that cabergoline is an effective, well tolerated therapy that should be considered in the management of acromegaly, especially if the pituitary adenoma cosecretes GH and PRL or if pretreatment plasma IGF-I levels are below 750 micrograms/L. BACKGROUND: Cabergoline is an ergotic dopamine agonist with D2 receptor activity and a very long half-life. Used in its neurological indication, cabergoline is known to induce cardiac valve regurgitations, essentially mitral and aortic valvular diseases, by its action on the 5HT2b receptors. While cabergoline can induce a suppression of cortisol secretion or a corticotroph tumor shrinkage, the sites of action remain unclear. Cabergoline is an N-acylurea derived from 9,10-dihydrolysergic acid, which is a potent prolactin inhibitor. More recently we have reported that cabergoline is a well-tolerated dopamine agonist in both young and elderly patients and has an acceptable side-effect profile. Cabergoline is a dopaminergic agonist with demonstrated efficiency of for the treatment of prolactin-secreting pituitary tumors. Cabergoline is a synthetic ergoline dopamine agonist with a high affinity for D(2) receptors indicated for use in both early and advanced Parkinson's disease and in hyperprolactinaemic disorders.Following oral administration, peak plasma concentrations of cabergoline are reached within 2-3 hours. We suggest that cabergoline is an adequate adjuvant treatment for Parkinson' disease. Cabergoline is a synthetic ergoline dopamine agonist with a high affinity for dopamine D2 receptors and a long elimination half-life. CONCLUSIONS: Cabergoline is an efficacious and well-tolerated option for the treatment of restless legs symptoms during the night and the day. Cabergoline is the most effective dopamine agonist and tumors that do not respond to bromocriptine or quinagolide frequently respond to cabergoline

Appendix A

			When fertility is desired, bromocriptine is generally preferable, but cabergoline is also likely safe; pergolide and quinagolide should not be used in this setting. Cabergoline is a direct dopamine receptor agonist, while reserpine depletes presynaptic stores of dopamine (as well as norepinephrine and serotonin).
calcium		Calcium channel antagonists are drugs currently used in the treatment of neurological and cardiovascular disorders and occasionally produce parkinsonism and movement disorders as a side effect. Some calcium channel blockers and H2 blockers induced or aggravated parkinsonism and other extrapyramidal symptoms. Our data suggest a predominant presynaptic effect on DA and 5-HT neurons; and could account for the longstanding parkinsonism induced by calcium antagonist in some patients as well as the depression observed in these subjects. The calcium (Ca) antagonist flunarizine hydrochloride (FNZ) has been reported to induce parkinsonism, especially in the elderly.	Calcium is an important mineral in homeostasis in all vertebrate animals. Calcium is an important second messenger in the rat pineal gland, as well as cAMP. Calcium is an important signaling molecule. Calcium is also involved in the depression of EP neuronal activity, since its removal during raised $K(e)(+)$ application prevented this attenuation and blocked the $I(h)$ sag. Calcium is the most universal signal used by living organisms to convey information to many different cellular processes.
calcium channel blocker		Some calcium channel blockers and H2 blockers induced or aggravated parkinsonism and other extrapyramidal symptoms.	Calcium channel blockers are the drugs of choice in the event of diabetes. Calcium channel blocker induced gingival overgrowth. Calcium-channel blockers were the class of anti-ischaemic drugs most prescribed (63%). Calcium channel blockers represent a pharmacologically non homogenic group. Calcium channel blockers are the most habitually used antihypertensive drugs in this population, although its long-term hemodimamycs effects could be deleterious especially in transplanted patients with chronic graft nephropathy. It is known that calcium channel blockers induce Parkinsonism. Calcium channel blockers were the most frequently used antihypertensive drugs.
calmodulin (→calmodulin dependent protein kinase ii)		Abnormal Ca2+-calmodulin-dependent protein kinase II function mediates synaptic and motor deficits in experimental parkinsonism.	Calmodulin is a ubiquitous Ca2+ binding protein that binds to ryanodine rectors (RyR) and is thought to modulate its activity. Calmodulin is a Ca2+-receptor protein and is regulated by the Ca2+-level [63].49.
calmodulin dependent protein kinase ii		Abnormal Ca2+-calmodulin-dependent protein kinase II function mediates synaptic and motor deficits in experimental parkinsonism.	Ca(2+)/calmodulin-dependent protein kinase II (CaMKII) is a major protein kinase that is capable of regulating the activities of many ion channels and receptors.
carbidopa		Carbidopa dosage modifies L-dopa induced side effects and blood levels of L-dopa and other amino acids in advanced parkinsonism.	Carbidopa (L-alpha-hydrazino-alpha-methyl-b-(3,4-dihydroxyphenyl) propionic acid is a known inhibitor of aromatic amino acid decarboxylase. The combination of carbidopa and levodopa (Sinemet) is a highly effective treatment for the symptoms of Parkinson's disease. Carbidopa induced the enhancement of serum prolactin at a later time and over a longer time span than benserazide.
carbolines		Endogenously occurring beta-carboline induces parkinsonism in nonprimate animals: a possible causative protoxin in idiopathic Parkinson's disease.	beta-Carboline alkaloids are a large group of natural and synthetic indole alkaloids with different degrees of aromaticity, some of which are widely distributed in nature, including various plants, foodstuffs, marine creatures, insects, mammalians as well as human tissues and body fluids. Beta-carbolines induce apoptosis in cultured cerebellar granule neurons via the mitochondrial pathway. beta-carboline alkaloids are found in several medicinal plants and display a variety of actions on the central nervous, muscular and cardiovascular systems Thus, beta-carbolines represent a new class of insulin secretagogues, although it remains unclear whether their action is mediated solely by I(3) sites in the beta cell.

Appendix A

		beta-Carbolines show structural resemblance to the neurotoxic N-methyl-4-phenyl-1,2,3,6-tetrahydropyridine and are metabolized to mitochondrial toxicants. Simple beta-carboline induced parkinsonian-like symptoms in mice via N-methylation.
carbon disulfide	Dopamine transporter binding study in differentiating carbon disulfide induced parkinsonism from idiopathic parkinsonism. Long-term exposure to carbon disulfide (CS(2)) may induce diffuse encephalopathy with parkinsonism, pyramidal signs, cerebellar ataxia, and cognitive impairments, as well as axonal polyneuropathy.	Carbon disulfide is a neurotoxic compound used in the production of viscose rayon, and is a major decomposition product of dithiocarbamates used in industry, agriculture, and medicine. Carbon disulfide induced polyneuropathy: sural nerve pathology, electrophysiology, and clinical correlation. For most non-polar or hydrophobic compounds, carbon disulfide was a versatile and effective solvent. Carbon disulfide is an exceptionally potent neurotoxicant. Carbon disulfide is a good solvent for non-polar selenium compounds like elemental selenium and selenium disulfide, but not for polar compounds like selenite and selenoproteins.
carbon monoxide	Treatment with diazepam and remission of the extrapyramidal symptoms in a case of parkinsonism caused by carbon monoxide poisoning	Carbon monoxide is a toxic gas with potentially lethal action, which forms as a result of incomplete combustion in conditions where there is a lack of oxygen and which, therefore, is present in varying percentages in environments where fire develops. Carbon monoxide is an insidious poison that accounts for thousands of deaths each year in North America. Carbon monoxide is the leading cause of poisoning injury and death worldwide. Carbon monoxide is a side product of enzymatic degradation of heme--a reaction catalyzed by heme oxygenase (HO).
ceramide	The synthetic ceramide analog L-PDMP partially protects striatal dopamine levels but does not promote dopamine neuron survival in murine models of parkinsonism.	Ceramide is a bioactive sphingolipid-derived second messenger that has been demonstrated to induce apoptosis and cell cycle arrest in various cancer cell culture systems. Ceramide induces apoptosis through caspase activation, cytochrome c release, and Bax translocation in HL-60 cells. Ceramide induces release of mitochondrial proapoptotic proteins in caspase-dependent and -independent manner in HT-29 cells. Of these, ceramide is a central metabolite and plays key roles in a variety of cellular responses, including regulation of cell growth, viability, differentiation, and senescence. Ceramide is a second messenger induced by various cellular insults that plays a regulatory role in apoptosis.
chloroquine	Chloroquine induced parkinsonism.	Chloroquine is an inexpensive antimalarial drug that also exerts anti-HIV activity. Chloroquine was the first drug of choice for malaria treatment in Nigeria at the time of this study. Chloroquine is one of the disease-modifying antirheumatic drugs (DMARDs) with anti-malarial effect. Chloroquine induced differential regulation of a plethora of genes implicated in immunity, apoptosis, the cytoskeleton, adhesion, and oxidative stress, confirming our previous findings [6] and further supporting the significant impact that chloroquine has on mosquito anti-Plasmodium defense processes. Chloroquine is a 4-aminoquinoline previously used in malaria therapy and now becoming an emerging investigational antiviral drug due to its broad spectrum of antiviral activities. Chloroquine is one of the antimalaria drugs, also used to treat rheumatoid arthritis and systemic lupus erythematosus (SLE). Chloroquine is a clinically approved drug effective against malaria. Chloroquine was the first line drug for uncomplicated malaria, and the recommended drug for home-base management of malaria in Ghana at the time of the study.
chlorpromazine	This finding is similar to that noted in parkinsonism caused by chronic chlorpromazine treatment. Both drugs induced significantly more parkinsonism than placebo, but differently so: chlorpromazine induced both types of parkinsonism hypo- and hyper-kinetic symptoms, whereas remoxipride induced hyperkinetic symptoms. Treatment of parkinsonism-like syndromes caused by reserpine & chlorpromazine.	Chlorpromazine is a potent and specific inhibitor of the mitotic kinesin KSP/Eg5 and inhibits tumor cell proliferation through mitotic arrest and accumulation of monopolar spindles. Chlorpromazine is a sedating drug, prone to cause movement problems. In 2003, in the UK, Chlorpromazine is a neuroleptic antipsychotic agent with a long history of clinical use. Chlorpromazine is the only drug that is registered for the treatment of persistent hiccups but it has many side effects.

Appendix A

chlorprothixene	Chlorprothixene (142 mg/day) had only a slight TD reducing effect and did not change parkinsonism.	Chlorprothixene was the only neuroleptic drug which like phentolamine (1-5 mg/kg) gave complete presynaptic alpha-antagonism. Chlorprothixene was the first neuroleptic of the thioxanthene group and was marketed in 1959 under the trade names of Taractan and Truxal.
cholecystokinin	Indeed, LID in parkinsonism can be modulated by drugs acting on different neurotransmitters including glutamate, gamma-aminobutyric acid, noradrenaline, acetylcholine, serotonin, adenosine, and cholecystokinin.	Cholecystokinin (CCK) is a brain gut peptide that plays an important role in satiety. Cholecystokinin (CCK) is the most abundant neuropeptide in the central nervous system. Cholecystokinin (CCK) is a peptide found in both gut and brain. Cholecystokinin (CCK) is a gut-brain peptide has been described to be able to induce mitosis according to recent studies. Cholecystokinin (CCK) is a gastrointestinal satiety signal released from the duodenum to terminate feeding, via CCK1 receptors.
Cholinesterase	In the first large placebo-controlled trial, the cholinesterase inhibitor rivastigmine improved cognition, daily functioning and psychiatric symptoms without worsening of parkinsonism.	Rivastigmine is also approved for the treatment of Parkinson's dementia. Rivastigmine is a dual cholinesterase inhibitor, being effective on both acetylcholinesterase and butyrylcholinesterase. Cholinesterases, in addition to their well-known esterase action, also show an aryl acylamidase (AAA) activity whereby they catalyze the hydrolysis of amides of certain aromatic amines. Cholinesterases are the main targets of organophosphorus compounds. Cholinesterases are a large family of enzymatic proteins widely distributed throughout both neuronal and non-neuronal tissues.
cinnarizine	Akathisia, parkinsonism and depression induced by cinnarizine: a case report Flunarizine and cinnarizine inhibit mitochondrial complexes I and II: possible implication for parkinsonism. We describe the production of an experimental model of parkinsonism induced by cinnarizine (CNZ) in three healthy sylvanna monkeys.	Cinnarizine, a piperazine derivative, is a widely prescribed medication for the treatment of vestibular disorders and motion sickness. Cinnarizine, a calcium antagonist that produces parkinsonism in humans, induces behavioural changes such as alopecia, buco-lingual dyskinesia and reduction of motor activity in female parkin knock out (PK-KO) mice but not in wild-type (WT) controls. Cinnarizine is a useful and well-tolerated drug in the treatment of acquired cold urticaria (ACU).
cisapride	We report one case of parkinsonism induced by cisapride and one case of Parkinson's disease whose symptoms were worsened by cisapride. However, the present cases showed that cisapride could be a dopamine receptor blocker, and either induce or worsen parkinsonism.	Cisapride is a gastrointestinal tract promotility agent that was frequently used in Canada before its withdrawal from the market in 2000, after completion of this study.Explicit criteriaCriteria for the appropriate prescription of cisapride were made available to us by the Quebec hospitals network on DUR [8]. The gastroprokinetic agent cisapride is a potent blocker of HERG currents and serious cardiac arrhythmias and deaths from TdP and ventricular fibrillation have been reported in patients taking cisapride. Cisapride is a commonly used therapy for gastroesophageal reflux in children.
clebopride	Persistent parkinsonism and tardive dyskinesia induced by clebopride.	Clebopride (3) is a substituted benzamide that although marketed for its stimulatory effects on gastric motility, is also a potent central dopamine antagonist.
clonazepam	Clonazepam proved more effective than lithium in controlling the symptoms of mania and caused fewer manifestations of parkinsonism.	Clonazepam (klonopin) is a popular prescription drug that has been implicated in the field of drug facilitated sexual assaults (DFSA). CONCLUSIONS: Clonazepam is the treatment of choice for patients with RBD. BACKGROUND: Clonazepam (Klonopin) is a benzodiazepine that has been used widely to treat seizures and conditions such as panic attacks and anxiety disorder. Clonazepam, a gamma aminobutyric acid (GABA) receptor agonist, is the treatment of choice for hypertonia and apnoeic episodes.
clozapine	Only the atypical antipsychotic clozapine improves psychosis without worsening of parkinsonism. Thus, antipsychotic action of clozapine does not affect the treatment of the underlying disease, i.e. relief of parkinsonism. As do other neuroleptics, clozapine can elicit sedation and asthenia, but corresponding to the motoric extrapyramidal syndrome, clozapine	Clozapine is an atypical antipsychotic with superior efficacy in the treatment of refractory schizophrenia. Clozapine is also used for other conditions such as mania, treatment-resistant depression and drug abuse.

Appendix A

	causes emotional indifference ("mental parkinsonism"), depression, and restlessness to a significantly lesser degree, which may be of importance in the higher compliance seen with this drug.	
cocaine	This study suggests that chronic heavy cocaine abuse does not cause parkinsonism. The possibility that chronic cocaine abuse might accelerate the development of parkinsonism is discussed.	Cocaine is a popular drug of abuse and despite impressive advances in the understanding of its physiological, pharmacological, and toxic effects, its mechanism of immunosuppression at the cellular level is not well understood. Also, cocaine acts as a local anesthetic by inhibiting sodium influx into cells. Cocaine is a Major Risk Factor for Antipsychotic Induced Akathisia, Parkinsonism and Dyskinesia.
Contraceptives	We report a case of parkinsonism induced by long term administration of an oral contraceptive.	Contraception is a powerful tool to promote equity between sexes; it improves women's status in the family and in the community. Contraception is not a new concept.
contrast agent	Contrast agent overdose causing brain retention of contrast, seizures and parkinsonism	Ultrasound contrast agents are useful in enhancing vascular Doppler signal and play an important role in liver transplantation assessment.
cs	Long-term exposure to carbon disulfide (CS(2)) may induce diffuse encephalopathy with parkinsonism, pyramidal signs, cerebellar ataxia, and cognitive impairments, as well as axonal polyneuropathy.	See carbon disulfide Carbon disulfide (CS2) is a man-made product utilized primarily in the manufacture of viscose rayon.
cyclophosphamide	In this study, we examined the quantitative prediction of drug-induced catalepsy by amoxapine, cinnarizine and cyclophosphamide, which have been reported to induce parkinsonism.	Cyclophosphamide is one of the most often used anticancer drugs. Cyclophosphamide is a cytotoxic agent that has been extensively investigated and is widely known to induce amenorrhea [6,7]. PURPOSE: Cyclophosphamide is a bifunctional alkylating agent long associated with immune activation.
cytochrome	Cytochrome P4502D and -2C enzymes catalyze the oxidative N-demethylation of the parkinsonism-inducing substance 1-methyl-4-phenyl-1,2,3,6-tetrahydropyridine in rat liver microsomes. Cytochrome P450 isozymes catalyzing 4-hydroxylation of parkinsonism-related compound 1,2,3,4-tetrahydroisoquinoline in rat liver microsomes. The drug 1-methyl-4-phenyl-1,2,3,6-tetrahydropyridine (MPTP), which induces parkinsonism in humans and in some animal models, is metabolized by cytochrome P450 db1 isozyme (the same enzymatic system implicated in 4-hydroxylation of debrisoquine).	Cytochromes P450 play a vital role in the steroid biosynthesis pathway of the adrenal gland. Cytochrome P450 is an important monooxygenase in biology. Cytochromes P450 is a family of heme proteins that metabolize xenobiotics including drugs.
cytotoxin	Persistence of antibody against cytotoxin-associated antigen (CagA) increases the predicted probability of being labelled as having parkinsonism.	The antigen, named CagA (cytotoxin-associated gene A), is a hydrophilic, surface-exposed protein of 128 kDa produced by most clinical isolates.
da	Although implantation of fetal dopamine (DA) neurons can reduce parkinsonism in patients, current methods are rudimentary, and a reliable donor cell source is lacking. Grafts of fetal neural tissue, rich in dopamine (DA) neurons, have previously been shown to improve the symptoms of parkinsonism,	Dopamine (DA) is a free radical scavenger that attenuates apoptosis. Recent studies have suggested that octopamine (OA) and dopamine (DA) play important roles in mediating the reward and punishment signals, respectively, in olfactory learning in insect. Dopamine, acting through D(1) receptors, is thought to play an important role in cognitive functions of the frontal cortex such as working memory. Dopamine is a retinal neuromodulator secreted from amacrine and interplexiform cells.

Appendix A

		both in humans and in animal models.	Dopamine is an important neurotransmitter that plays important roles in various physiological and pathological processes, such as Parkinsons disease. Dopamine is a key neuromodulator of locomotory circuits, yet the role that dopamine plays during development of these circuits is less well understood. Dopamine is necessary to endogenous morphine formation in mammalian brain in vivo. Dopamine is the main neurotransmitter present in dopaminergic neurons of the ventral midbrain, where dysfunction of these neurons can lead to Parkinson's disease and schizophrenia.
	dbs	The mechanisms by which STN DBS improves parkinsonism remain speculative. Bilateral STN DBS improves parkinsonism considerably more than unilateral STN DBS; bilateral simultaneous electrode implantation may be the most appropriate surgical option for patients with significant bilateral disability. Bilateral STN DBS may improve off parkinsonism more than other procedures and might also improve on-period motor function	Subthalamic nucleus (STN) deep brain stimulation (DBS) is also a promising treatment. STN-DBS is an effective treatment for elderly patients with advanced PD. STN-DBS is the prevalent surgical therapy for PD and has shown efficacy, but behavioural disorders, including cognitive problems, depression and suicidality have been reported. While DBS is an approved adjunct therapy for severe, medication-refractory movement disorders, it remains investigational in neuropsychiatry. DBS is an efficient treatment for motor complication of PD that can no longer be controlled by drug treatment. DBS is an effective surgical treatment for movement disorders with sustained long-term benefits.
	debrisoquin	The drug 1-methyl-4-phenyl-1,2,3,6-tetrahydropyridine (MPTP), which induces parkinsonism in humans and in some animal models, is metabolized by cytochrome P450 db1 isozyme (the same enzymatic system implicated in 4-hydroxylation of debrisoquine).	See MPTP Debrisoquine is an antihypertensive drug that is metabolized by cytochrome P4502D6. Debrisoquine was a weak, noncompetitive inhibitor of alfentanil metabolism and of the formation of its major metabolites, with Ki values between 2.00 and 3.21 mM. Debrisoquine is a substrate of CYP2D6.
	decanoates (→ fluphenazine)	A double-blind, cross-over trial of the effectiveness of piribedil, procyclidine and placebo in the control of parkinsonism induced by fluphenazine decanoate was conducted in sixteen cases of chronic schizophrenia.	luphenazine decanoate was the most frequently employed parenteral long-acting antipsychotic preparation. On the basis of a comparison to a study of fluphenazine enanthate patients, the author concludes that fluphenazine decanoate is the drug of choice in terms of incidence and severity of EPS.
	donepezil	Donepezil improves cognition, and seems to be well tolerated and not to worsen parkinsonism in patients with cognitive impairment. In three of nine patients, treatment with donepezil resulted in worsening of parkinsonism, which in each case responded to levodopa/carbidopa. In consideration of clinical course, her catatonia and worsened parkinsonism was thought to be induced by donepezil and she was stopped the administration of donepezil.	Donepezil is the drug most frequently used to treat cognitive symptoms in Alzheimer disease. Donepezil is an acetylcholinesterase inhibitor that is used to treat Alzheimers disease. Donepezil is a reversible, primarily non-competitive, selective inhibitor of AChE used in patients with Alzheimers disease for the improvement of cognitive deficits. Donepezil may induce P50 amplitude reduction by means of enhanced dopamine release.
	Dopamin	Unilateral implantation of dopamine-loaded biodegradable hydrogel in the striatum attenuates motor abnormalities in the 6-hydroxydopamine model of hemi-parkinsonism. The present experiment indicates that dopamine released from the graft improved the symptoms of parkinsonism in the monkey.	See definitions DA
	dopamine antagonists	Dopamine antagonists reduced all types of LID but usually aggravated parkinsonism.	These results demonstrate that dopamine antagonists or dopamine depletion blocks photoreceptor degeneration and that dopamine is necessary for photoreceptor degeneration in the rd mouse retinal organ culture model, indicating that dopamine antagonists may represent a therapeutic strategy in retinal degenerative disease. Membrane lipid peroxidation increases membrane order while dopamine antagonists show a disordering effect of membrane

		phospholipids.
dopamine d1 receptor	Both the dopamine D2-receptor agonist quinpirole and the dopamine D1-receptor agonist SKF 82958 ameliorated the parkinsonism in a dose-dependent manner with a slight induction of hyperactivity.	SKF-82958 is a subtype-selective estrogen receptor-alpha (ERalpha) agonist that induces functional interactions between ERalpha and AP-1. Therefore, SKF-82958 is an ERalpha-selective agonist.
dopamine d2 receptor	Both the dopamine D2-receptor agonist quinpirole and the dopamine D1-receptor agonist SKF 82958 ameliorated the parkinsonism in a dose-dependent manner with a slight induction of hyperactivity.	The D2 family agonist quinpirole, which induced mild dyskinesia on chronic treatment, did not produce BOLD changes in the striatum or motor cortex.
dopamine d4 receptor	Dopamine D4 receptors may alleviate antipsychotic-induced parkinsonism.	The dopamine D4 receptor (DRD4), a well-characterized, polymorphic gene, is an attractive candidate for contributing risk to disordered eating and anorexia nervosa (AN). Recently, a specific dopamine D4 receptor (DRD4) agonist was shown in rats to induce penile erection through a central mechanism. OBJECTIVE: The dopamine D4 receptor (DRD4) is a candidate gene for increasing genetic susceptibility to schizophrenia. The dopamine D4 receptor (DRD4) is the most important gene in psychiatric genetics since its involvement in the physiology of behavior, pharmacology response and psychopathology. The dopamine D4 receptor is a G protein-coupled receptor that binds with high affinity various antipsychotics. The dopamine D4 receptor (DRD4) may play a role in the pathogenesis of neuropsychiatric disease and in the action of dopaminergic drugs. The dopamine D4 receptor (D4R) is expressed at highest levels in the prefrontal cortex and is the predominant D2-like receptor localized in this brain area.
dopamine receptor	The findings suggest that parkinsonism was caused by the brain tumor, which damaged both the presynaptic dopaminergic nigrostriatal neurons and the postsynaptic dopamine receptors.	Dopamine receptors play a critical role in the cell signalling process responsible for information transfer in neurons functioning in the nervous system. Dopamine receptors are involved in the regulation of renal hemodynamics and may play a role in diabetes-induced hyperfiltration. Dopamine receptors belong to the superfamily of G protein-coupled receptors and play a crucial role in mediating the diverse effects of dopamine in the central nervous system (CNS).
dops	Especially in akinetic crisis and in combination with L-Dops amantadine improves the major symptoms of parkinsonism if L-Dopa alone is no more sufficient.	l-dops amantidine – no definition found
ethylenes	We recently demonstrated that pretreatment with N-(2-chloroethyl)-N-ethyl-2-bromobenzylamine (DSP-4) exacerbates experimental parkinsonism induced by methamphetamine.	N-(2-chloroethyl)-N-ethyl-2-bromobenzylamine (DSP-4) is a selective noradrenaline (NA) uptake blocker, capable of inducing a long-lasting depletion of NA in some noradrenergic axon terminals originating from the locus coeruleus in rodents. N-(2-chloroethyl)-N-ethyl-2-bromobenzylamine (DSP4) induces a degeneration of noradrenergic axons originating in the locus coeruleus. DSP-4 [N-(2-chloroethyl)-N-ethyl-2-bromobenzylamine] is a potent neurotoxin highly selective to the locus coeruleus noradrenaline (NA) system.
famotidine	Famotidine induced parkinsonism in a case of essential tremor	Famotidine is a histamine H2-receptor antagonist that inhibits stomach acid production, and is commonly used in the treatment of peptic ulcer disease (PUD) and gastroesophageal reflux disease (GERD/GORD). Famotidine, belonging to H2-antagonist group, is a compound containing a thiazolic moiety and it is used in peptic ulcer therapy. Famotidine induced a profound inhibition of gastric secretion and increased collagen secretion but it did not affect cell proliferation. Famotidine is a potent highly selective H2 receptor antagonist which crosses the blood-brain barrier.
flunarizine	Flunarizine and cinnarizine inhibit mitochondrial complexes I and II: possible implication for parkinsonism. The calcium (Ca) antagonist flunarizine hydrochloride (FNZ) has been reported to induce	Flunarizine is a highly potent inhibitor of cardiac hERG potassium current. Flunarizine is a selective calcium entry blocker poorly water-soluble. Flunarizine is the drug of first choice in the treatment of migraine-related disorders. Flunarizine is an antagonist of L-, T- and N-type calcium channels, which permits calcium entry into cells via a voltage-dependent

Appendix A

		parkinsonism, especially in the elderly. The authors studied 19 patients with parkinsonism induced by flunarizine.	mechanism.
	flunarizine hydrochloride	The calcium (Ca) antagonist flunarizine hydrochloride (FNZ) has been reported to induce parkinsonism, especially in the elderly.	No definition found for flunarizine hydrochloride
	Fluorine (→ cinnarizine and flunarizine)	Potentialities of cinnarizine [1-(diphenylmethyl)-4-(3-phenyl-2-propenyl)piperazine, CZ] and its fluorine derivative flunarizine [1-[bis(4-fluorophenyl)-methyl]-4-(3-phenyl-2-propenyl)piperazine, FZ] to induce parkinsonism as an adverse effect were evaluated pharmacokinetically and pharmacodynamically in rats.	Fluorine is a highly sensitive probe to monitor the conformation and dynamics of the side chains in native state. A common strategy to study enzyme catalyses is to use fluorinated substrate analogues as mechanistic probes, since fluorine is an effective hydroxyl group mimic and can also be used to replace a hydrogen atom.
	fluoxetin	Exacerbation of parkinsonism caused by fluoxetine	Fluoxetine is a biologically active pharmaceutical chemical that has been detected at parts-per-trillion levels in surface waters in North America and Europe. Fluoxetine is an antidepressant that acts as a selective serotonin reuptake inhibitor (SSRI). Fluoxetine is a selective serotonin reuptake inhibitor (SSRI) broadly used in the treatment of human mood disorders and gastrointestinal diseases involving the serotoninergic system.
	fluphenazine (→ fluphenazine decanoate/ enanthate)	In a 12-week controlled study ethopropazine was compared to benztropine in the treatment of parkinsonism induced by fluphenazine enanthate in 60 schizophrenic outpatients. A double-blind, cross-over trial of the effectiveness of piribedil, procyclidine and placebo in the control of parkinsonism induced by fluphenazine decanoate was conducted in sixteen cases of chronic schizophrenia.	Fluphenazine was an effective drug for tic suppression in 24/31 patients. Flupentixol specifically antagonizes dopamine and noradrenaline, whereas fluphenazine was a more potent antagonist of dopamine than of the other transmitters.
	fluphenazine decanoate	A double-blind, cross-over trial of the effectiveness of piribedil, procyclidine and placebo in the control of parkinsonism induced by fluphenazine decanoate was conducted in sixteen cases of chronic schizophrenia.	fluphenazine decanoate is the drug of choice in terms of incidence and severity of EPS. All neuroleptics tested (haloperidol, sulpiride, flupentixol decanoate, perphenazine enanthate, fluphenazine decanoate, palmitic ester of pipotiazine) induced a marked behavioral supersensitivity to intraaccumbens opiate infusion.
	fluphenazine enanthate	In a 12-week controlled study ethopropazine was compared to benztropine in the treatment of parkinsonism induced by fluphenazine enanthate in 60 schizophrenic outpatients.	No definition found for flunarizine enanthate
	fluspirilene	Fluspirilene induced more parkinsonism than chlorpromazine, but less drowsiness, dizziness, and dry mouth.	fluspirilene was a potent displacer of [3H]-PN-200-110 binding to rat cerebral cortical membranes (EC50 30 nM), albeit with a low Hill slope (0.66), and was more potent than other lipophilic diphenylalkylamines such as flunarizine and lidoflazine. fluspirilene is an efficient inhibitor of the voltage dependent Ca2+ channel, achieving a half-maximal effect near 0.1-0.2 nM and nearly complete blockade at 1 nM. fluspirilene is a useful drug in the treatment of schizophrenics without having to admit them to hospital initially.
	fungicide	Agricultural exposure to the organomanganese fungicide MANEB (manganese-ethylene-bis-dithiocarbamate) may induce an	Maneb is a dithiocarbamate fungicide that contains manganese. Paraquat and maneb induced neurotoxicity. Maneb, manganese ethylene-bis-dithiocarbamate, is a fungicide pesticide used in the agriculture and bulb flower culture sector.

Appendix A

	extrapyramidal syndrome resembling parkinsonism.	Maneb is one of Ethylenebisdithiocarabamate (EBDCs).
gamma aminobutyric acid	Indeed, LID in parkinsonism can be modulated by drugs acting on different neurotransmitters including glutamate, gamma-aminobutyric acid, noradrenaline, acetylcholine, serotonin, adenosine, and cholecystokinin.	Gamma-aminobutyric acid (GABA) is the main chemical inhibitory neurotransmitter in the brain. Gamma-aminobutyric acid is an inhibitory neurotransmitter, synthesized by two isoforms of glutamate decarboxylase (GAD), GAD65 and -67. gamma-Aminobutyric acid is an inhibitory transmitter of spinal interneurons that functions both pre- and postsynaptically.
gdnf	GDNF did not improve parkinsonism, possibly because GDNF did not reach the target tissues--putamen and substantia nigra.	GDNF is a fast-acting potent inhibitor of alcohol consumption and relapse. GDNF is a key component to preserve several cell populations in the nervous system, including dopaminergic and motor neurons, and also participates in the survival and differentiation of peripheral neurons such as enteric, sympathetic and parasympathetic. GDNF is a potent neurotrophic factor that protects catecholaminergic neurons from toxic damage and induces fiber outgrowth. Glial cell line-derived neurotrophic factor (GDNF) is a growth factor that plays a role in the development and survival of the enteric nervous system.
glutamate receptor	However, the mechanisms by which activation of glutamate receptors produce parkinsonism are unknown.	Glutamate receptors are the predominant mediators of excitatory synaptic signals in the central nervous system and are important in learning and memory as well as in diverse neuropathologies including epilepsy and ischemia. Glutamate receptors play a major role in neural cell plasticity, growth, and maturation. The fact that glutamate receptors are a particularly ancient intercellular signaling molecule suggests a potential role in the transition from single celled to multicellular organisms.
glyphosate	03 For three patients, the diagnose of secondary parkinsonism was supported by clinical data: the first had the onset of the symptoms after the exposure to an herbicide (glyphosate); the second after vaccination against measles; the third after coma due to encephalitis.	Glyphosate is the worlds most important herbicide, with many uses that deliver effective and sustained control of a wide spectrum of unwanted (weedy) plant species. Glyphosate is a highly effective broad-spectrum herbicide, yet it is very toxicologically and environmentally safe. Glyphosate is the only herbicide that targets 5-enolpyruvyl-shikimate-3-phosphate synthase (EPSPS), so there are no competing herbicide analogs or classes. INTRODUCTION: Glyphosate is a broad-spectrum, non-selective herbicide and commonly used to eliminate weeds in agricultural and forest settings.
gm1 ganglioside	GM1 ganglioside treatment promotes recovery of striatal dopamine concentrations in the mouse model of MPTP-induced parkinsonism.	The sialoglycosphingolipid GM1 is important for lipid rafts and immune cell signaling. GM1 increases catalase activity in cerebral cortices in vivo, but the mechanisms underlying this effect of GM1 are not known. GM1 is a marker for membrane raft-containing membrane fractions. GM1 in the inner membrane of the NE is tightly associated with a $Na(+)/Ca(2+)$ exchanger whose activity it potentiates, thereby contributing to regulation of $Ca(2+)$ homeostasis in the nucleus. Monosialoganglioside (GM1) is a glycosphingolipid present in most cell membranes that displays antioxidant and neuroprotective properties.
guanosine 5 triphosphate	We describe a 54-year-old man with dominant adult-onset dopa-responsive dystonia (DRD) with parkinsonism caused by an Arg184His mutation in guanosine 5'-triphosphate cyclohydrolase I (GCH-I).	GTP cyclohydrolase I (GCH) is the enzyme in the first and rate-limiting step for the biosynthesis of tetrahydrobiopterin (BH4) which is an essential cofactor for tyrosine hydroxylase.
h2	Some calcium channel blockers and H2 blockers induced or aggravated parkinsonism and other extrapyramidal symptoms.	Proton pump inhibitors (44.9%), lifestyle modifications (28.7%), and H2 blockers (11.8%) are the three most commonly used therapeutic modalities for NCCP. However in morphological examination, the primary culture of parietal cells with three types of H2-blocker (cimetidine, ranitidine, famotidine) induced same damage to the cells. In H2 blockers induced movement disorders, renal and liver dysfunction is the risk factor of them, but the mechanism is not clearly understood. Currently, H2-blockers and sucralfate are the only agents approved by the Food and Drug Administration for maintenance therapy of duodenal ulcer disease.
haloperidol	Secondary parkinsonism may be caused by certain drugs (e.g.,	Haloperidol is a classical neuroleptic drug that is still in use and can lead to abnormal motor activity such as tardive dyskinesia (TD) following

Appendix A

	metoclopramide and haloperidol) or by cerebrovascular disease (e.g., multiple lacunar strokes). By contrast, haloperidol produced significantly more parkinsonism than placebo and risperidone (2, 6 and 16 mg), with no effect on tardive dyskinesia. The test medications, haloperidol and zuclopenthixol, caused a significant suppression of TD and a significant increase of parkinsonism.	repeated administration Besides, haloperidol also induced oxidative damage in all regions of brain which was prevented by rutin, especially in the subcortical region containing striatum. 7 Furthermore, we have shown that haloperidol induces neurotoxicity of neuronal cells via NMDA receptor complex, accompanied by dissociation of Ras-GRF from membranes and activation of c-Jun-kinase. Haloperidol is a typical antipsychotic with potent dopamine D(2) receptor antagonism.
herbicide	For three patients, the diagnose of secondary parkinsonism was supported by clinical data: the first had the onset of the symptoms after the exposure to an herbicide (glyphosate); the second after vaccination against measles; the third after coma due to encephalitis. While the cause of Parkinson's disease (PD) remains unknown, recent evidence suggests certain environmental factors, such as well water drinking, herbicides and pesticides exposure, and neurotoxins, may trigger the chain of oxidative reactions culminating in the death of dopaminergic neurons in substantia nigra to cause parkinsonism.	Glyphosate is the worlds most important herbicide, with many uses that deliver effective and sustained control of a wide spectrum of unwanted (weedy) plant species. Glyphosate is a highly effective broad-spectrum herbicide, yet it is very toxicologically and environmentally safe. Glyphosate is the only herbicide that targets 5-enolpyruvyl-shikimate-3-phosphate synthase (EPSPS), so there are no competing herbicide analogs or classes. INTRODUCTION: Glyphosate is a broad-spectrum, non-selective herbicide and commonly used to eliminate weeds in agricultural and forest settings.
hydrogels	Unilateral implantation of dopamine-loaded biodegradable hydrogel in the striatum attenuates motor abnormalities in the 6-hydroxydopamine model of hemi-parkinsonism.	No definition found for hydrogel
insecticide	From an experimental point of view, a new model of parkinsonism induced by rotenone, a diffuse insecticide, has been proposed, and in vitro studies have provided proof that several pesticides stimulate the formation of alpha-synuclein fibrils (one of the principal constituents of Lewy bodies).	Rotenone is a widely used pesticide. Rotenone is a mitochondrial complex I inhibitor that also stimulates the production of ROS above physiologic levels [65]. In addition, rotenone induced production of reactive oxygen species (ROS), and pretreatment with N-acetylcysteine abrogated ferritin H mRNA induction by rotenone, suggesting that this response is oxidative stress-mediated.
iron	Intranigral iron injection induces behavioral and biochemical "parkinsonism" in rats.	Iron is an essential element in all living organisms and is required as a cofactor for oxygen-binding proteins. Iron is an essential nutrient for almost all organisms, but at the same time excess iron is toxic to generate radicals and damages important macromolecules.
isatin	These findings suggest that JEV-infected rats may serve as a model of Parkinson's disease and that exogenously administered isatin and selegiline can improve JEV-induced parkinsonism by increasing DA concentrations in the striatum. Isatin (100 mg/kg per day for 1 week, intraperitoneal injection) improved the bradykinesia observed in the JEV-induced parkinsonism rats.	Isatin is an endogenous oxidized indole that influences a range of processes in vivo and in vitro. Isatin has anxiogenic, sedative, anticonvulsant activities and acts as a potent antagonist at atrial natriuretic peptide receptors in vitro.
Isoquino-lines	This isoquinoline induced parkinsonism in rat after injection in the striatum, and the behavioral, biochemical and pathological changes were very similar to those in Parkinson's disease.	Isoquinoline is a possible anti-psoriatic agent in coal tar.
$\frac{1}{+}$	A number sign (#) is used with this	Na+K+-ATPase is a plasma membrane-associated protein complex,

Appendix A

	entry because rapid-onset dystonia-parkinsonism (DYT12) is caused by mutation in the gene encoding the alpha-3 subunit of the N,K-ATPase (ATP1A3; 182350).	expressed in most eukaryotic cells.
kappa opioid receptor	The selective kappa-opioid receptor agonist U50,488 reduces L-dopa-induced dyskinesias but worsens parkinsonism in MPTP-treated primates.	The kappa opioid receptor (KOR) system seems to play a role in stress responsivity, opiate withdrawal and responses to psycho-stimulants, inhibiting mesolimbic dopamine. kappa-opioid receptors (KORs) represent the principal site of action of dynorphin and related neuropeptides.
l alanine	Repeated dietary consumption of the neurotoxic amino acid beta-N-methylamino-L-alanine (BMAA), found in the seeds of Cycas circinalis, has been postulated as causing both amyotrophic lateral sclerosis (ALS) and the parkinsonism-dementia syndrome (PD) that were formerly very prevalent among the indigenous people of the Marianas Islands.	Beta-methylamino-L-alanine (BMAA) is a neurotoxic amino acid that can be produced by cyanobacteria in aqueous environments. We demonstrated that L-BMAA is a full-agonist of the Qp receptor, but with a low potency. BMAA was found to induce selective motor neuron (MN) loss in dissociated mixed spinal cord cultures at concentrations (approximately 30 muM) significantly lower than those previously found to induce widespread neuronal degeneration.
l deprenyl	In addition L-deprenyl has been shown to delay the necessity for L-dopa treatment in patients with early parkinsonism.	L-Deprenyl induced rapid increases in NO production in brain tissue and cerebral blood vessels. L-deprenyl induces aromatic L-amino acid decarboxylase (AADC) mRNA in the rat substantia nigra and ventral tegmentum.
l dopa	L-dopa alone improved the parkinsonism, but induced hyperactivity and dyskinesia, depending on the dose applied. Also when infused directly into the dopaminergic neurons, rotenone produced parkinsonism which was antagonized by L-DOPA.	L-DOPA is an endogenous ligand for OA1. Chronic L-dopa treatment is associated with L-dopa induced dyskinesia (LID). 8 L-DOPA is also the precursor to dopamine, a neurotransmitter produced by dopaneurgic neurons from tyrosine.
lergotrile	Effects of lergotrile on schizophrenia & drug induced parkinsonism.	The results are consistent with the idea that lergotrile is a direct acting dopamine agonist. Lergotrile was an agonist with therapeutic properties marred by prominent hepatotoxicity.
levodopa	Levodopa therapy can ameliorate tetrabenazine-induced parkinsonism. Long-term clinical follow-up with late neuropsychological evaluation revealed post-encephalitic parkinsonism, which worsened very slowly and was improved by levodopa.	Levodopa is the most effective agent to alleviate motor dysfunction in Parkinsons disease but its long-term use is associated with the development of dyskinesias. Levodopa is the gold standard drug for the symptomatic control of Parkinsons disease (PD). Levodopa is the most effective drug for treating Parkinson's disease. OBJECTIVES: Levodopa is the immediate precursor of dopamine and the substrate for DOPA decarboxylase, an enzyme subject to regulation in living brain.
maneb	Agricultural exposure to the organomanganese fungicide MANEB (manganese-ethylene-bis-dithiocarbamate) may induce an extrapyramidal syndrome resembling parkinsonism.	Maneb is a dithiocarbamate fungicide that contains manganese.
manganese	Exposure to high levels of manganese can cause neurotoxicity with the development of a form of parkinsonism known as manganism. Manganese as environmental factor is considered to cause parkinsonism and induce endoplasmic reticulum stress-mediated dopaminergic cell death.	8 Manganese is an essential nutrient for humans that has to be maintained at proper levels for normal brain functioning. Manganese is an abundant element. These results suggest that manganese is a unique metal that induces the synthesis of hepatic MT completely depending on the production of IL-6 without accompanying liver injury. CONTEXT: Manganese is a trace element, essential for physiologic functioning but neurotoxic at high doses.
mao a	The data of [3H]harman displacement support the hypothesis of a high-affinity binding site of the neurotoxin MPP+ located on mitochondrial MAO-A with a	MAO-A is the primary enzyme metabolizing catecholamines and dietary amines, and its role in skeletal muscle remains largely unexplored.

Appendix A

		significant influence on the development of MPTP induced parkinsonism	
melatonin (↑ melatonin receptor)		The view that melatonin may be unfavorable in the case of parkinsonism, was further supported by respective experiments using the (putative) melatonin receptor antagonists ML-23 and S-20928, which, again, improved motor functions and, in the case of ML-23, prevented 6-OHDA-induced mortality [309,310]	Melatonin is a biogenic amine, known from almost all phyla of living organisms. Extensive literature suggests that melatonin play a role against the degenerative effect of central neurotoxins by its acting as free radical scavenger. Melatonin is an endocrine output signal of the clock and provides circadian information as an endogenous synchronizer which stabilizes and reinforces circadian rhythms.
melatonin receptor		The view that melatonin may be unfavorable in the case of parkinsonism, was further supported by respective experiments using the (putative) melatonin receptor antagonists ML-23 and S-20928, which, again, improved motor functions and, in the case of ML-23, prevented 6-OHDA-induced mortality [309,310].	No definitions found for ML-23 or S-20928
meperidine		MPTP, a meperidine analog, causes parkinsonism in human and nonhuman primates. Abuse of 4-propyloxy-4-phenyl-N-methylpiperidine, a meperidine congener, produced parkinsonism in a 23-year-old man.	PURPOSE: Meperidine is a commonly used analgesic despite unique disadvantages compared with other opioid analgesics. Meperidine is an opioid analgesic metabolized in the liver by N-demethylation to normeperidine, a potent stimulant of the central nervous system.
methamphetamine		We recently demonstrated that pretreatment with N-(2-chloroethyl)-N-ethyl-2-bromobenzylamine (DSP-4) exacerbates experimental parkinsonism induced by methamphetamine. Persistent reductions of DAT density in methamphetamine and methcathinone users are suggestive of loss of DAT or loss of DA terminals and raise the possibility that as these individuals age, they may be at increased risk for the development of parkinsonism or neuropsychiatric conditions in which brain DA neurons have been implicated.	8 Methamphetamine is a drug that is often consumed at dance parties or nightclubs where the ambient temperature is high. Methamphetamine is a profoundly addictive drug that seriously impacts health, families, businesses, social services, and the environment. Methamphetamine is a popular addictive drug whose use is associated with multiple neuropsychiatric adverse events and toxic to the dopaminergic and serotonergic systems of the brain. Methamphetamine induces autophagy and apoptosis in a mesencephalic dopaminergic neuronal culture model: role of cathepsin-D in methamphetamine-induced apoptotic cell death. Methamphetamine is an amphetamine analogue which also has some limited therapeutic uses, primarily in the treatment of ADHD and obesity. For instance, methamphetamine was shown to induce substantial nigrostriatal dopaminergic terminal damage, including an increase in glial fibrillary acidic protein, a marker for astrocyte proliferation.
metoclopramide		Secondary parkinsonism may be caused by certain drugs (e.g., metoclopramide and haloperidol) or by cerebrovascular disease (e.g., multiple lacunar strokes).	Metoclopramide is a dopamine receptor antagonist used in animals as both an antiemetic and a gastroprokinetic agent. Metoclopramide is a dopamine receptor antagonist that is used to treat diabetic gastroparesis, chemotherapy-induced nausea, and migraines.
minocycline		Furthermore, Minocycline has been shown to block microglial activation of 6-hydroxydopamine and 1-methyl-4-phenyl-1,2,3,6-tetrahydropyridine-lesioned parkinsonism animal models and protect against nigrostriatal dopaminergic neurodegeneration.	Minocycline is a potent inhibitor of microglia and may have a role as a neuroprotective agent that ameliorates brain injury after hypoxia-ischemia in neonatal animal models. Minocycline is a semisynthetic second-generation tetracycline that exerts anti-inflammatory and antiapoptotic effects that are completely separate from its antimicrobial action
mitochondrial protein		However, no primary gene defects affecting mitochondrial proteins causing mendelian transmission of parkinsonism have been characterised.	mitochondrial proteins are known to play a key role in mammalian cell apoptosis and a number of mitochondrial proteins, appear to be able to activate the apoptotic process directly Mitochondrial proteins may also play a role in the development of the sporadic kidney tumor oncocytoma [4]. Although mitochondrial proteins play well-defined roles in caspase activation in mammalian cells, the role of mitochondrial factors in caspase activation in Drosophila is unclear.
mk 801		MK-801 prevents 1-methyl-4-phenyl-1,2,3,6-tetrahydropyridine-induced parkinsonism in primates.	MK-801 is a high affinity antagonist which blocks glutamate-mediated neuroplasticity and behavioural sensitization to other psychostimulants. MK-801 is a use-dependent open channel NMDA receptor blocker,

Appendix A

	In fact, MK-801 exacerbated the symptoms of parkinsonism.	which enters the channel only after its activation but then becomes trapped inside the pore to "irreversibly" block the receptor as long as the receptor is not re-activated to release the blocker [36,37]. Since MK-801 is an irreversible open channel blocker, we took advantage of this fact to differentiate between synaptic and extrasynaptic NMDA receptors. MK-801 is a selective NMDA channel blocker.
monoamine oxidase inhibitor	Pretreatment with monoamine oxidase inhibitors prevents this cell death and associated parkinsonism by blocking the oxidation of MPTP to a toxic intermediate.	Monoamine oxidase inhibitors are the antidepressant of choice for atypical bipolar depression. Monoamine oxidase inhibitors are also effective treatments for outpatients who have failed to respond to tricyclic antidepressants.
mpp	1-Methyl-4-phenylpyridinium (MPP(+)) and manganese are dopaminergic neurotoxins causing a parkinsonism-like syndrome. Complex I inhibitors, including MPP+, are known to induce both apoptosis in cell culture and parkinsonism in man and other primates.	MPP+ is one of the most potent dopamine (DA)-releasing agents. MPP is a heterodimer; its alpha and beta subunits are homologous to the core II and core I proteins, respectively, of the ubiquinol-cytochrome c oxidoreductase complex. MPP+ is a neurotoxin and an inducer of parkinsonism.
mptp	1-Methyl-4-phenyl-1,2,3,6-tetrahydropyridine (MPTP) is known to cause parkinsonism in humans and this fact is a major incentive for using this toxin as an animal model to study the pathogenesis of Parkinsons disease (PD). MPTP selectively targets and damages the dopaminergic neurons causing parkinsonism in humans and other primates [18, 19].	MPTP is used to induce experimental models of Parkinsons disease [92,93]. In conclusion, the data suggest that MPTP is a good model to study the early impairment associated with Parkinson's disease and phosphatidylserine did not improve the memory impairment induced by MPTP. MPTP is a neurotoxin thought to damage dopaminergic neurons through free radical formation. Treatment of mice by 1-methyl-4-phenyl-1,2,3,6-tetrahydropyridene hydrochloride (MPTP) is a well established animal model for Parkinsons disease (PD)
muscarine	Although dopamine D2 receptor blockade continues to be a dominant feature of successful neuroleptics, the concomitant blockade of muscarinic or serotonergic S2 receptors helps to prevent neuroleptic-induced parkinsonism for some atypical neuroleptics (clozapine, thioridazine, risperidone).	Muscarinic receptors are the predominant cholinergic receptors in the central and peripheral nervous systems. These findings suggest that muscarinic receptors play important roles in animal models to examine sensory gating which is known to be disrupted in schizophrenic patients, and hence activation of muscarinic receptors may provide an alternative approach for the treatment of psychotic symptoms in addition to classical antipsychotics. Muscarinic receptors are a functionally important family of G-protein-coupled receptors. Since muscarinic receptor antagonists are the only effective drug treatment to date, it is logical to assume that muscarinic receptors play an important role in the pathogenesis of OAB.
n hexane	n-hexane induces parkinsonism in rodents.	n-Hexane is a saturated aliphatic hydrocarbon widely used in industry. n-Hexane is an isomer of hexane and was identified as a peripheral neurotoxin in 1964. OBJECTIVE: n-Hexanal is a major component in emissions from stored wood pellets. CONCLUSIONS: n-hexane can induce a series of damages in ovary or testis of SD rats, and lipid-preoxidation may be one of the effect process.
n methyl (r) salsolinol	Endogenous N-methyl(R)salsolinol, which caused parkinsonism in rats by injection in the striatum, was found to induce apoptosis in dopaminergic neuroblastoma SH-SY5Y cells. As an endogenous MPTP-like neurotoxin, N-methyl(R)salsolinol was proved to induce parkinsonism in rats and apoptosis in dopaminergic neurons.	An endogenous dopaminergic neurotoxin, N-methyl(R)salsolinol, an MAO-A inhibitor, reduced membrane potential, DeltaPsim, in isolated mitochondria, and induced apoptosis in the cells, which 5-hydroxytryptamine, an MAO-A substrate, prevented. An endogenous dopaminergic neurotoxin, N-methyl(R)salsolinol, was found to induce apoptosis in human dopaminergic SH-SY5Y cells by step-wise activation of apoptotic cascade; collapse in mitochondrial membrane potential, DeltaPsim, activation of caspases, and fragmentation of DNA.
nadh	While NADH may yet prove to ameliorate parkinsonism, recommendations for its use in PD are premature.	NADH is the major electron acceptor during ATP synthesis. NADH is the reduced form of NAD+, and NAD+ is the oxidized form of NADH, A coenzyme composed of ribosylnicotinamide 5-diphosphate coupled to adenosine 5-phosphate by pyrophosphate linkage.
naloxone	Naloxone reduces levodopa-induced dyskinesias and apomorphine-induced rotations in	Naloxone is an opioid receptor antagonist with effects on the EEG and behavior in animals and humans and has been used clinically in drug-abuse treatment.

Appendix A

		primate models of parkinsonism.	Naloxone acts as an antagonist of estrogen receptor activity in MCF-7 cells. Naloxone is an antagonist that can reverse the side effects of morphine.
neomycin		The increased excretion of m-hydroxyphenylacetic acid in the urine of patients with parkinsonism being treated with L-dopa was reduced by gut sterilization with neomycin.	Neomycin is a large, positively charged, aminoglycoside antibiotic that has previously been shown to induce a voltage-dependent substate block in the cardiac isoform of the ryanodine receptor (RyR2). Neomycin is the most effective of the aminoglycosides tested; it stimulates splicing of Cr.psbA2 at micromolar concentrations, and, in this respect, is >100-fold more effective than spermidine. Neomycin is the most effective aminoglycoside (groove binder) in stabilizing a DNA triple helix
nerve growth factor		Non-chromaffin tissue plus nerve growth factor reduces experimental parkinsonism in aged rats.	Nerve growth factor (NGF) is a strong inducer of axon growth and survival in the dorsal root ganglia (DRG). Nerve growth factor in serum is a marker of the stage of alcohol disease. Nerve growth factor is a potential therapeutic target in breast cancer. Nerve growth factor induces endothelial cell invasion and cord formation by promoting matrix metalloproteinase-2 expression through the phosphatidylinositol 3-kinase/Akt signaling pathway and AP-2 transcription factor. Nerve growth factor is released by IL-1beta and induces hyperresponsiveness of the human isolated bronchus.
neuronal nitric oxide synthase		Inhibition of neuronal nitric oxide synthase prevents MPTP-induced parkinsonism in baboons.	nNOS (neuronal nitric oxide synthase) is a constitutively expressed enzyme responsible for the production of NO* from L-arginine and O2. Neuronal nitric oxide synthase is the dominant nitric oxide supplier for the survival of dorsal root ganglia after peripheral nerve axotomy.
neuropeptide		It is suggested that an early developmental abnormality in the DA system could permanently alter the neuropeptide systems, which in turn could influence the progression and expression of the DA-deficiency state parkinsonism, Lesch-Nyhan disease, or both.	Many neuropeptide systems subserving sex-typical behavior are dependent on sex steroids for both their organization early in life and activation during maturity. Over a decade of research has demonstrated that species differences in neuropeptide systems play significant roles in the behavioral divergence of these species.
neurotoxin		1-Benzyl-1,2,3,4-tetrahydroisoquinoline (1BnTIQ), an endogenous neurotoxin, is known to cause parkinsonism in rodents and nonhuman primates. While the cause of Parkinson's disease (PD) remains unknown, recent evidence suggests certain environmental factors, such as well water drinking, herbicides and pesticides exposure, and neurotoxins, may trigger the chain of oxidative reactions culminating in the death of dopaminergic neurons in substantia nigra to cause parkinsonism.	Neurotoxins are a varied group of compounds, both chemically and pharmacologically. Neurotoxins represent tools to help elucidate intra- and extra-cellular processes involved in neuronal necrosis and apoptosis, so that drugs can be developed towards targets that interrupt the processes leading towards neuronal death.
nicotine		Nicotine prevents experimental parkinsonism in rodents and induces striatal increase of neurotrophic factors. Nicotine activates the dopaminergic system and acts to alleviate hypokinetic disorders (parkinsonism).	Nicotine is a well studied pleiotropic agent which occurs naturally in tobacco smoke and has been largely accused for many of the adverse effects of smoking on the cardiovascular system, including autonomic imbalance, endothelial dysfunction and coronary blood flow dysregulation. Although not the only constituent of tobacco smoke, there is now abundant evidence that nicotine is a neural teratogen. Nicotine is an anti-inflammatory, but the association between smoking and asthma is highly contentious and some report that smoking cessation increases the risk of asthma in ex-smokers.
nitric oxide synthase		Inhibition of neuronal nitric oxide synthase prevents MPTP-induced parkinsonism in baboons.	Nitric oxide synthases are a family of enzymes capable of converting L-arginine to L-citrulline with the subsequent release of nitric oxide (NO). Because inducible nitric oxide synthase is the key enzyme responsible for the generation of nitric oxide in patients with intra-amniotic infection, we used immunohistochemistry to localize it on human fetal amnion.
no		No NO prevents parkinsonism.	Nitric oxide is a signalling molecule which has a portfolio of potential antiatherosclerotic effects. In the brain, nitric oxide acts as a neurotransmitter; in the immune

Appendix A

		system, nitric oxide acts as a mediator of host defense; in the cardiovascular system, nitric oxide mediates the protective effects of the intact endothelium, acting as an endogenous antiatherogenic molecule. Nitric oxide (NO) is believed to play a role in mechanical signal transduction, and there is also significant evidence of its role in cartilage and meniscus degeneration. Nitric oxide (NO) is postulated to play a key role in the pathophysiology of renal failure in sepsis.
noradrenalin	Indeed, LID in parkinsonism can be modulated by drugs acting on different neurotransmitters including glutamate, gamma-aminobutyric acid, noradrenaline, acetylcholine, serotonin, adenosine, and cholecystokinin.	Noradrenaline is one of major neurotranmitters that modulate repetitive firing in the cerebral cortex. BACKGROUND: In mammals and humans, noradrenaline is a key modulator of aggression. Noradrenaline is necessary for the hedonic properties of addictive drugs. Noradrenaline is a neurotransmitter closely connected with the processing of stimuli eliciting these emotions.
ochratoxin a	Can low level exposure to ochratoxin-A cause parkinsonism?	Ochratoxin A is an important mycotoxin that can enter the human food chain in cereals, wine, coffee, spices, beer, cocoa, dried fruits, and pork meats. Ochratoxin A is a mycotoxin produced by widespread mold fungi of the genera Aspergillius and Penicillium.
oh	In 4 such patients, OH (orthostatic hypotension)had preceded parkinsonism, and in 4 others, OH had dominated the early clinical picture, even after cessation of levodopa treatment for the movement disorder. Transmitter-loaded polymeric microspheres induce regrowth of dopaminergic nerve terminals in striata of rats with 6-OH-DA induced parkinsonism.	Orthostatic Hypotension is a sudden drop in blood pressure upon assumption of upright posture. Objectives: Orthostatic hypotension is a known complication of pancreas transplant. Orthostatic hypotension is a well-defined clinical consequence of spinal cord injury (SCI), particularly in those with tetraplegia.
olanzapine	RESULTS: Pharmacological treatment with olanzapine produced marked parkinsonism, agitation and confusion. Olanzapine can worsen parkinsonism.	CONCLUSIONS: This study suggests that olanzapine is an effective treatment option for schizophrenia patients requiring a switch from risperidone. Olanzapine is a thienobenzodiazepine which has been studied extensively for the treatment of schizophrenia, and which more recently has been indicated for the treatment of bipolar disorder. Olanzapine is a second-generation antipsychotic with mood-stabilizing properties and antagonistic activity at several dopamine receptors.
oral contrace ptives	We report a case of parkinsonism induced by long term administration of an oral contraceptive.	Oral contraceptives are the second most popular contraceptive method after female sterilization in the US. Oral contraceptives are the most commonly used reversible method, the choice of 16% of women of reproductive age.
oxides	Recently, the neurotoxicity of dopamine quinone formation by auto-oxidation of dopamine has been shown to cause specific cell death of dopaminergic neurons in the pathogenesis of sporadic PD and dopaminergic neurotoxin-induced parkinsonism. Inhibition of neuronal nitric oxide synthase prevents MPTP-induced parkinsonism in baboons.	Oxidized metabolites of dopamine, known as dopamine quinone derivatives, are thought to play a pivotal role in the degeneration of dopaminergic neurons. Dopamine quinones activate microglia and induce a neurotoxic gene expression profile: relationship to methamphetamine-induced nerve ending damage. The neurotoxicity of dopamine (DA) quinones that appears in dopaminergic neuron-specific oxidative stress has recently been shown to play a role in the pathogenesis and/or progression of Parkinson disease.
paraquat	Rotenone and paraquat are shown to induce parkinsonism in multiple animal models and in human.	Paraquat is a contact herbicide (one that kills plants by contact rather than being taken up in the roots and acting systemically) that is extensively used in agriculture, as it is fast-acting and non-persistent in the environment. Paraquat is a well-characterized genotoxic agent that generates intracellular superoxide. Paraquat is a bipyridyl herbicide and in appropriate and careful usage, will not be health threatening. By 24 h, paraquat decreased mitochondrial complex I activity and mitochondrial transmembrane potential and induced the release of cytochrome c from mitochondria. These data demonstrate that paraquat induces oxidative stress in keratinocytes leading to increased expression of antioxidant genes. Paraquat induced catalase (CAT) activity at low concentrations (1muM),

Appendix A

		whereas at higher concentrations, inhibition was observed.
pargyline	Pargyline caused no changes in baseline behaviors, but significantly reduced haloperidol-induced acute dystonia (AD) (-67%, P less than 0.002) and parkinsonism (-56%, P less than 0.005). Pargyline prevents MPTP-induced parkinsonism in primates.	Pargyline is a lipophilic amine with a low pKa-value of 6.6 and undergoes extensive metabolism. Pargyline was a relatively more potent inhibitor of MAO than chlordimeform, but not more efficacious.
parkin	BACKGROUND: Mutations in the parkin gene cause autosomal recessive early-onset parkinsonism. Mutations in the parkin gene cause autosomal recessive, juvenile-onset parkinsonism.	Parkin is a cytosolic, 52-kDa E3 ubiquitin ligase responsible for targeting specific substrates for proteasomal degradation (Imai et al., 2000; Shimura et al., 2000; Zhang et al., 2000). Parkin was localized in mitochondria of proliferating cells and was also shown to play a role in mitochondrial biogenesis by regulating both transcription and replication of mtDNA (Kuroda et al. 2006).Loss-of-function mutations in parkin cause autosomal recessive juvenile parkinsonism (Kitada et al. 1998). Parkin is the gene product identified as the major cause of autosomal recessive juvenile Parkinsonism (AR-JP).
pergolide	Increase of L-dopa/benzerazide and pergolide did not improve his parkinsonism and his disinhibited behaviors became worse.	Pergolide is an ergot derivative dopamine agonist used in the treatment of Parkinson's disease and restless legs syndrome. INTRODUCTION: Pergolide is a widely used antiparkinsonian dopamine agonist. Pergolide is an inhibitor of voltage-gated potassium channels, including Kv1.5, and causes pulmonary vasoconstriction.
pesticide	Chronic treatment with the pesticide rotenone has been reported to induce parkinsonism in rats. The observations that rural residence and pesticide exposure increase the risk of developing PD, and that a synthetic drug, 1-methyl-4-phenyl-1,2,3,6-tetrahydropyridine, can cause parkinsonism, suggest that at least a subset of PD may be caused by a toxin.	Pesticides are an essential tool in integrated pest management. Organo-phosphorus pesticides down-regulate or competitively bind to muscarinic receptors in brain [as reviewed by Jett and Lein (2007)], and by analogy, organophosphorus pesticides may interact directly with neuronal M2 receptors to block their function and increase vagally induced acetylcholine release from parasympathetic nerves, thus potentiating vagally induced bronchoconstriction.As in the lungs, all doses of parathion slightly shifted vagally induced bradycardia to the right, although the effect was not dose related or significant.
phenothiazines	This is a review of reserpine, haloperidol, and various phenothiazines that produce parkinsonism and other movement disorders.	Phenothiazine is an aromatic tricyclic compound that first emerged from the furtive chemical activity surrounding the aniline dye industry at the latter half of the 19th century. Phenothiazines induce apoptosis in a B16 mouse melanoma cell line and attenuate in vivo melanoma tumor growth. Phenothiazines were the only other class of anthelmintics tested which inhibited specific [3H]paraherquamide binding.
piperazine	Potentialities of cinnarizine [1-(diphenylmethyl)-4-(3-phenyl-2-propenyl)piperazine, CZ] and its fluorine derivative flunarizine [1-[bis(4-fluorophenyl)-methyl]-4-(3-phenyl-2-propenyl)piperazine, FZ] to induce parkinsonism as an adverse effect were evaluated pharmacokinetically and pharmacodynamically in rats.	BACKGROUND: Piperazine is a secondary heterocyclic amine that may give rise to occupational asthma of uncertain mechanism. Piperazine is a GABA (gamma-amino-butyric acid) agonist at receptors on nematode muscles and causes flaccid paralysis. Piperazine is an ideal desulfurizing agent but the heat-stable salts formed in desulfurization have caused secondary pollution and waste of resources.
poisons	Manganese poisoning may cause extrapyramidal signs such as parkinsonism, dystonia and chorea. Treatment with diazepam and remission of the extrapyramidal symptoms in a case of parkinsonism caused by carbon monoxide poisoning	See carbon monoxide and manganese definitions Carbon monoxide (CO) poisoning is an important cause of mortality and late neurological sequelae such as memory loss, personality changes, psychosis, dementia, and so on. Carbon monoxide (CO) poisoning is the leading cause of death from intoxication. Carbon monoxide (CO) poisoning is the most common form of lethal poisoning.

Appendix A

poly(adp ribose) polymerase	Poly(ADP-ribose) polymerase activation mediates 1-methyl-4-phenyl-1, 2,3,6-tetrahydropyridine (MPTP)-induced parkinsonism.	Poly(ADP-ribose) polymerase-1 (PARP-1) is a nuclear DNA-binding protein that has been shown to play a relevant role in cell necrosis and organ failure in various diseases associated with inflammation.
pramipexole	Cabergoline and pramipexole fail to modify already established dyskinesias in an animal model of parkinsonism.	Pramipexole is a non-ergot dopamine agonist shown to be efficacious in the treatment of Parkinsons disease (PD). Pramipexole is an oral, non-ergoline dopamine agonist with selectivity for the dopamine D(3) receptor, which was recently approved in the EU and the US for the treatment of idiopathic restless legs syndrome (RLS) in adults. Pramipexole is a non-ergoline dopamine agonist with a high selectivity for D(2) and D(3) receptors.
proteasome	These data suggest that systemic administration of proteasome inhibitors to normal adult rats does not reliably cause an animal model of parkinsonism.	In eukaryotic cells, proteasomes play an essential role in intracellular proteolysis and are involved in the control of most biological processes through regulated degradation of key proteins. In these processes, proteasomes are the essential components of the pathway that provides specific degradation of ubiquitinated substrates.
Psychotropic drug	More than half of the cases of parkinsonism seen in a neurology practice are drug induced or aggravated, generally by psychotropic drugs.	Psychotropic drugs show a large variation in response and side effects. Psychotropic drugs play a major role in primary care management of mental disorders.
pyridines	Study of the nongenetic causes of Parkinsons disease (PD) was encouraged by discovery of a cluster of parkinsonism produced by neurotoxic pyridine 1-methyl-4-phenyl-1,2,3,6-tetrahydropyridine (MPTP) in the 1980s.	See definition for MPTP Pyridine is a clear liquid with an odor that is sour, putrid, and fish-like. Pyridine is a simple heterocyclic aromatic organic compound that is structurally related to benzene, with one CH group in the six-membered ring replaced by a nitrogen atom.
pyridostigmine	A case report of pyridostigmine induced parkinsonism	Pyridostigmine is a short-acting inhibitor of cholinesterase (ChE) used as a pretreatment against potential nerve agent exposure during the Persian Gulf War. Pyridostigmine is a reversible cholinesterase (ChE) inhibitor that is associated with neurologic dysfunction involving both central and peripheral nervous systems Pyridostigmine is an anticholinesterase that stimulates GH secretion, probably by inhibition of hypothalamic somatostatin secretion. We conclude that, in general, at this dose pyridostigmine is a safe drug for asthmatics;
pyridoxine	Pyridoxine improves drug-induced parkinsonism and psychosis in a schizophrenic patient.	We conclude that pyridoxine is an effective, safe, well-tolerated, and relatively inexpensive adjunct to routine antiepileptic drugs for treatment of recurrent seizures in children. Pyridoxine appears to play a role in the resistance of the filamentous fungus Cercospora nicotianae to its own abundantly produced strong photosensitizer of singlet molecular oxygen (1O2), cercosporin.
quetiapine	CONCLUSIONS: Quetiapine was well-tolerated and did not worsen parkinsonism. Quetiapine may produce lower incidences of using medication for extrapyramidal side effects such as parkinsonism, akathisia and dystonia Atypical antipsychotic medications such as quetiapine have a reduced likelihood of causing adverse drug-induced parkinsonism and therefore a possible role in treating psychotic symptoms in patients with PD.	Quetiapine is an atypical antipsychotic with good tolerability, but has recently been associated with respiratory dysfunction. Quetiapine and the olanzapine-fluoxetine combination are also effective for treating bipolar depression, while olanzapine, quetiapine and aripiprazole are effective during the maintenance phase. Quetiapine is a dopamine D2 and serotonin 5-HT2 antagonist with antipsychotic and mood-stabilizing properties.
quinone	Recently, the neurotoxicity of dopamine quinone formation by auto-oxidation of dopamine has been shown to cause specific cell death of dopaminergic neurons in the pathogenesis of sporadic PD and dopaminergic neurotoxin-induced parkinsonism.	See definition for "dopamine quinone" Quinones are essential components of the respiration chain that shuttle electrons between oxidoreductases. uinones represent a very important class of compounds found in nature and for the chemically synthesized drugs.

Appendix A

quinpirole	Both quinpirole and SKF 82958 alone improved the parkinsonism with a slight induction of the hyperactivity and dyskinesias. Both the dopamine D2-receptor agonist quinpirole and the dopamine D1-receptor agonist SKF 82958 ameliorated the parkinsonism in a dose-dependent manner with a slight induction of hyperactivity.	Quinpirole induced locomotion, sniffing, and oral behaviors, all of which were attenuated by AP5 co-infusion in the intact rats. The D2 family agonist quinpirole, which induced mild dyskinesia on chronic treatment, did not produce BOLD changes in the striatum or motor cortex. SKF-82958 is a subtype-selective estrogen receptor-alpha (ERalpha) agonist that induces functional interactions between ERalpha and AP-1. Therefore, SKF-82958 is an ERalpha-selective agonist.
rabies vaccines	Modern rabies vaccines produced in cell cultures rarely cause neurologic complications, among which Guillain-Barre syndrome and parkinsonism.	The RabAvert rabies vaccine (Chiron Corporation, Emeryville, California, United States) is a sterile freeze-dried vaccine obtained by growing the fixed-virus strain Flury LEP in primary cultures of chicken fibroblasts. Currently, the vaccinia-rabies glycoprotein recombinant virus vaccine (V-RG) is the only licensed oral rabies vaccine in the US.
remoxipride	Remoxipride caused less parkinsonism than the prior neuroleptic therapy and appeared to have little masking effect on tardive dyskinesia. Remoxipride was found to cause less parkinsonism than the prior neuroleptic therapy and appeared to have little masking effect on tardive dyskinesia.	Remoxipride is a novel substituted benzamide that more effectively blocks mesolimbic than striatal D2 dopamine receptors. Remoxipride is a selective dopamine D2 antagonist with virtually no activity on other transmitter receptors. Remoxipride is a substituted benzamide of the same class as sulpiride, and has a pharmacodynamic profile consistent with central antidopaminergic activity.
reserpine	Treatment of parkinsonism-like syndromes caused by reserpine & chlorpromazine.	As reserpine is an adrenergic neuron blocker, these results suggest that catecholamines may play an essential role in the maintenance or control of NaK ATPase activity, and that the stria vascularis may be one of the target organs of catecholamines. In conclusion, the supersensitivity induced by reserpine is related only to alpha(1D)-adrenoceptors, even in tissues where this receptor subtype is already present and functional. CONCLUSION: Reserpine induced behavioral depression partially via brain interleukin-1 beta generation. METHOD: Parkinson's disease model mice induced by reserpine was used and by HPLC-ED the levels of Dopamine (DA) and its metabolites were determined. These results demonstrate that reserpine acts at the gene or the mRNA level to induce dopamine supersensitivity in striatal dopaminoceptive neurons.
ribavirin	Recovery after L-DOPA treatment in peginterferon and ribavirin induced parkinsonism.	Ribavirin is a guanosine analogue that has little antiviral activity when used alone, but considerably enhances the efficacy of conventional and pegylated interferon in the treatment of hepatitis C virus (HCV). Ribavirin is the only effective drug currently available against acute RSV bronchiolitis. Ribavirin is an antiviral drug that is effective against HCV only when combined with interferon.
ribose (→ Poly(ADP-ribose) polymerase)	Poly(ADP-ribose) polymerase activation mediates 1-methyl-4-phenyl-1, 2,3,6-tetrahydropyridine (MPTP)-induced parkinsonism.	Poly(ADP-ribose) polymerase is involved in sensing DNA single-strand breaks and inducing DNA repair via poly(ADP-ribosyl)ating various DNA-binding and DNA-repair proteins. Poly(ADP-ribose) polymerase is a B-MYB coactivator. Poly(ADP-ribose) polymerase is a regulator of chemokine production: relevance for the pathogenesis of shock and inflammation. Poly(ADP-ribose) polymerase is a 113-kDa nuclear enzyme that binds to both damaged DNA and to RNA associated with actively transcribed regions of chromatin
riluzole	Riluzole prevents MPTP-induced parkinsonism in the rhesus monkey: a pilot study.	Riluzole is the only medication approved for the treatment of ALS and has been registered as a neuroprotective agent in several countries. These results suggest that riluzole is a potential antiepileptic drug with activity against limbic seizure and absence seizure. Riluzole is a neuroprotective drug that blocks glutamatergic neurotransmission in the central nervous system. Riluzole is a presynaptic inhibitor of glutamate release with neuroprotective properties.
risperidone	Results indicated that risperidone at 6 mg/day had the most beneficial effect on TD, especially on the BLM syndrome, without inducing significant parkinsonism while	Risperidone is an atypical antipsychotic drug with combined dopamine-2/serotonin-2 (D(2)/5-HT(2)) antagonist activity that has been effective in reducing cocaine use in some animal studies. Risperidone is a commonly used medication for the treatment of bipolar disorder and schizophrenia in children and adolescents.

Appendix A

rivastigmine		treating psychotic symptoms. This antidyskinetic effect was greater than with either placebo or haloperidol.	
		In the first large placebo-controlled trial, the cholinesterase inhibitor rivastigmine improved cognition, daily functioning and psychiatric symptoms without worsening of parkinsonism.	Rivastigmine is a newer-generation inhibitor with a dual inhibitory action on both acetylcholinesterase (AChE) and butyrylcholinesterase (BChE) enzymes, and is used for the treatment of AChE- and BChE-related diseases such as brain Alzheimers disease and cardiovascular disease.
rotenone		Rotenone and paraquat are shown to induce parkinsonism in multiple animal models and in human. Chronic treatment with the pesticide rotenone has been reported to induce parkinsonism in rats.	Rotenone is a mitochondrial complex I inhibitor that also stimulates the production of ROS above physiologic levels [65]. Rotenone is a widely used pesticide.
salsolinol		Salsolinol causing parkinsonism activates endoplasmic reticulum-stress signaling pathways in human dopaminergic SK-N-SH cells. Endogenous N-methyl(R)salsolinol, which caused parkinsonism in rats by injection in the striatum, was found to induce apoptosis in dopaminergic neuroblastoma SH-SY5Y cells.	Salsolinol is an endogenous catechol isoquinoline detected in humans. Salsolinol induces a decrease in cyclic AMP at the median eminence and an increase at the adenohypophysis in lactating rats. Salsolinol is a putative endogenous neuro-intermediate lobe prolactin-releasing factor. Salsolinol is a dopaminergic active compound which binds to the D(2) receptor family, especially to the D(3) receptor with a K(i) of 0.48+/-0.021 micromol/l.
selegiline		Selegiline can prevent the parkinsonism caused by MPTP in animals; similar findings have been reported with other toxins like 6-OHDA and DSP-4, that destroys noradrenergic nuclei. These results suggested that exogenously administered isatin and selegiline can improve JEV-induced parkinsonism by increasing DA concentrations in the striatum.	In mice, selegiline was a potent inhibitor of nicotine metabolism in hepatic microsomes and cDNA-expressed CYP2A5; Selegiline is an MAO-B inhibitor with antioxidant and neurotrophic properties. Selegiline is a monamine oxidase type B (MAO-B) inhibitor that incorporates a propargyl ring within its molecular structure. The results show that selegiline can induce neuronal phenotype associated with neurotrophic factor expression.
serotonin		Clinicians should be aware that serotonin noradrenaline reuptake inhibitors as well as selective serotonin reuptake inhibitors can cause parkinsonism. Indeed, LID in parkinsonism can be modulated by drugs acting on different neurotransmitters including glutamate, gamma-aminobutyric acid, noradrenaline, acetylcholine, serotonin, adenosine, and cholecystokinin.	Serotonin is a major regulator of structural brain plasticity, which may occur following cortical resection in humans. Serotonin is one of the important neurotransmitter and neuromodulator so far studied in crustacean models. Serotonin is a classical neurotransmitter of central nervous system, and it is connected to the control of appetite and satiet
sertraline		Sertraline induced parkinsonism.	Sertraline is a selective serotonin reuptake inhibitor. Sertraline is an effective antidepressant for postmenopausal women with MDD. Sertraline is the only treatment for major depressive disorder studied in a placebo-controlled trial of patients with ACS and found to be safe and effective.
smoke		Accordingly, smoking appears to reduce neuroleptic-induced parkinsonism.	Smoking is a leading cause of morbidity and mortality globally. Smoking is a major risk factor for many chronic diseases.
sn		The gradual loss of striatal dopamine and dopaminergic neurons residing in the substantia nigra (SN) causes parkinsonism characterized by slow, halting movements, rigidity, and resting tremor when neuronal loss exceeds a threshold of approximately 80%.	The substantia nigra (SN) is a midbrain center composed of dopaminergic (DA-) and gamma aminobutyric acid (GABA-)ergic (GABA-) neurons. Substantia Nigra was the brain area exhibiting the highest levels of HO-2, constitutive and inducible Hsp70, GSSG, peroxides, iron, and calcium, in contrast with the lowest content in GSH, GSH/GSSG ratio and glutathione reductase activity, compared to the other cerebral regions examined. Substantia nigra is a mesencephalic structure inserted along several circuits which appear to play a key role in epilepsy. Selective damage of mitochondrial complex I within the dopaminergic neurons of the substantia nigra is the central event during Parkinson

Appendix A

soot			disease.
	soot	The possibility that parkinsonism might be caused by environmental MPTP present in soot formed from partial combustion of coal has been assessed.	Soot is not a homogenous substance and several factors determine its properties. The data demonstrate that soots are cytotoxic and that cytotoxicity is not related to PAH content but is related to ROS generation, suggesting that soot induces cellular oxidative stress and that cell viability assays can be indicators of ROS production.
	sphingolipid	Oral administration of semisynthetic sphingolipids promotes recovery of striatal dopamine concentrations in a murine model of parkinsonism.	Sphingolipids represent a class of membrane lipids that contain a hydrophobic ceramide chain as its common backbone structure. Sphingolipids are an amazingly complex family of compounds that are found in all eukaryotes as well as some prokaryotes and viruses. Sphingolipids are essential structural components of membranes and are found to be enriched in lipid rafts [18].
	sulpiride	Sulpiride, a selective D-2 dopamine receptor blocker, is able to suppress TD without producing a reciprocal aggravation in parkinsonism, although in vulnerable patients it may induce/aggravate parkinsonian symptoms.	Sulpiride is a substituted benzamide with selective dopaminergic blocking activity. Sulpiride is a safe and effective pharmacotherapeutic treatment for the acute management of schizophrenia.
	synuclein	OBJECTIVE: Recently, genomic multiplications of alpha-synuclein gene (SNCA) have been reported to cause hereditary early-onset parkinsonism. Association between cardiac denervation and parkinsonism caused by alpha-synuclein gene triplication.	Synucleins are a family of highly conserved small proteins predominantly expressed in neurons. Here we report that synucleins are a novel class of GRK substrates. These results strongly support the idea that α-synuclein is the pathogenic protein of Parkinsons disease.
	tau protein	Recently it was shown by several research groups that mutations in the gene encoding for the tau protein associated with microtubuli on chromosome 17 caused a distinct form of dementia named frontotemporal dementia and parkinsonism (FTDP-17).	Tau protein is a major microtubule (MT)-associated brain protein enriched in axons. Tau protein is a neuronal microtubule-associated protein (MAP), which localizes primarily in the axon. By the early 1990s, it was clear that tau protein is the major component of the paired helical filament and that the latter is made of all six tau isoforms, each full-length and hyperphosphorylated.
	terguride	Terguride also improved the parkinsonism but did not induce the hyperactivity and dyskinesias. Terguride alone ameliorated the parkinsonism without inducing any sign of excitability, irritability, or aggressiveness (hyperactivity).	Terguride is the transdihydroderivative of lisuride (Dopergin). Terguride is an ergoline derivative with mixed agonistic/antagonistic dopaminergic activity. Terguride is a prototype drug belonging to a recently characterized class of compounds, dopamine partial agonists, which appear to possess a unique pharmacological profile in altering dopamine neurotransmission, where these drugs act as antagonists in conditions of high dopaminergic tone.
	tetrahydro-isoquinolines	1-Benzyl-1,2,3,4-tetrahydroisoquinoline (1BnTIQ), an endogenous neurotoxin, is known to cause parkinsonism in rodents and nonhuman primates. Chronic administration of 1-benzyl-1,2,3,4-tetrahydroisoquinoline, an endogenous amine in the brain, induces parkinsonism in a primate.	Chronic administration of 1-benzyl-1,2,3,4-tetrahydroisoquinoline, an endogenous amine in the brain, induces parkinsonism in a primate. 1-Benzyl-1,2,3,4-tetrahydroisoquinoline is specifically increased in the cerebrospinal fluid of patients with Parkinson's disease and induces parkinsonian features in the monkey and mouse. 1BnTIQ is an endogenous amine in the brain and the 1BnTIQ content increases in the patients with PD.
	thyrotropin releasing hormone	Sustained release dosage of thyrotropin-releasing hormone improves experimental Japanese encephalitis virus-induced parkinsonism in rats.	Thyrotropin-releasing hormone (TRH) is a well-characterized regulator of the hypothalamic-pituitary-thyroid endocrine axis. Thyrotropin-releasing hormone (TRH) is a tripeptide that is widely distributed in the brain including the hippocampus where TRH receptors are also expressed. In amphibians, thyrotropin-releasing hormone (TRH) is a potent stimulator of alpha-melanotropin (alpha-MSH) secretion, so TRH plays a major role in the neuroendocrine regulation of skin-color adaptation.
	trazodone	Can trazodone induce parkinsonism?	Trazodone is an antidepressant agent used in Spain since 1975. Trazodone is a commonly prescribed off-label for sleep disturbance in alcohol-dependent patients, but its safety and efficacy for this indication is unknown. Trazodone is a unique antidepressant, which blocks the postsynaptic serotonin (5-HT) receptors, 5-HT(2A) and 5-HT(2C), and weakly inhibits presynaptic 5-HT transporters.

Appendix A

trh	Effects of TRH-SR (sustained release microspheres of TRH) which is encapsulated in copoly (dl-lactic/glycolic acid) using an in-water drying method were investigated in experimental Japanese encephalitis virus (JEV)-induced post-encephalitic parkinsonism rats by a pole test and high performance liquid chromatography (HPLC) with an electrochemical detector (ECD).	Thyrotrophin-releasing hormone (TRH) is known to play an important role in the control of food intake and energy metabolism in addition to its actions on the pituitary-thyroid axis. TRH is the most proximal member of the hypothalamic-pituitary-thyroid (HPT) axis. The acute effects of TRH are likely to be centrally mediated and independent of its role in the control of the production of thyroid hormones
trimetazidine	Trimetazidine is known to induce parkinsonism but choreiform disorders have not yet been described with this drug. Trimetazidine induces parkinsonism, gait disorders and tremor.	Trimetazidine is an anti-ischemic agent that is used to treat angina and it has cardioprotective effects without inducing any significant hemodynamic changes. Trimetazidine is an anti-ischemic agent that improves the myocardial metabolism and that can be especially useful in the ischemic myocardium of diabetic patients.
triphosphate	We describe a 54-year-old man with dominant adult-onset dopa-responsive dystonia (DRD) with parkinsonism caused by an Arg184His mutation in guanosine 5'-triphosphate cyclohydrolase I (GCH-I).	See GCH-I definitions Triphosphate is an intermediate in the biosynthesis of Folate, the metabolism of Purine, the metabolism of Porphyrin and chlorophyll, the metabolism of Pyrimidine and the metabolism of Thiamine.
ubiquitin	BACKGROUND: Autosomal recessive juvenile parkinsonism (AR-JP) is caused by mutations in the parkin gene which encodes an E3 ubiquitin-protein ligase. Authors suggest that PARK2 functions as a ubiquitin ligase and a mutation would induce ubiquitin-proteasome dysfunction resulting in autosomal recessive juvenile parkinsonism.	Ubiquitin is an essential, highly-conserved small regulatory protein in eukaryotic cells. Ubiquitin is a 76 amino acid polypeptide that is highly conserved among eukaryotes and is attached to the substrate (protein targeted for degradation) by a process called ubiquitination.
ubiquitin protein ligase	BACKGROUND: Autosomal recessive juvenile parkinsonism (AR-JP) is caused by mutations in the parkin gene which encodes an E3 ubiquitin-protein ligase.	Ubiquitin-protein ligases (E3s) are responsible for target recognition and regulate stability, localization or function of their substrates. The ubiquitin protein ligases (or E3) are in charge of substrate specificity and therefore play a pivotal role in the pathway.
vaccines	Modern rabies vaccines produced in cell cultures rarely cause neurologic complications, among which Guillain-Barre syndrome and parkinsonism. For three patients, the diagnose of secondary parkinsonism was supported by clinical data: the first had the onset of the symptoms after the exposure to an herbicide (glyphosate); the second after vaccination against measles; the third after coma due to encephalitis.	Vaccination is the most effective means to control infectious diseases. Vaccines are one of the most cost-effective medical interventions and protect the individual and the community against vaccine preventable diseases.
valproate	Valproate induced parkinsonism	BACKGROUND: Valproate is a first-line antiepileptic agent and is also used in the treatment of bipolar disorder and migraine. Valproate is a small (144 Da), water-soluble molecule with a volume of distribution of only 0.1–0.4 l/kg.
venlafaxin	Reversible and dose-related parkinsonism induced by venlafaxine	Venlafaxine is a serotonin-noradrenaline reuptake inhibitor antidepressant. Venlafaxine is metabolized primarily by CYP2D6 and is a substrate of P-glycoprotein. Venlafaxine is an approved antidepressant that is an inhibitor of both serotonin and norepinephrine transporters.
veralipride	Veralipride, an antidopaminergic drug commonly prescribed to counteract postmenopausal symptoms, may cause reversible parkinsonism.	Veralipride is a substituted benzamide which is used for the treatment of menopausal hot flushes. Veralipride is a benzamide derivative effective in the treatment of menopausal syndrome. Because it is well tolerated, effective, and devoid of adverse metabolic

Appendix A

	This seems to be a case of parkinsonism induced by veralipride, a drug known to cause other extrapiramidal signs such as bucco-facial or limb dyskinesia.	side-effects, we conclude that veralipride is the best non-hormonal treatment for menopausal disorders presently available.
VPA	VPA induced parkinsonism is not so rare and has been under-reported and under-recognized. When we are confronted with the patients who develop parkinsonism after VPA administration, the possibility of VPA induced parkinsonism should be considered in the differential diagnosis.	In conclusion, VPA is a powerful antiproliferative agent in estrogen-sensitive breast cancer cells, making this drug of clinical interest as a new approach to treat breast cancer. Actually, in MCF-7 cells, VPA induces apoptosis, down-regulates Bcl-2 and up-regulates Bak expression. RESULTS: In our study we show that VPA is a potent inducer of neuro-endocrine transdifferentiation (NET) in androgen receptor null PCa cells, both in vitro and in vivo.
zuclopent hixol	The test medications, haloperidol and zuclopenthixol, caused a significant suppression of TD and a significant increase of parkinsonism.	Zuclopenthixol is the cis(Z)-isomer of clopenthixol, a neuroleptic of the thioxanthene group, used for treating people with psychotic symptoms. Zuclopenthixol is a thioxanthene derivative which acts as a mixed dopamine D1/D2 receptor antagonist.

APPENDIX B

*Borrelia induced phenotypes supported by **more than three** / three/ two/one evidence sentences;*

lyme disease	thyroiditis autoimmune	scleroderma	hodgkin lymphoma
infection	severe combined immunodeficiency	retrobulbar neuritis	hepatitis
borreliosis	pneumonia	radiculopathy	hearing loss sensorineural
fever	osteomyelitis	purpuras thrombocytopenic	hearing loss
relapsing fever	neurologic manifestations	purpura thrombocytopenic	glomerulonephritis
arthritis	neuritis	polyneuropathy	glioma
infectious disease	necrosis	polyneuritis	focal infection
multisystem disorder	meningoencephalomyelitis	pneumonitis	fibrosis
tick borne disease	lymphocytomas	pneumonia mycoplasma	facial paralysis
tick borne fever	lyme neuroborreliosis	plasminogen	erythema chronicum migrans
erythema	infection borrelia	peripheral neuritis	encephalitis tick borne
facial palsies	immunodeficiency	paralysis	dog disease
meningitis	human ehrlichiosis	panuveitis	disease thyroid
inflammation	ehrlichiosis	pain cranial	disease joint
infection tick borne	combined immunodeficiency severe	non hodgkin lymphoma	dermatosis
spirochetal infection	chronic inflammation	neuropathy painful	dementia
inflammatory disorder	central nervous system infection	neuropathies multiple cranial	death
chronic disease	borrelia infection	nervous system disorder	cerebral infarction
inflammatory response	autoimmune disease	myositis	cattle disease
inflammatory disease	zoonosis	myocarditis	cardiomyopathy
disease transmitted by tick	weakness muscle	mycoplasma pneumoniae pneumonia	cardiac abnormalities
systemic infection	toxicity	mycoplasma pneumoniae infection	canine disease
Carditis	tick borne encephalitis	muscle weakness	blindness
apoptosis	tick bite	mixed infection	bite
skin manifestations	thyroiditis	meningoencephalitis	bannwarth syndrome
radiculitis	thyroid disease	meningitis aseptic	bacteremia
persistent infection	thrombocytopenic purpura	malignancy	av block
neutrophil migration	thrombocytopenia	localized infection	autoimmune thyroiditis
neuropathy	systemic vasculitis	lobar pneumonia	autism
manifestation skin	system disorder of nervous system	joint injury	aseptic meningitis
joint inflammation	syphilis	joint disease	arthropathy
infectious disorder	synovitis	jarisch herxheimer reaction	anetoderma
encephalomyelitis	spirochetal disease	injury	amyloid beta deposits
encephalitis	skin lesion	infective pneumonia	aging
bacterial infection	skin disorder	infection mycoplasma	acute inflammation
vasculitis	seronegative arthritis	infarction	acrodermatitis
uveitis	sensorineural hearing loss	hypertension	abortion
tumor			

Appendix B

PUBLICATION RECORD

Stümpflen, Volker; Barnickel, Thorsten; Nenova, Karamfilka *Large Scale Knowledge Representation of Distributed Biomedical Information Scaling Topic Maps.*, Lecture Notes in Artificial Intelligence, Vol. 4999, pp. 116-127, *Scaling Topic Maps*, Third International Conference on Topic Map Research and Applications, TMRA 2007 Leipzig, Germany, October 11-12, 2007, ISBN: 978-3-540-70873-5

Barnickel, Thorsten; Weston, Jason; Collobert, Ronan; Mewes, Hans-Werner; Stümpflen, Volker; *Large Scale Application of Neural Network Based Semantic Role Labeling for Automated Relation Extraction from Biomedical Texts;* PLoS ONE, 2009

Die VDM Verlagsservicegesellschaft sucht für wissenschaftliche Verlage abgeschlossene und herausragende

Dissertationen, Habilitationen, Diplomarbeiten, Master Theses, Magisterarbeiten usw.

für die kostenlose Publikation als Fachbuch.

Sie verfügen über eine Arbeit, die hohen inhaltlichen und formalen Ansprüchen genügt, und haben Interesse an einer honorarvergüteten Publikation?

Dann senden Sie bitte erste Informationen über sich und Ihre Arbeit per Email an *info@vdm-vsg.de*.

Sie erhalten kurzfristig unser Feedback!

VDM Verlagsservicegesellschaft mbH
Dudweiler Landstr. 99   Telefon +49 681 3720 174
D - 66123 Saarbrücken   Fax   +49 681 3720 1749
www.vdm-vsg.de

Die VDM Verlagsservicegesellschaft mbH vertritt

Printed by Books on Demand GmbH, Norderstedt / Germany